BRINGING THE WORLD
INTO FOCUS

THE STORY OF VOSH

Volunteer Optometric Services to Humanity

by Michel Listenberger, OD, FVI

authorHOUSE®

AuthorHouse™
1663 Liberty Drive
Bloomington, IN 47403
www.authorhouse.com
Phone: 1 (800) 839-8640

Published by AuthorHouse 04/22/2017

ISBN: 978-1-5246-7226-3 (sc)
ISBN: 978-1-5246-7224-9 (hc)
ISBN: 978-1-5246-7225-6 (e)

Library of Congress Control Number: 2017903450

This book was generously underwritten
by the following donors:

Elsa Branson and Walter Branson, FVI
Charles Gray, OD, FVI
C. Ellis Potter, OD, FAAO, FVI
Greg Pearl, OD, FVI
Tom Pruett, OD
Natalie Venezia, Esq., FVI
Ellen L. Weiss, OD, FVI
Harry I. Zeltzer, OD, DOS, FAAO, FVI
University of Houston School of Optometry
University of Missouri School of Optometry

(FVI indicates Fellow of VOSH/International)

Major contributors to the historic record

Dale Cole, OD, FVI, Past Historian
C. Ellis Potter, OD FAAO FVI,
editor Kansas Optometric
Journal
Dr. Harry Zeltzer, personal files
Natalie Venezia, Esq., FVI
Consultation with most of the
living Past Presidents of
VOSH/International.

This book is dedicated to the memory of

Dr. Franklin Harms

The "Father" of Volunteer Optometric Services to Humanity

Dr. Franklin Harms From left to right: Doctors Abrahams, Enns, Benelli, Landes, Harms and Morlong. (Courtesy of Dr. Morlong)

And written to honor all who have served VOSH

VOSH is not only dedication.
    VOSH is not only passion.
        VOSH is not only a shared vision.
VOSH is a life-changing quest reaching the core meaning of life.

You can see it in the walk;
    You can see it in the talk.
VOSH stirs in the heart and shows by a sparkle in the eye.

VOSH Logo

VOSH, as its name indicates, provides
Volunteer Optometric Services to Humanity around the world.
VOSH has grown to become the largest Non-Government
Organization in the world volunteering
direct, professional eye care,
free to millions in need. It consists of 5,000 eye care professionals
and volunteers in 81 Chapters including North America,
South America, Africa, Asia, and Europe.

BRINGING THE WORLD INTO FOCUS
The Story of VOSH

Contents

Foreword

My first introduction to Volunteer Optometric Service to Humanity was in the fall of 1979 when I joined. Little did I know that VOSH/International was being formed at the very same time. Although I did not know the founder of VOSH, Dr. Franklin Harms, over the years I have known or met all of the Presidents of VOSH/International. Writing this book has been a sentimental journey.

My first VOSH mission to Haiti was lead by Dr. Walter Marshall, one of the founders of VOSH/International. Like most first-time VOSHers, I was totally immersed in the cultural shock and overwhelming needs in Haiti. And as fortune would turn, one of our team members died that week of cardiac failure. He was unable to access immediate care. That too, hit all of us hard. It forced us to swallow the reality of why we were there and what we were doing – in the context of ultimate life's values. And today, years later, it connects, VOSH is less about your resume and more about your eulogy.

After that mission, it seems, I inherited a similar single-mindedness that was demonstrated by our founder Dr. Harms. That VOSH focus set me toward the task of creating VOSH-Michigan. While attending my first International Meeting to get more information, I first met then International President Dr. Bud Falkenhain. He, too, had that same internal focus toward this VOSH cause that was greater than any of us.

In writing this account an effort has been made to carefully get the most accurate and relevant history while citing specific sources along the way. Having been involved for many years, I feel positive about bringing continuity and perspective to voluminous archives. I remember being personally intrigued along the way by the mood, the feeling, the priorities and the 'buzz' of highly enthusiastic volunteers. As each decade passed it became fascinating to see what motivated people why they did what they did – dedicating themselves to embrace the culture, objectives and priorities of VOSH/International.

So this begins our story together as we strive to answer the question, "Why would anyone put their life on hold, paying their own expenses, traveling to the other side of the world, to give others they don't even know, the gift of sight?"

A Whole New World

While on a VOSH mission in Mexico I met a nine year-old "princess" who showed me a "whole new world."

I was working in a crowded exam room with a group of eye doctors. The room was dark; I was sweaty and my mouth was dry from talking with too many people. An endless line of patients and their children keep coming through the clinic. By the afternoon of the second day, hundreds of faces start to take on a numerical identity. "How many have we seen?" "How many are still waiting?"

Just as my mind began to drift to the endless line of patients, I felt a gentle tug on my sleeve. It was my wife, Judy. She whispered to me to come outside. As I entered the sunlight I shielded my eyes and refocused on the little nine year-old girl standing next to her mother. She was wearing a sundress, she had dark hair tied with a ribbon, large dark eyes framed by a round pair of brown glasses, and her eyes were reaching into mine. She was clutching in her fist a bouquet of wilted flowers that she had picked along the roadside. She offered them to me as a gift.

It turned out that the day before, I had examined her and given her first pair of glasses, which because of the power, opened up a whole new world of sight to her. She and her mother had taken a bus ride three hours each way to come to our clinic the day before. They were so appreciative that they took the same three hour trip back to say thank you with flowers. The day before she was a number in a long line; today she was an angel from God bringing a vision of the heart, revealing to me a vision of who we are and why we do what we do – giving me a vision of a "Whole New World."

> *A whole new world, a hundred thousand things to see.*
> *I'm like a shooting star, I've come so far,*
> *I can't go back to where I used to be.*

These words from Disney's "A Whole New World" by Tim Rice suggest the excitement and wonder that captures the hearts of VOSHers from their first mission forward. Experiences like these change one forever.

The Creation of VOSH
Beginnings

Dateline 1969

Imagine Dr. Franklin Harms, safely buckled into his airline seat as he left a life-changing experience in Haiti. He turns his head and strains to see the Island of Hispaniola disappear into the horizon. How could he leave so many people without a hope of good vision? How could he convince other eye care professional to meet these dire needs?

He sits silently in his seat; his heart still racing. How incredible that any optometrist in Kansas could give the gift of sight to those most in need all around the globe! Then reality hit. Why would any eye doctor leave his livelihood in private practice and put their lives on the line in places like Haiti?

Leading up to 1969

In the years following World War II servicemen flooded optometry schools aided by generous government programs re-training Americans in professional endeavors. In the 1960's optometrists emerged as primary eye care providers.

In 1961 President John F. Kennedy created the Peace Corps. The sixties were a time of peace and love. "Flower power" and "Bohemian poverty" were embraced among other unorthodox lifestyles. The country itself was moving from volunteers supporting service men and women toward volunteers working to meet the needs of others in poverty both at home and in foreign lands. Inequality and violence were quickly dominating social consciousness.

Eye care professionals responded in their own ways by sharing their gifts of providing eyesight to those less able to access eyecare and eye wear. Optometrists around the country began organizing short mission trips from a single weekend to a few weeks traveling to areas mostly in the western hemisphere south of the United States. Providers would usually work on their own or with churches or local service organizations. At the same time optometrists were encouraging other eye care professionals to join them in traveling to remote areas, giving eye care to people suffering from vision problems that kept these individuals from performing tasks that made them meaningful contributors in their own communities.

SOSH (Student Optometric Service to Haiti also called SVOSH) was founded at the Pennsylvania College of Optometry by Algernon Phillips, OD, then a fourth year optometry student. SOSH conducted its first mission in 1968. Algernon was a Haitian American who took SOSH teams to Northern Haiti.

It is also acknowledged that New England College of Optometry soon after organized a SOSH Chapter.

Although eye care missions were increasing in popularity, no large organizational system was in place to grow, assist and sustain the movement. Would the world benefit if someone stepped forward to lead such a movement?

Dr. Harms – Prelude to an Organization

In 1968, Dr. Franklin Harms of Hillsboro, Kansas read an article by Dr. Reynold F Swanson, a Florida optometrist, regarding one of Dr. Swanson's many eye projects in Haiti. Dr. Swanson had been organizing missions in Haiti since 1962. In 1969, Franklin went with Dr. Swanson on a mission to Haiti. According to Dr. Harms this was when he began building a consortium of other optometrists who would serve the eye care needs of those in foreign lands – those having the greatest need for eye care.

Co-founder Dr. Dave Reynolds (1st Treasurer of Kansas VOSH) comments, "In the later part of the 1960's the late Dr. Franklin Harms of Hillsboro, Kansas traveled outside the USA on church mission trips, not as an optometrist, but as a church member doing missionary work. During these trips he realized the tremendous need for eye care in developing countries and eventually joined forces with a Florida OD who spent some time in Haiti doing eye exams. After that experience, Dr. Harms began the process of developing the idea of an organization of optometrists who would travel into developing areas of the world and provide much-needed eye care to the people of those countries. Dr. Harms was a spiritual person who believed that his career in optometry was meant to allow him to serve others in a humanitarian way and he began to look for other like-minded Kansas ODs to join him in this project....

...It was decided that we (VOSH) would work through mission groups, service organizations and other church affiliated entities who could help identify the areas of Caribbean and Central American countries where the need was greatest, in places where we would be welcomed by those groups, and could provide sponsors in country. In keeping with the spirit of the name, this project was to be strictly voluntary and the participants would provide their own transportation and equipment, as well as lodging and meals as necessary." *(Quote by Dave Reynolds, OD, FAAO in the Kansas Optometric Journal, January-March 2004.)*

Planting the "seeds" of professional maturity and core values in fellow optometrists

*Dr. Harms sets the stage for volunteering among fellow optometrists in this speech entitled "**Professional Maturity**" presented to the Kansas Optometric Association, 1978*

"The following remarks are based on the assumption that professional men who are involved in the healing arts, whether it be optometry, dentistry, or medicine, chose their profession

3

because they wanted to be involved in rendering a specialized service to humanity. I feel confident that this assumption is correct. Many of my colleagues have expressed interest in extending their service beyond the realm of their own office and community. Whether it be foreign service or with underprivileged groups within our country, it could range from a short-term service of several days to a longer-term service of several weeks to a long-term service of a year or more. This is a real encouraging trend. It is a sign of Optometry reaching a higher level of professional maturity. We should do all we can to encourage this type of philosophy.

In more recent years quite a few Optometrists from the United States have rendered foreign Optometric services, and have felt greatly enriched and rewarded because of it. Medicine and dentistry are doing a considerable amount of this type of work now, and there are opportunities where Optometry can cooperate with these other disciplines and go out as inter professional teams. I recently learned about a foursome medical practice in Indiana in which one of the practitioners takes his turn in doing foreign medical service each year, while he continues to share in the income of the practice while he is gone. Numerous Optometrists are associating into joint practices, which would make the long-term type of service more feasible. The Christian Medical Society, which is a nation-wide organization with headquarters in Los Angeles, California, does a lot of medical work abroad and more recently it has involved dentistry in its projects. One of the medical doctors, who is a member of this organization, informed me that they would like to involve Optometrists in some of their projects. It is gratifying to see that in recent schools of Optometry, and together with a faculty member, have gone out to render foreign Optometric service for several weeks between semesters or during the summer months. In most of these projects the students raised their own money to finance it, but the experience and inspiration which they gained was invaluable. I consider the opportunity which I had two years ago of serving on an interprofessional team in Haiti one of the most rewarding experiences of my professional career.

Since there is considerable interest among Kansas Optometrists to extend their services to others in this manner, I would like to propose to the Executive Board of the Kansas Optometric Association that they give consideration to the possibility of appointing an ad hoc committee, which would be charged with the responsibility of doing some research on this and developing a plan of action. If such plan could be initiated, and if Kansas Optometrists would make themselves available when possible for this type of service, it would pay good dividends. It would mean enrichment and renewal for the Optometrist who volunteers his services. It would give our profession a new challenge. Yes, it would even speak to our restless "Now Generation," and tell them that Optometry is a segment of the "establishment" who are concerned about human needs, and do something about it!

I am proud to be an Optometrist – especially a Kansas Optometrist. I sincerely believe that we are ready to meet the challenge of extending our services in this manner. History might well identify this as another chapter which provided a new dimension and additional professional maturity to Kansas optometry."

That speech set the stage that Dr. Harms used to build an organization. Many, many conversations expanded upon this vision. His compassion and persistence proved to be a powerful force in bringing volunteers to action.

Formation of VOSH Kansas

Building consensus with Kansas OD's
The following speech helped secure at least thirty-five optometrist's interest in serving. *(Except from Dr. Franklin*

Harms in the November 1973 Journal of the American Optometric Association, Vol. 44, No. 11.)

"A plan and name for such an organization was recommended to the KOA (Kansas Optometric Association) Board, which was adopted. It was later decided that VOSH would possibly function most effectively under the Kansas Optometric Foundation, Inc., of which now it is a department.

It must be explained that Kansas optometrists do not take any credit for having originated the idea of eye projects, because they have not. It is men like Dr. Reynold F. Swanson, who has been on 12 consecutive projects to Haiti, and many others, who have been an inspiration and help to us. A number of our optometric colleges have carried out projects like this, of which "SOSH" of Pennsylvania College of Optometry and the New England College of Optometry are good examples. The American Optometric Student Association (AOSA, which is made up of about 3,000 student members from our optometric colleges,) now has a committee which is projecting and planning similar projects. Medicine and dentistry have done a lot of this type of service through organization such as the Christian Medical Society, Medical Missions, Good Samaritans, Health Care Missions, Project Concern, Hope, MAP, and many others. Vision care often has not been included. But there is a real need for it.

What is unique about the Kansas Project is that, to my knowledge, it is possibly the first attempt to organize professional manpower on a statewide basis by a state professional association for such volunteer services. It has been a real inspiration to find optometrists from all over the state volunteering to assist in every phase of the VOSH program, including 8 optometrists who want to fly their private planes into Mexico to participate in a series of "Fly-In" eye projects. The Board of Directors of both the Kansas Optometric Association and the Kansas Optometric Foundation has been most helpful and cooperative."

A First! Volunteer Optometric Services to Humanity is formed in Kansas

In January of 1972 nine optometrists lead by Dr. Harms met to organize. A plan and name for this organization were recommended to the Kansas Optometric Association Board and it was decided that the project would be identified as Volunteer Optometric Services to Humanity commonly identified with the acronym VOSH. Shortly after, it was decided that VOSH would function most effectively under the Kansas Optometric Foundation, Inc. As such, the first VOSH Organization came into being as a department of the Kansas Optometric Foundation. This move served them well as they did not need to incorporate, yet they acquired the non-profit charitable contribution status. Kansas VOSH became the first to organize professional manpower on a statewide basis by a state professional organization for such volunteer services.

The initial Kansas VOSH committee consisted of the following ODs: Franklin Harms, Hillsboro, chairman; N.E. (Norm) Abrahams, Hillsboro, secretary; O.R. (Rich) Morlong, Clay Center, treasurer; Jack Landes, Wichita; David Reynolds, Topeka; and Herb White, Dodge City, ophthalmic materials section; Robert Whittaker, Augusta, and M.D. Torrence, Hutchinson, needs section; and David Benelli, Pittsburgh, portable equipment section.

Transition from VOSH organization to first outreach mission

Dr. O.R. (Rich) Morlong, the founding treasurer of VOSH-Kansas reflects on this historic time as the group moved toward organizing their first mission trip. He shares, "At the Kansas Optometric Association (KOA) Convention April 1972 the VOSH Committee was busy trying to get it together.

We decided a face-to-face meeting was necessary after a busy Convention so I volunteered to host a committee meeting at our house in Clay Center, Kansas. This would have been early summer 1972.

Drs. Harms, Abrahams and Landes flew to Clay Center and we sat around a card table in our living room and discussed costs, logistics, would we be accepted by foreigners, and a million 'what-ifs'. It finally got down to "I'll go if you'll go." We all shook hands and agreed it was a go. The balance of the team going somewhere was to be Dr. Benelli, Dr. Morlong and Dr. Jim Enns the trip's ophthalmologist from Newton Kansas. VOSH was alive! The team members were all committee members which really helped future trips.

Dr. Harms had been talking with a Seventh Day Adventist group looking for a suitable site with needs. He settled on Montemorelos, Mexico and things moved rapidly.

The ophthalmic materials section was notified it was to be a go and to get glasses gathered and processed. We had discussed at my house what the Rx priorities might be and nobody knew. We soon discovered that Mexican myopes were scarce as 'hen's teeth'.

It was now October 1972 and my next recollection is being inside the aircraft hangar in Hillsboro Kansas loading gear into Dr Abrahams' shiny Cherokee hours before daylight. At the same time Dr Jim Enns, the expedition's ophthalmologist, was loading gear into a brand new Bellanca aircraft at Newton. Shortly we were airborne and the project was actually happening."

This as well as the next section came from a series of telephone interviews with Dr. Morlong as well as references from several articles in the Kansas Optometric Journal (Jan-March 2004).

First VOSH Mission

VOSH Kansas was ready to go. The founding members were ready to do what they only heard Dr. Harms talk about.

The first mission was a fly-in to Montemorales, Mexico in the fall of 1972. One of the optometrists and one of the ophthalmologists volunteered to fly their own private planes. Literally barrels of glasses were taken on this first trip. The glasses were collected by Kansas Lions Sight Foundation, Kiwanis and Rotary clubs.

According to Dr. Norm Abrahams, optometrist and one of the two Kansas pilots recalls, "When the team arrived at the border in Redosa, Mexico, customs agents could not believe this group would take all those glasses into Mexico and not try to sell them for a profit. For this reason, the team was forced to leave one person behind (known thereafter as 'the hostage') and he was replaced with an armed Mexican representative. Dr. Rich Morlong, another team member, recalled the guard having guns strapped all over himself. During the flight, the Mexican guard, who apparently had never been in a plane previously, was hanging out the window, pointing his gun at everything and acting like he was shooting it."

After a long flight the plane approached the dirt landing strip just outside of town. Dr. Morlong recalls that as they approached the landing strip, they realized that it was covered with small Mexican burros. When the pilots saw this they called each other on their radio. Dr. Jim Enns, the ophthalmologist and second pilot decided he would "buzz" the landing strip to chase the burros away. Dr. Morlong later commented, "Those burros moved so fast they likely ended up somewhere in South America." Once the Mexican officials were convinced the VOSH team was truly in the country to give vision to those in-need, one of the pilots was allowed to go back and claim the 'hostage'."

(Courtesy of Dr. Morlong)

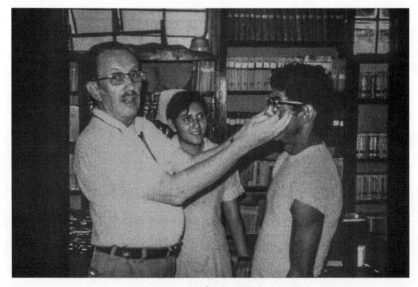

(Courtesy of Dr. Morlong)

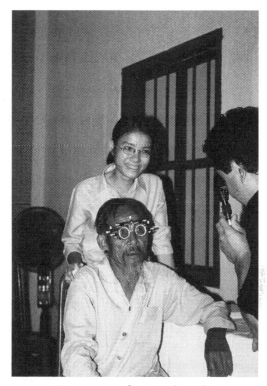

(Courtesy of Dr. Dale Cole)

(Courtesy of Dr. Dale Cole)

Eyeglass acquisitions in 1972

Dr. Herb White, as a founding member of VOSH Kansas, was in charge of the ophthalmic materials section located in his home town of Dodge City, Kansas. In the _Kansas Optometric Journal_ Jan-March 2004 Dr. White explains how VOSH-Kansas got the glasses for their mission trips.

"Dr. Frank Harms called me in October of 1972. He asked if I was interested in joining the Haiti VOSH Mission sponsored by the Seventh Day Adventists. I replied that I was and that I wanted my oldest daughter, Julie, to join us. Because of my seventeen years of experience with the Lions Vision Committee he further asked if I would help to get their assistance in collecting recycled glasses.

The Lions members had already set up a collection program for old glasses in this period. The local Lions collected and sorted out unusable lenses, frames and cases. They also divided the gold from the plastic because all the gold was sent to the Kansas Lions Sight Foundation who used the funds for a money making project. To get the Lions' cooperation it was my job to meet with the KLSF. They were as enthusiastic about helping the needy of the third world as we were. The directors, Gib Shafer (Jayhawk Optical) and Newt Bressie (McPherson Lion), were particularly helpful.

Before each VOSH Mission, the Optometrists planning to go (on the trip) were held responsible for neutralizing, labeling and preparing glasses for shipping. When we got to our destination the glasses were randomly placed on several tables. In the case of Haiti, we had 3,700 pairs.

After they got the results from the optometrists' retinoscope Rx, one OD, one optician, and several helpers would sort through the piles of glasses to pick out the best Rx for the needy patient.

This is how dispensing was handled in the very beginning."...

..."Obviously, the equipment and supplies we would take on trips had to include eyeglasses. The Lions Clubs had been collecting used spectacles and it was decided to follow this model of obtaining eyewear as the cost of providing new lenses and frames would be prohibitive, not to mention the almost impossible logistics of sending prescriptions back to the project areas. A drive was initiated asking Kansas optometrists to start collecting used eyeglasses from their patients and the labs were asked to contribute any old or discontinued frames and reject lenses. Many offices participated in the collection of used spectacles and most ODs noticed an immediate interest on the part of their patients and their desire to be at least passive participants in such a worthwhile endeavor. The task of collecting, neutralizing and categorizing the used eyewear fell on the shoulders of the doctors who were going to be going on the trips and many "neutralizing" sessions were held throughout the state thus bringing many ODs and their staff together for a common purpose. The power of positive public relations appeal was evident even before the first trip out of the country."

C. Ellis Potter, OD, FAAO, FVI, wrote further about these beginning efforts to create VOSH. He was also responsible for collecting and securing a large number of articles about the formation of VOSH-Kansas in the <u>Kansas Optometric Journal</u>, of which he was editor. He writes;

*"VOSH is a story of idealistic service to mankind.
It is another of the great stories of the Kansas Optometric heritage.
It, in many respects, seems like a fantasy, but it is a true story.
Those of you who have participated in VOSH know its impact."*

Led by the Kansas Chapter, trips in the early days were organized by one to two optometrists with the guidance of Dr. Harms. Following the death of Dr. Harms, Dr. Landes, along with Dr. Bill and Susan Bendelman of Wakeeney, Kansas, took over the leadership roles. Upon the passing of Dr. Landes in 1984, Dr. Don Kuehn of Russell, Kansas and Dr. Dale Cole of Salina, Kansas became co-chairmen and continued to serve in that capacity. Assisting the leadership on the Kansas VOSH committee were Drs. David Crum of August, and Ellis Potter of Iola, Steve Flory of Lawrence, Eldon Gray of Kinsley, Dennis Hoss of Lawrence, and Randy Pohlenz of Topeka.

This **personal testament to Dr. Harms** was written by his co-founder and key VOSH partner Norm Abrahams, OD from North Newton, Kansas. Norm's words follow as they were printed in the Kansas Optometric Journal January-March 2004.

"My friend Franklin Harms, OD, has been described as being organized, detail oriented and enthusiastic.

I agree with all of these descriptions of the man who had the vision of VOSH, but I would add another characteristic: he was persuasive. He would stop at nothing if he had an idea that he knew would work. His late night phone calls have become legend, partially because it was an uninterrupted time to talk, but also because many times he would talk and talk until he persuaded you, either to do a job, join a team, or help in other ways.

I practiced in the same town as my friend, and although we were friendly competitors, our friendship grew quite close with the VOSHers. Our common religious background as Mennonites and our creed to help the unfortunate were, in part, our underlying motivation. He and I would frequently meet to exchange ideas, to find ways to organize, and to foster the program. Dr. Harms was the driver. He had the ideas and the vision. I worked more as a recorder of the progress of the mission trips.

The name VOSH (Volunteer Optometric Service to Humanity) seemed to come without thought, discussion or debate. It contained everything that the organization meant: Volunteers, Optometrists, Humanitarian Service.

After his trip in 1969 with the medical group mission to Haiti, a multidisciplinary group of doctors, he returned charged with the idea that Kansas Optometrists could do something similar. He promoted the idea every chance he could; chiefly at the Kansas Optometric Convention, zone meetings and study groups. He worked day and night promoting it to Kansas Optometrists and eventually to the American Optometric Association. With the VOSH REPORTS at the Kansas Optometric Association meetings there was tremendous interest, much inquiry and great response. It was such a good idea that there was never any trouble securing volunteer doctors. The project grew and grew.

My personal satisfaction and best memories of my VOSH experience are:

1. To have my family accompany me on almost every trip and
2. As a pilot, to combine my interest in flying with service. I remember distinctly that the landing strip of the first mission was a cow pasture. The cows had to be shooed away before we could take off.

My family and I are thrilled and rewarded from our experience. It has been among the best things I have ever done, inside or outside of Optometry.

Franklin would have been pleased with the success of VOSH, but he wouldn't be surprised, for he had the vision that the program would work."

"Your career is not complete until you have participated in a VOSH eye care mission." Dr. Franklin Harms

Kansas VOSH had been successfully formed with great leadership and a good solid start, but, what is to be done within the other states? What about the rest of the world? Where do we go from here?

The 1970's

By the mid 1970's the war in Vietnam had ended and increased attention shifted toward women's liberation, nuclear proliferation, and environmentalism. Our daily lives became punctuated with Lava Lamps, pet rocks and the iconic yellow "smiley face." If you were a young adult you might have slept in a water bed, sat in a bean bag chair and maybe even had a disco ball hanging from your ceiling.

The late 1970's fostered a renewed influence of conservatism and growing interest in non-profit organizations serving others.

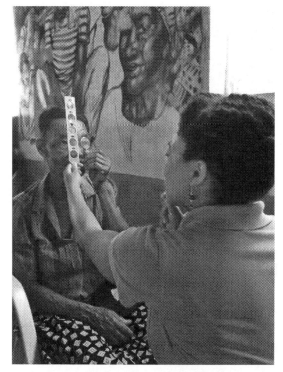

(Courtesy of Dr. Dale Cole)

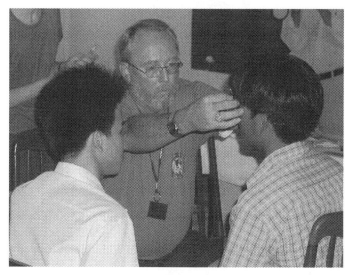

(Courtesy of Dr. Dale Cole)

Becoming VOSH/Interstate
1975

By this time state chapters were springing up around the nation. It became clear that uniting forces provided an opportunity to share ideas and resources.

The next step in the evolution of VOSH started in January of 1974 following an article written by Dr. Harms in the November, 1973 issue of the _Journal of the American Optometric Association_.

"In February 1974, a nationwide VOSH conference in Wichita, KS drew eye care professionals from around America. Eighteen states were represented at this landmark VOSH event. Attendees included fifty optometrists, opticians and ophthalmologists. Four strong chapters had already formed and brought strong leadership to the group:

- VOSH-Kansas: Franklin Harms, OD, Chairman
- VOSH-Indiana: Walter Marshall, OD, Chairman
- VOSH-Minnesota: Russell Dorland, OD, Chairman
- VOSH-Iowa: Stephen B. Rose, OD, Chairman
- Two student groups, both Volunteer Optometric Services to Haiti groups, were in existence at the time at New England College of Optometry and at Pennsylvania College of Optometry.

In September 1975, a nationwide symposium took place in Kansas City, Missouri and VOSH was officially organized on a national level as VOSH/Interstate.

Dr. Harms continued to work tirelessly to advance VOSH/Interstate, both administratively and in the field. Not surprisingly just three years later, in 1978, thirty nine states boasted active chapters. Dr. Harms' comment to any optometrist he ran into was, 'Your optometric career is not complete until you have participated in a VOSH eye care mission."

Dr. Stephen Rose tells of the formation in his article "VOSH Revisited" in the Journal of the American Optometric Association, Vol. 55, #9, September, 1984.

"**VOSH/Interstate** was formed to coordinate, develop and inform new state chapters. By 1976 Illinois, Missouri and Arkansas had developed their own chapters and taken "I Care" missions. A multitude of other states would soon follow either with their own missions or providing personnel for other states' missions.

Growth pangs of VOSH/Interstate now created some serious logistical problems. This was and is of course an organization staffed by volunteers, who albeit eager to serve, must also make a living – VOSH feeds the soul, not the pocket. As the need rapidly rose in the middle 70's the ability to handle the "traffic" simply became too great for the financial and personnel pool. Dr. Harm's dream of creating a nationwide organization to serve thousands of disadvantaged people around the world had materialized, but without the finances and paid staff to handle this burgeoning giant, the effectiveness of VOSH/Interstate became doubtful. As many as forty states were now to a greater or lesser degree requesting information and guidance. The effort to keep VOSH/Interstate running smoothly became too great. In 1978 Dr. Harms died. (It was also stated that he died from a heart attack while preparing a mailing of VOSH information to potential volunteers.) Many believe from overwork and frustration in not being able to carry the burden of his creation. No man could have."

Founding of VOSH/International
1979

"Volunteer Optometric Services to Humanity (VOSH) is a federation of American optometrists dedicated to the improvement of vision of disadvantaged people around the world."

Until this time in history, VOSH-Kansas was a committee under the Kansas Optometric Foundation and VOSH/Interstate was a group of interested optometrists from a number of states. The movement was building momentum and became poised for an official organization as a non-profit corporation with officers and bylaws on its own volition.

VOSH/International was founded, becoming a legal entity in 1979 (July resolution and October Incorporations papers received).

Dr. Stephen Rose continues in the <u>Journal</u> <u>of</u> <u>the</u> <u>American</u> <u>Optometric</u> <u>Association</u> Volume 55, Number 9, September, 1984:

"A letter dated September 18, 1978 from David Reynolds, OD, editor of the <u>Kansas</u> <u>Optometric</u> <u>Journal</u> to Eugene McCrary, OD, chairman, AOA (American Optometric Association) International Affairs Committee with copies to other AOA and VOSH/Interstate officers may have been the stimulus that kept VOSH going."

"New officers were elected and an advisory committee appointed. Legal matters pertaining to establishment of VOSH as a non-profit corporation as well as financial assistance was donated by VOSH-Indiana. Bylaws were established. Additional financial aid was supplied by VOSH-Illinois, VOSH-Minnesota, and the North Central States optometric Conference. State membership and International received a dues increase. Dr. Ray Mienheartt, Brazil, Indiana, volunteered his printing skills to disseminate information to anyone requested it and VOSH/ Interstate became VOSH/International."

First Bylaws of VOSH/International (1980)

The primary source of this section came from email communication and phone conversations with Dr. Bud Falkenhain.
It had been self-evident that VOSH/International understood that to be independent they needed their own bylaws to legally operate as a corporation. The original founders understood that now was the time for movement to another level with more sustainability, directionality, and continuity.

The conversations and opinions of the founders expressed feelings of how this new organization should be structured. The American Optometric Association supported this independence and agreed to provide the assistance of Tom Eichhorst, Legal Counsel for the American Optometric Association in St. Louis, Missouri.

In the summer of 1979 the first set of bylaws for this new VOSH Organization were created. The framers of the bylaws included, Tom Eichhorst, legal counsel for the American Optometric Association, Dr. Walter Marshall of Indiana VOSH, Dr. Bud Falkenhein of Missouri VOSH, and Dr. McCrary, American Optometric Association Chairman of International Affairs. Several others contributed to the process as well.

Over a four month period these creators of the first bylaws met in Tom Eichorst's office in St. Louis. They gathered with a daunting task laying before them - creating the blueprint for which VOSH/International was being defined for the foreseeable future. Being the first time in a unique circumstance, these early pioneers set about the task of determining the language that would embody our first operational bylaws.

Dr. Falkenhain felt strongly, and the others agreed, that the Presidency should be a two-year term. They also felt that in order to maintain a regular rotation of talent and ideas, the Presidency would be limited to a one term maximum.

The contingent agreed which created a functioning Board of Directors of their own non-profit corporation.

Leading up to this time VOSH was rather informal and basic, being propelled forward by a strong sense of mission, purpose and vision. In 1979, VOSH/International was created – it grew its own programs and governance.

The original 1979 bylaws, although not available in the records, most original items are reflected in the 1982 set of bylaws available in VOSH Archives include:

- Chapters, including SVOSH, were the members (not individuals), each having one vote. A quorum was defined as one-fifth of the member chapters.
- International Board of Directors (all of which are officers) consists of five members with 3-year terms each. The Board elects one-year term President, President Elect, 1st Vice President, 2nd Vice President and Secretary-Treasurer. (Presidents will have 'moved up' in a four-year ascending rotation)
- General membership (one voting representative per chapter) meetings were conducted annually with the President's option to call emergency meetings.

Note: In 1991 the Bylaws were changed so that chapters had representation on the expanded board with supervisory powers of finances, budgets, policies and elections. The "Executive Committee (officers)" was given the power of conducting business. In both cases the International President was the 'Chief Executive Officer' (CEO).

First Articles of Incorporation: VOSH/International
(October 12, 1979)

During formation of VOSH/International, Indiana provided legal counsel as well a financial support for the administration of the expansion of VOSH. With this commitment Dr. Walter Marshall of Indiana-VOSH proceeded with the incorporation of "Volunteer Optometric Services to Humanity – International" (VOSH) under the laws of Indiana. Articles of Incorporation were issued October 12, 1979.

Dr. Stephen Rose talks about the early years of VOSH/ International *in his article "**VOSH Revisited**" in the September 1984 issue of the Journal of the American Optometric Association, Volume 55, Number 9.*

"April 20, 1980 the officers of VOSH/International and leaders of the active VOSH states were invited to conference in Chicago, Illinois by officers of the Illinois Optometric Association. Purpose of the conference was to explore the possibility of expanding the scope of VOSH/International.

Dr. Al Bucar, then trustee of the American Optometric Association and currently president of the AOA, suggested that VOSH/International could increase its visibility and effectiveness by becoming one of the task forces of the American Optometric Association. This had been proposed to him by the executive director of the AOA. Project ORBIS, AID (Agency for International Development), SEE (Surgical Eye Expeditions), and military air transportation were the principal areas discussed."

Notes from phone conversations with Dr. Falkenhain, November 2-15, 2015: Dr. Bud Falkenhain also attended this meeting and suggests that at the meeting onset, VOSH felt that it offered a lot to the American Optometric Association as a humanitarian gesture or outreach function. He suggests that the American Optometric Association Trustee Dr. Bucar was reluctant to have VOSH operate under the jurisdiction of the AOA – possibly because of missions outside of American jurisdiction, possible liability issues, and the charitable purpose VOSH represented.

So in summation, it is most likely that, although individual opinions varied, both parties embraced their own independence and moved on amicably.

Dr. Rose goes on to explain the formation of VOSH/ International in the September 1984 issue of the <u>Journal of the American Optometric Association</u>, Volume 55, Number 9.

"Very little action resulted from this meeting. The reason was simple: the concept of VOSH mandates its independence – a singular approach to solving the problems for which it was created . . . to be not the arm of any other primary organization . . . to create its own light, not pale in the shadow of others. This concept has been maintained, but, now, with a difference. VOSH is no longer an organization providing only better vision to the less fortunate people of the world; it has become an organization of men, women and young people who are looked upon as caring about others without ulterior motivation. The image that VOSH creates, therefore, reflects upon America and upon the profession of optometry. Consequently, VOSH should not ignore this reflection but work to make it even better. This will be achieved through better cooperation with the American Optometric Association and state and federal agencies, but still as an independent body."

This issue of VOSH/International's relationship with the American Optometric Association was revisited several times in the few years following its formation. Ultimately the relationship evolved to be most beneficial to both organizations and to the eye care profession as a whole. VOSH became known as the volunteer outreach partner to the American Optometric Association in the eyecare profession. VOSH owes its existence, largely to the networking opportunities presented by the relationship.

VOSH Through the Years
With Presidential Insights

With the formation of VOSH/International the 1980's emerged. It was a time of Yuppies, Reaganomics, Madonna and Ray-Ban sunglasses. AIDS was a lingering fear as globalization spread both in international corporations and VOSH. Americans moved toward conservatism as populations migrated away from the North and Midwest toward the South and Southwest.

New electronic devices made it possible to record video with a VCR and even to have our own personal computer! Information technology is born!

Providing islands of care in a sea of poverty

Dr. Bud Falkenhain and Dr. Russ Dorland sat in a voluminous, empty lecture hall following a full day of meetings. This was when they first met back in 1975 at the "Heart of America" Conference in Kansas City. Both were tired; their thoughts flickered as their shared excitement for what VOSH was doing ignited their conversation. They talked for two and a half hours about VOSH – its challenges and opportunities as well as a nettle of frustrations.

VOSH Chapters were beginning to gather momentum in several states with many others showing interest. VOSH/Interstate having recently formed had little or no resources just an idea driven by Dr. Franklin Harms with a very powerful vision!

Just as mission trips were self-organized and self-funded, so too was the administrative outreach to other states self-organized and self-funded. As momentum grew, this put a great deal of stress on individual time and finances. Late at night in that empty lecture hall Dr. Dorland expressed some frustration with his spending twelve thousand dollars for secretarial assistance to help reach out to other states promoting VOSH. He had hoped that the American Optometric Association would help defray those expenses but that was not to be. VOSH was on its own.

1979-81 Dr. Russ Dorland becomes first President of VOSH/International

As history unfolds, Russ and Bud took the leadership torch of VOSH from the "father" of VOSH Dr. Franklin Harms. Dr. Russ Dorland became the first President under the new corporate entity VOSH/International. His administrative actions set the course for future administrations.

As the early 1980's emerged as many as thirty-nine states had either formed or expressed a serious interest in forming VOSH chapters. Dr. Russ Dorland shared this vision and connected with volunteers for eye care missions. Being the President, he led with a well-mannered, well-dressed confident presence.

Dr. Dorland knew Dr. Harms from the beginning being a classmate of his in optometry school. Very early in Dr. Dorland's career he participated as a Mennonite in many church mission trips. While on these missions he noticed that women were having a difficult time seeing to sew. In these poorer communities sewing was a primary way in which women served the needs of their family and their community. Russ thought to himself, if I can put a few pair of reading glasses in my suitcase each trip, I can help these ladies, enabling them to return to their avocation of contributing through sewing.

Reflecting, he shared "this is the whole idea about how VOSH came about!" He told this and other stories about VOSH as he projected his vision to others in the eye care fields.

VOSH was preparing for a long record of reaching out across the world, correcting vision for those who could not afford nor have access to eyecare and glasses.

The first International President died on December 22, 1989, just eight years after his presidency. The following farewell address tells what kind of man he was. In remembrance of the first VOSH/International President, this "Farewell to a Founding Father" was printed in the VOSH/International Newsletter, April 1990.

Russ Dorland, OD Farewell to a Founding Father First President of VOSH/International

"It is with great sadness that Minnesota VOSH announces the death of its founding father and its greatest leader, Dr. Russ Dorland. Russ died of cancer December 22, 1989. He was 67. What else can you say, but Russ did it all. He was an optometry school classmate of Dr. Franklin Harms, the founder of VOSH/International. He led Minnesota VOSH for many years and was the first president of VOSH/International. He was the person responsible for helping to start several other state chapters and the fire that got VOSH's first foreign chapter going in England, called Vision Aid Overseas, an organization that now carries out several missions a year on its own. He was the person who led Minnesota VOSH's greatest adventures into Africa and India. And even though married and several children still at home, he spent three months in a refugee camp in Thailand, caring for Cambodian refugees. He was truly a caring man. Russ was the guy who put Minnesota on the map in VOSH circles and earned us the respect we still have today. We will never be able to replace Russ, for he accomplished in his 67 years more that what an average man could only hope to in 150 years. And Russ enjoyed it all. You could tell it the in the sparkle that he always had in his eyes and the big smile on his face. He is survived by his wife Dolores and twelve children. We miss him a lot."

Vision Aid Overseas (VAO)

Perhaps Dr. Russ Dorland's greatest legacy he left to the world was in spreading the VOSH concept to Europe and Africa. Vision Aid Overseas (VAO) never officially was a part of VOSH, but they were born of VOSH. The standard VOSH model of growth became VAO's beginning. That model was to invite eye care professional from other states on a mission with you; after spending a week living and working together, you not only get the passion, but you get the knowledge of implementation.

VAO formed in 1985 becoming an independent British version of VOSH. VAO, in its first ten years has conducted 45 overseas projects with an emphasis on Cameroon, Gambia, Ghana, Kenya, Malawi, Sierra Leone, Swaziland, Tanzania, and Uganda. Dr. Darrell Groman, a VOSH board member from Ohio went to England to share in the celebration of VAO's tenth anniversary. Upon returning he wrote an article in the *VOSH/ International Newsletter, July 1996 entitled "Vision Aid Overseas observes Tenth Anniversary."* In this article he writes about the formation of VAO.

"The late Dr. Russell Dorland, first president of VOSH/ International and director of VOSH-Minnesota, organized this mission with an unusual international team of optometrists from Australia, Denmark, the United Kingdom, and the United States. Brian Ellis of Essex, England served as co-leader. Forty-five volunteers divided up to serve simultaneously in six mission cities across Tanzania. The sixteen individuals from the United Kingdom returned home with such enthusiasm, that they organized their own group, named Vision Aid Overseas. Brian Ellis served as Founder Director of Vision Aid Overseas."

Legacy

Dr. Harms' and Dr. Dorland's legacy is showing VOSH how to change the world – share the mission experience – create new leaders – and in turn new leaders create new leaders.

1981-83 Dr. Bud Falkenhain is second President of VOSH/International

In 1977 Dr. Franklin Harms called Dr. Bud Falkenhain. Bud had known Dr. Harms from several previous discussions at optometric conferences. He was curious to know why Dr. Harms was calling him. Dr. Harms lead by asking, "Would you like to go to Nicaragua?" Bud said "Yes, I would." Franklin replied "Well, you've got two weeks to get five hundred pairs of glasses," then proceeded to explain the details to Bud.

This forthright experience of seeking volunteers was pretty common in those days. Dr. Falkenhain went to Nicaragua, gave his life to helping people see, and brought VOSH back to Missouri. Dr. Falkenhain eventually became the second President of VOSH serving 1981 to 1983.

As President, Dr. Falkenhain continued the primary strategy of building, supporting and sustaining State Chapters of VOSH because State Chapters were organizing and conducting vision care missions. Support included communication by providing materials written by Dr. Harms explaining details of organizing mission trips, supply acquisition, chapter organization models and other items that would help state VOSH chapters be successful.

Under this leadership an effective strategy to building chapters was encouraged.

Interested optometrists from other states were invited to join mission trips so they would be personally exposed to the passion of giving sight and the skill set to organize. This system became widely successful continuing for many years as the main strategy for building new chapters and for creating new mission outreach trips.

Dr. Falkenhain early on felt that an ideal would be for one chapter to be connected to one country in service. After choosing Missouri's one county, El Salvador, a rampant civil war broke out before their first mission trip. Needless to say, that unanticipated experience put a stop to that approach.

Also in the early 1980's the VOSH Board encouraged other countries to form their own VOSH Chapter and conduct their own missions. Although this didn't happen until the following decade, this seed of future growth became firmly planted.

U.S. President Ronald Reagan recognizes Dr. Bud Falkenhain and VOSH/International with "Outstanding Volunteer Award"

The primary source of this section came from email communication and phone conversations with Dr. Bud Falkenhain.

In 1985 Dr. Falkenhain, while routinely going through his mail, noticed that one letter stood out. He looked closer; that letter was from the White House. Well, he thought this was a "big deal" and quickly opened it. He slowly read the letter; it was from President Ronald Reagan at the White House. It explained that he, and VOSH/International, was being chosen to be recognized with the "Outstanding Volunteer Award" to be presented at the White House in Washington, D.C. He thought again "this is a big deal"!

The letter explained that sixteen people in America were chosen to receive an "Outstanding Volunteer Award" from the President. His was in the "International" category. Other winners that year included "The Olympic Committee" for the Los Angeles Olympics and "MADD," headquartered in Philadelphia. Several years later "Doctors without Borders" won the award in the same International category.

This award was to recognize a volunteer in an organization that had contributed not only in a meaningful and influential way but also in an originally unique manner.

Soon after he received a phone call from the White House giving him the details about his travel arrangements and what would be happening during his visit to Washington, D.C. Arrangements were made for Dr. Falkenhain and his wife Linda to stay in a hotel within walking distance to the White House.

Before the presentation along with many United States Senators and Representatives they attended several receptions to honor the recipients.

On the day of the presentation, Dr. Falkenhain remembers George Romney coming and picking he and his wife up from the hotel and escorting them as he walked with them to the White House and through security. Also walking with them was a lady from the selection committee. She said that "the committee had a hard time deciding whether to give you (VOSH) or the American Red Cross recognition. They ended up choosing you and VOSH because yours was such a new and unusual concept."

When they arrived Dr. Falkenhain and Linda were escorted to the East Room and seated at a table of eight with others including the then Vice President George H. W. Bush.

When Dr. Falkenhain was called forward he walked onto the stage and shook hands with President Ronald Reagan who proceeded to talk about Dr. Falkenhain, VOSH and the unique way in which they were addressing the eye care needs of the world. Throughout the ceremony fifty to sixty members of the Press Corp flashed photos from behind a roped-off area.

Three winners including Dr. Falkenhain and VOSH were invited to be interviewed on the "Today Show" by Willard Scott. They stayed in town to do this interview on the following day. It was a success! The VOSH name became known by millions!

1983-85 Dr. Stephen Rose assumes VOSH/ International Presidency

Dr. Rose was active in his church and interested in doing what he could for humanity. One evening in the early 1970's he attended a talk at the church where he was a member. The talk was delivered by a local dentist who had recently returned from a foreign mission trip to provide dental services. Dr. Rose listened and became intrigued by what he was hearing. He thought to himself that this same kind of program would work with optometry and eye care.

Soon after he saw an article in the American Optometric Association Journal and he called the contact who happened to be Dr. Franklin Harms. Not only did Dr. Rose get information by talking on the phone with Dr. Harms but also attended a meeting in Kansas to learn more about how to organize an eye care mission.

Preparing himself Dr. Rose next reached out to contact fellow optometrists. It took him about nine months to build a core group and to develop plans. He also contacted "Medical Group Missions" who agreed to sponsor him and his Iowa optometrists.

Dr. Stephen Rose led his first VOSH mission to the Dominican Republic with a group of Iowa optometrists (1973 or 1974) which became known as VOSH-Iowa. With this act he established his commitment to a cause greater than himself.

After participating in a number of missions, Dr. Stephen Rose took the presidency of VOSH/International in 1983. His primary purpose was to build more VOSH Chapters in other states. As part of this larger purpose his administration sought out more contacts internationally that needed and would host eye care missions in other countries. During the early 1980's the focus was to develop hosts and sponsors to serve Mexico and other Central and South American countries. Outreach to Jamaica also occurred since it also seemed to have access for teams and needs similar to what was seen in Haiti.

During this time VOSH/International had on-site Annual Meetings in the fall as well as a mid-year Board of Directors meeting. In 1984 VOSH/International met in Chicago, Illinois.

In 1984 Dr. Stephen Rose gave this **status report** for VOSH/International *reprinted in his article "VOSH Revisited" in the September 1984 issue of the Journal of the American Optometric Association, Volume 55.*

"VOSH/International is now beginning to utilize its resources without jeopardizing its independence. The communications, legal and informational resources of AOA have been made available. National, international and church agencies are utilized as the need exists or opportunity arises.

Lions clubs, both domestic and foreign, are very effective as collectors of old glasses and as hosts in the countries visited.

(As of 1984) The administrative structures of VOSH/International consists of five officers: President, Stephen B. Rose, OD; President Elect Thomas Henley, OD; 1st Vice President, Charles Gray, OD; 2nd Vice President, Glade F. Whitworth, OD; Secretary-Treasurer, Jon Thayer, Sr., OD; and advisory committee chaired by the immediate past president, V.E. Falkenhain, OD, and AOA staff liaison, Alice Martin; and a newsletter editor, Ray Mienheartt, OD. Officers are elected for one year with staggered terms. No two officers can be elected from the same state. Only states and optometric schools with VOSH/International membership can vote, with only one vote per state or school.

Financial support comes from many sources – all quite limited. State membership at $50.00 provides about 20% of the income. Personal memberships are $15.00 which produces another 20%. Several state VOSH chapters and private individuals provide the remaining 60%.

Annual budget runs around $3,000. This is a very limiting factor, but, hopefully will be surmounted this year. Renewed emphasis on membership structure similar to optometric state and national membership is in process. Private donations are being sought on a much broader scale.

With the exception of the communist and arctic countries, VOSH has served in most of the geographical areas of the world requiring optometric care. Greatest emphasis, of course, has been in the Caribbean and Latin American area simply because access makes it more affordable.

All VOSH missions have been successful. This is measured in terms of helping people and cooperation of host groups. "Yankee, go home" is never encountered. In fact just the opposite! VOSH teams are always invited back to the same site time after time. Some teams have returned to the same site every year.

Payment of services rendered is in the gratitude from the people served. No language barrier exists here. No one misunderstands the big smile, warm hug, tears of joy, and the "muchas gracias, amigos" said in a hundred different dialects. The hundreds of people standing in line when you arrive at the work site at 8 o'clock in the morning, and the same numbers appearing every morning for the next five days straight. The impact of this experience as a VOSH team member is never forgotten. The people served will never forget. No one can deny the rationale of VOSH: 'to share my experience, my professional knowledge, my waking hours and my love demands much: for when I share the richness of these, I share my life.'"

1985-87 Dr. Tom Henley continues VOSH tradition as International President

Dr. Tom Henley is a friendly, outgoing, relaxed person who appears to enjoy being with people. He, too, shared his passion for VOSH as President.

By this time Dr. Michel Listenberger had been on six VOSH missions and had just formed the Michigan chapter of VOSH. Both Dr. Rose and Dr. Henley were primary "go-to" people for accessing materials and resources to make the new Michigan chapter successful. They supplied documents on how to get a new chapter started, how to run a mission, and how to approach and arrange local hosts including sample letters.

Dianne Johnson wrote this inspirational editorial in the VOSH/International Newsletter: "With the holiday season behind us, VOSHers turn their attention towards missions. I would like to focus attention on the mission leaders. Not enough is said or done in appreciation of the mission leaders who could be called the 'unsung heroes' of our organization.

Like the captain of a ship, the mantle of leadership falls on the mission leader and carries with it awesome responsibilities. Many hours go into the organization of every detail. They begin with establishing a rapport, by mail and telephone, with the host person or organization in the country where the leader has chosen a mission site. It is also imperative for the leader to create an understanding of our special 'gifts' and unique needs to most effectively execute our visionary mission.

Without a 'visionary team' there's no mission. The leader gathers his team with careful consideration for the acceptable balance between optometrists and support personnel. They must keep in mind there are always far more support personnel on the waiting list than there are OD's, again, hours of letter writing and phone calls! Oh! the phone bills. The personalization of a phone call is often more effective than a letter.

Many mission participants are drawn to a particular mission because of the personality and leadership qualities of the mission leader, as well as the location of the mission. The leader is also responsible for the neutralization of the eyeglasses and the packing of the crates and other equipment needed for a successful mission. Now as for the bookkeeping; due to new IRS requirements, the bookkeeping associated with a mission can be a nightmare. Even putting together a rooming list can be tricky.

The mission leader must have a good working relationship with a travel agent with whom he will speak at least twice a week for several months prior to the mission. Once the group is underway, the leader assumes the role of our tour conductor with all the potential, beyond his control, unforeseen occurrences (complicated by anywhere from ten to forty personalities) not the least of which is the actual physical safety of the group.

During the six plus months that it takes to put a mission together, the leader has been reading and listening to all media coverage of the political atmosphere of the country in which his mission is being hosted. The leader is always prepared to cancel or abort a mission if he sees the safety of his group of visionaries may be compromised. These can be heavy decisions considering the usual mission locations. Guerilla warfare, internal unrest, revolution, the most volatile of hot-spots around the globe are, have been or will be eye care mission sites where else are we more needed?

Have I completely discouraged you? I hope not. Because hand in hand with the worry, work, stress and devotion by the mission leaders comes this enormous sense of pride in a job well done. The pride is experienced by every single mission participant each as if he had done it all by himself. But reward for all the work. I feel I can say this with conviction as I have many times, been a mission leader. Each time, as the mission approaches and I'm very stressed out about it, I think I'm not going to put myself in this position again.

However, after a successful and satisfying mission is completed and I've rested a few weeks, I can hardly wait to get started on the next one.

So, I'm sending a special thanks to all of you mission leaders and I challenge new leaders, to share in this special achievement."

The Annual Meetings during this period were generally one day long and attended by 25-35 people, most of whom were chapter representatives. Meetings during these years generally included a VOSH Board meeting the night before a full-day conference. Typically the agenda included chapter reports,

International business and several speakers of VOSH interest. The afternoons were generally breakout sessions or roundtable discussions to facilitate the sharing of information.

One of the ideas that excited Dr. Henley was the Membership Certificates given to every VOSH Member for display in their office. To be placed on the certificates VOSH had "Flag Stamps" from most of the countries in the world. For each mission in which a member participated, he or she would get a stamp of that country to be affixed to their Membership Certificate.

1987-89 Dr. Charles Gray becomes VOSH/ International President

This section came from recollection of Dr. Gray at annual VOSH meetings and from phone interviews with Dr. Gray in 2015 as well as excerpts from 1987-89 VOSH/International Newsletters, Editor Dianne Johnson.

Dr. Charles Gray, a personable, quiet, soft spoken, unassuming man with a talent for organization came to be the President of VOSH/International using these traits to lead VOSH through its next few years.

Dr. Gray began his eye care missions in VOSH-Nebraska. He participated in three VOSH missions; Honduras, Costa Rica and Dominican Republic. Previously he served as Vice President of VOSH/International.

In addition to optometry he brought experience from being the president of the Nebraska Optometric Association. He also served several administrative positions in his local community including the Lion's Club, Sertoma, and Big Pals / Little Pals. His administrative skills grew as he served on the Council of the North Central States where he met fellow VOSHer Dr. Phil Hottel. The two of them became great friends and shared ideas about VOSH. Dr. Hottel later became President of VOSH/International as well.

As President, Dr. Gray's vision of VOSH/International as an administration was to serve as a "parent" organization whose primary role can and should be to coordinate activities and guide the state chapters in principles of the Volunteer Optometric Services to Humanity concept as conceived and promulgated by the founder Dr. Franklin Harms.

During this administration there was constant communication with the twenty-two state chapters, nine student chapters and four International chapters of VOSH. Dr. Gray began a comprehensive collection of statistics and information from the individual chapters and organized a mission calendar. This was widely distributed in order to be helpful to every chapter and sent to every member to keep them informed of the comprehensive activities of VOSH as a complete organization.

Communications during these years were primarily delivered via telephone calls with an occasional mailing through the United States Post Office. Dr. Gray kept the VOSH Advisory Board fully informed as well. One of Dr. Gray's most rewarding calls was to Dr. Greg Pearl. He invited Greg to bring California into the VOSH/ International organization with their affiliation. Greg took the challenge and with the help of others California became a new international VOSH chapter.

During his leadership Dr. Gray spent much time reaching out to optometrists to become involved in eye care mission. Dr. Gray along with his wife Eula, Dr. John Lancaster and Editor Dianne Johnson organized and hosted many displays. VOSH/ International had a booth or table at the major optometric conferences in Chicago, New York and Boston. The basic display tables consisted of tri-fold cardboard table displays with pictures of VOSH missions as well as information to pass out to optometric attendees.

The movement toward VOSH establishing permanent eye clinics began during this administration. Dr. Gray also oversaw development of permanent eye clinics in Mexico, Honduras and Guatemala. Dr. Jim Sanderson assembled forms and guideline materials into a "Mission Manual". This included sample letters to foreign hosts and sponsors.

One of Dr. Gray's primary endeavors was to seek out grant moneys. Applications were made too many sources including a nomination of VOSH to receive a $200,000 grant by being named "Lion's International Humanitarian of the Year". VOSH did not win but was a finalist. A valued assistant, Candy, worked with Rick Myrick to put together a grant request which was awarded to VOSH from the "Mary Lynn Richardson Foundation". Along with the grant came $3,500 to help develop a permanent eye clinic in Mexico.

In 1988 the VOSH/International Annual Meeting was at the Adam's Mark in St. Louis, Missouri. In 1989 the Annual Meeting was at the Hilton Flamingo in Las Vegas, Nevada.

Nearing the end of Dr. Charles Gray's term as VOSH/International President he shared the following words. "The two years of my presidency is nearly over. It seemed to go very fast and I enjoyed the opportunity to serve. We have seen a good growth in the organization membership and I think a spirit of cooperation between the different chapters....Eula and I presented the VOSH/International booth at the American Optometric Association Convention in New York. We had a lot of interest and gave out VOSH brochures. Several people who had been on VOSH missions before stopped at the booth to recall their missions.....I appreciate all the support that you have given me in the past two years and hope you will continue to give Dr. Wayne Vander Leest as much help. We can always do better if we try harder and remember the goals of VOSH. Again, I thank you for the opportunity to serve as president of VOSH/International."

1989-91 Dr. Wayne Vander Leest takes the reins as the next President

Dr. Wayne Vander Leest came on the scene as an energetic, personable," never-met-a-stranger" young doctor. He was considered among the "movers and shakers" and so with expectant anticipation he took the leadership for the next two years. He made quite an impression relating to VOSHers by leading meetings often wearing suspenders over a flannel shirt.

Wayne was a Magna Cum Laude graduate of Illinois College of Optometry participating as a member of the Student Volunteer Optometric Services to Humanity in his first mission to Haiti with Dr. Walt Marshall. He followed that with ten missions to Mexico, eight of which as a mission leader while becoming President of VOSH-Iowa for five years until being elected President VOSH/International.

When he was installed as International President in Las Vegas in 1989 he felt that he wanted to make VOSH more cohesive and efficient. There were, however, a lot of independent chapters with many very independent and highly motive leaders. Dr. Vander Leest believed that this was the overall paradigm uniquely indicative of VOSH around the country at the time.

So he started thinking about some of the ways to create a more cohesive and effective business model, something structured like the operations of his optometric practice. He thought this could include the formation of a "buying group" to leverage access to supplies and equipment. He also felt that rather than "reinventing the wheel" he would standardize planning guides for use by all chapters. That could include "How to Organize a Chapter", "How to Lead a Mission", and "How to Develop Good Mission Hosts Abroad." He felt that overall this structure could be assisted with streamlining the Governance of VOSH/International including re-working our International Constitution and Bylaws.

Upon being elected President of VOSH/International Dr. Wayne Vander Leest gave his first *"President's Message" in the VOSH/International Newsletter,* excerpts of which follow:

"VOSH is a great organization and I appreciate the opportunity to serve as President. The Board of Directors is made up of dedicated, veteran VOSH doctors, with who I look forward to working. We look forward to our responsibilities in directing and helping VOSH.

Before talking about the future, I want to pay tribute to the great success and growth of VOSH/International under the wonderful leadership of our past presidents. I say 'Thank you' and highly commend the efforts of Dr. Russ Dorland, Dr. V.E. Falkenhein, Dr. Steve Rose, Dr. Tom Henley, and Dr. Charles Gray. They had a lot of help from some wonderful people and with the direction of these men VOSH has become what it is today and has a tremendous future.

One thing we can be sure of in life is that nothing stays the same or is constant. All things, including organization, must always be changing to meet new demands and needs. Hopefully the changes made to meet those demands and needs, will be made judiciously and with the betterment of the organization first and foremost. As I begin the upcoming two years there are several things I am mindful of:

- Change is sometimes slow and not always easy
- It is my and the Board's responsibility to always do what is best for the organization and acceptable by the majority of the membership
- VOSH/International's role is to help the state chapters by promoting cooperation, communication, and coordination between them I have some grand dreams in mind for VOSH, but, also, some more specific goals. For example:
- Establish an organizational structure to VOSH/International with far more people participating and helping VOSH grow
- More state VOSH chapters

- Large supply purchasing coordinated between all state chapters
- Grants, booth space and support from various foundations, regional and national optometric meetings and conventions
- There were three functioning governing units
  - o Executive Committee consisted of International officers made operational decisions and recommendations to the Board of Directors
  - o Board of Directors set policies, meetings, budgets and elected officers. The Board consisted of each International officer and a representative of each chapter
  - o The General Sessions were not for business but for education, resource distribution and sharing of ideas

There are many, many more areas where VOSH/International can grow and change. The ideas, goals, and brainstorming will only be limited by each one of us and our willingness to work and to help achieve those dreams and goals. VOSH can grow tremendously. The time is right for us to make some large strides. I and the Board appeal to you for your help and continued voluntarism, whether it be on missions, at home within your state chapter, or on the national level. Many of you are helping in various capacities already. If you are, wonderful; if you are not and would like to increase your participation, please contact your state VOSH director or myself and I'm sure a way can be found for you to help.

It is an exciting time of the year for VOSH, with many missions upcoming. Much work has been done and is being done to make these missions successful. I wish every mission the very best and look forward to hearing reports about each of them."

An enhanced set of committees were appointed. Dr. Jim Wellington took the lead in building supply sources and resources sharing ideas in addition to developing a VOSH supplies catalogue that state chapters could use. Dianne Johnson continued a lead role in editing and publishing the VOSH/International Newsletters that was mailed to leaders and members – more than four hundred. So much mail was directed to her that the VOSH Board established her home address in Taylorville, Illinois as a permanent VOSH mailing address. VOSH "How-to" guides were updated and shared with all chapters.

At this time VOSH continued to develop and enhance the working relationship with Lions Clubs International's recently released "SightFirst" program – a global sight conservation and blindness prevention effort. One component of SightFirst was a used eyeglass recycling project to meet the needs of people who need eyeglasses in developing countries as well as exploring options for low-cost eyeglass production facilities overseas. At the time two Lions SightFirst Eyeglass Recycling Centers were established – one in Muncie, Indiana and another in Sonoma, California.

Midway through his first fast-paced year Dr. Vander Leest paused to reflect upon progress toward goals of cohesiveness and efficiency. He considered that perhaps his goals may have been a little altruistic. Volunteers are independent and often work "outside-the-box" as to uniformity. It was, indeed, hard to create the standard business model with all the independent, free-wheeling diversity of leaders organizing missions and leaders running chapters. "Maybe we need more money for professional staff to make this work," Wayne ponders. "Was it an error in my thinking?" "Was I too ambitious?" "Was I too naïve to think we could bring uniformity to VOSH?"

The next annual VOSH/International meeting at the New England College of Optometry was quickly approaching. This was a good time for Dr. Vander Leest to consider the structural considerations for the administration of VOSH by taking a good look at the current VOSH/International Constitution and Bylaws.

After a number of discussions both informally in groups and officially at Board meetings, Dr. Michel Listenberger was appointed along with Dr. Darrell Groman to coordinate the input from these discussions with the re-writing of the VOSH/ International Constitution and Bylaws. This was a year-long process with mid-year Board review and notice to members about an impending vote for adoption at our next annual meeting.

Voting was to occur at the next annual meeting in 1991. This annual meeting was hosted by The Ohio State University, College of Optometry in Columbus, Ohio. The proposal for the new Constitution and Bylaws was brought to the delegates. About seventy-five percent of the changes related to rewriting procedures that were already in use even though they were not in print. The substantive changes that were made included:

- Allowing a more representative form of administration. Not only will each chapter have a vote but a specifically assigned representative of their views on the Board
- Increasing proactive with Vice-Presidents taking thoughts, ideas and initiatives directly back to the chapter representatives. Also to seek International leaders from the state chapters.
- Electing the International President a year before taking office in a progressive system being a year as "elect", two years as President followed by a year as "past" on Board. This replaced a system of being elected 4 years in advanced and moving up through a series of automatic chairs.

After a year of working on this initiative inspired by Dr. Vander Leest and the Board of Directors the new Constitution and Bylaws were adopted.

As the term of Dr. Vander Leest progressed toward an end, he reflected again upon his goals and objectives for VOSH/

International. Certainly he celebrated in the progress that was made and all of the many, many great things that volunteers did throughout the years. This experience led him to the realization that these innovative, independent, spirited leaders are what brought growth and progress to VOSH all around the world. This was exactly the spirit that empowered individuals to succeed, not to comply, but to be motivated by their own vision, not someone else's.

Years later in a statement he said; "Leading volunteers is in some ways is like raising children. It is frustrating when you try to make them conform to your ideal behavior patterns. It makes much more sense to let them go to find their own successes and achievements – the president or parent being there, of course, to provide resources, coaching and feedback."

Dr. Wayne Vander Leest left his heritage to the future of the VOSH/International Presidency. He remains proud to still be at the heart of VOSH.

This section primarily came from the author working with Dr. Vander Leest on re-writing of the bylaws. Also significant input came from phone interviews with Dr. Vander Leest and excerpts from VOSH/International Newsletters by Editor Dianne Johnson.

VOSH Meeting Dynamics

During the 1980's and 1990's it was a tradition with some exceptions that the VOSH/International annual meeting was conducted in conjunction with a school of optometry.

These annual meetings would often begin on a Friday afternoon in which the current optometry students would conduct a tour of their school for anyone who would be interested. These tours were usually quite well attended. Then around 5 PM members would host a reception for attendees. The International Board would also meet either in the morning or in the evening on Friday as well. General membership meetings were on Saturday and often conducted within the facilities of the optometry school. The advantages to this system of hosting the annual meeting were:

- Connectivity to optometry students who would hopefully learn about and consider VOSH as part of the future optometry career
- Education and information to attendees about the innovations schools were teaching to the next generation of optometry
- Cost effectiveness in many cases although with some schools of optometry costs could still be a factor because of travel and expenses.

VOSH would also have a mid-year Board of Directors meeting in the late winter or early Spring. These would be a full day and be coordinated with various large optometry conferences. VOSH would have a display at these conferences and talk with other optometrists about VOSH in the days preceding or following the Board meeting.

The 1990's

The 1990s began as we learned about the internet by reading a book and ended the decade by being fearful about how Y2K (Year 2000) programming could shut down our world!

It was a time of multiculturalism and alternative media. We reached out to learn about other people; we embraced diversity yet ethnic wars and conflicts ravaged people around the globe. Cable TV and the World Wide Web put us in touch with an ever expanding presence. In the 1990's the pace of news, outreach, and information quickened.

To find an answer in 1990 you went to your local library, reference the card catalogue for sources, hunted through the stacks, searched the source index, turned to the referenced chapter and read a few pages. If you didn't find the answer you were looking for; you started over.

By the end of the 1990's our entire world started to become accessible; our encyclopedias started to gather dust.

In VOSH, the tedium of organizing an eye care mission was eased. We began to use the internet to communicate instantly with people in other countries. We extended our reach and sought diverse, interesting, and previously inaccessible work sites. During the 1990's VOSH's diversity and outreach expanded as well.

1991-93 Dr. Jim Hess takes over as next VOSH/International President

Changing of the VOSH/International Presidency seemed seamless as Dr. Jim Hess succeeded Dr. Wayne Vander Leest as President. Jim, along with Wayne, were both 1979 graduates of Illinois College of Optometry. And yes, both first became involved with VOSH as students.

As the early VOSHers continued to invite and coax optometrists to participate in an eye care mission, more embraced the ideals of VOSH and committed themselves to the organization, administration and growth of VOSH/International. Jim's first experience in Honduras inspired him to respond, "That was a wonderful mission and filled me with the spirit."

Dr. Hess's interest and experience grew as he established himself as an optometrist in his native Minnesota. Here Dr. Hess was inspired even more by Dr. Russ Dorland, the founder of VOSH-Minnesota and the first elected President of VOSH/International. Dr. Hess participated in fifteen missions before being elected International President himself.

Of particular and historic note, is that Dr. Jim Hess co-led a VOSH mission to Tanzania that included a group of British optometrists. Following that mission those British optometrists formed our sister organization, VISION AID OVERSEAS (VAO) in the United Kingdom.

As Dr. Hess took office in October 1991 as President of VOSH/International he addressed the Annual Meeting participants by announcing the theme for his term of office. He committed to moving our organization forward under the acronym/slogan "**S.U.R.G.E.**" which emphasized the concepts:

- **S** – Strengthen
- **U** – Uniformity
- **R** – Results
- **G** – Growth
- **E** – Enjoyment

One of President Hess's first challenges was to implement the new Constitution and Bylaws adopted as he assumed office. He was the last President that came up through-the-ranks under the old system requiring 4-5 two-year terms after being elected and he recalls spending about thirteen years in this progression.

With the governance change Dr. Hess assigned Vice Presidents and other board members specific jobs. One primary change was that everyone on the Board had specific chapters in which to communicate keeping open, direct contact between the International Board and the chapter officers.

In addition to this direct link, Board members were also given specific tasks and committee assignments such as donations, supplies, outreach, "Gift of Sight" and others.

Transition to this new governance was facilitated by Dr. Maggie Corbin of Ohio. She would very promptly and emphatically let anyone know what was required under our new Constitution and Bylaws. This was one of those dynamics remembered later in reflection – her passion and enthusiasm was, indeed, quite inspirational and it did make the transition to this new form of governance quick and effective.

After the new plan began to settle in, Dr. Hess reflected that he seemed to be spending a lot of his time "putting out fires."

One of those "fires" was the growing use of the automatic refractor to be used on VOSH mission trips. There were people that complained of their unreliability, taking the professionalism out of eye care and the difficulty getting this equipment through customs. Others like Dr. Sol Rocke were supporters of the automatic refractor. After a year or so of opinions, Dr. Hess seemed to put this one to rest in his editorial *published in the VOSH/International Newsletter.*

"I feel the autorefractor is one of the most important tools we can take on a VOSH trip. It has the capacity to see so many more patients in a day than the average optometrist can, and it doesn't get tired or get Montezuma's Revenge. I have been fortunate to have had an auto refractor on more than half of the fifteen VOSH trips I have been on, and I find them more accurate than a retinoscope."...

"On the average, each autorefractor can examine close to 700 patients in an average work day. This takes the workload off the optometrists who can devote more of their time to doing primary care procedures or can help in dispensing."...

..."The auto retractor, I wouldn't leave home without one!"

Dr. Sol Rocke added that "The automatic refractor is only a starting point for an eye examination. The subjective response of the patient coupled with the professional judgment of the examiner will provide the patient with an adequate prescription."

Another one of those "fires" that was smoldering for over a year was the concern over Lions International introducing a new program called "Gift of Sight." It became a heated discussion at the 1992 Annual Meeting at the University of California at Berkeley Optometry School.

The issue was summarized in this Newsletter opinion: "While speaking with optometrists across the nation, I'm hearing a rising and alarming concern about the endorsement of a segment of their profession by a service organization, at the exclusion of all others of their profession; namely the Lions/

Lenscrafter alliance." Several strong voices swayed the delegates both ways.

Caught in this position, Dr. Hess approached the American Optometric Association (supported by VOSH board action) by accepting an invitation to a meeting of their Interprofessional Relations Committee in Washington, D.C. After extensive discussion and sharing of overall dynamics and objectives, VOSH did see that it was in our best interests to support and work with the Lions "Gift of Sight" program even though it was connected to a corporate interest.

The end result was that good working relationships were restored among VOSH/International, Lions International and the American Optometric Association as they are integrally bound in purpose.

Celebrating the Twentieth Anniversary of VOSH

Dr. Jim Hess thought it would be a good idea to celebrate the history of VOSH with a 20th Anniversary Celebration at the VOSH Annual Meeting in Chicago, Illinois, October 9, 1993. Dr. Alfred Rosenbloom, President of VOSH/Illinois (and future Board member of VOSH/International) hosted the annual meeting and 20th Anniversary Celebration. In conjunction with the celebration Dr. Darrell Groman, historian, wrote a brief history of the formation of VOSH.

Dr. Jim Hess wrote in his **President's Message – 20 Years of Giving and two years of Surging**: "VOSH/International is turning twenty years old, and I feel it is time to celebrate our accomplishments by having a little celebration. We are putting together a really fun weekend. It's a time to reminisce, meet new people, match faces with names, and just plain have fun."

An editorial by Diane Johnson added: "Yes, one man's vision can make a difference! Twenty years after Dr. Franklin Harms envisioned a Volunteer Optometric Services to Humanity (VOSH) and more than 900 volunteer members, 18 state chapters, one International chapter, at least one spin-off organization (VAO) and hundreds of eye care missions later – wouldn't he be proud?"

President Bill Clinton sent VOSH a letter of commendation: "I am pleased to send my greetings to all those gathered to celebrate the 20th anniversary of Volunteer Optometric Services to Humanity.

Your organization is an excellent example of Americans working together to help not only Americans but also others around the world. The gift of better vision is, in essence, the gift of hope to many individuals. Your generous donations of time and supplies assist those people who gave the greatest needs and the least access to the proper services. I appreciate the many people who donate their used eyeglasses, and I commend the dedicated optometrists who travel to foreign missions to serve their fellow human beings. Your dedication is an inspiration to us all.

I send my best wishes for a memorable anniversary year and for continued success in your future endeavors."

-   Bill Clinton, President of the United States

As Dr. Hess left office he reflected on all the positive things that were accomplished during the previous two years. Nine hundred and fourteen members in eighteen chapters carried out the work of VOSH. In 1992 alone VOSH conducted twenty-one foreign missions, examined 42,543 patients and dispensed 37,839 pairs of glasses.

Also in the prior two years VOSH-Northwest and its eye care clinic at the Union Gospel Mission in Spokane, Washington were recognized by the **United States President George Bush**, being named one of his "Thousand Points of Light." The mission served the needs of the homeless of the inland northwest. It was founded by VOSH's clinic director Dr. Walt Michaelis.

VOSH Donations Collection Center becomes very successful

Diane Johnson, in addition to her duties as VOSH Newsletter Editor, also coordinated the VOSH Collection Center in Taylorville, Illinois. At this time the Center was accepting donations from a wide variety of sources.

Dianne worked diligently to reach out to a wide variety of sources for eyeglasses. They include:

- Thousands of private individuals who cared enough to donate their used eyeglasses either directly to VOSH or to one of the numerous groups who collected eyeglasses and then forwarded them to VOSH
- Temples and churches of all denominations
- Service organizations including:
  o Kiwanis
  o Lions and Lady Lions
  o Moose
  o Rotary
- Direct donations of supplies from optical labs:
  o Pech Optical
  o Rite-Style Optical
  o Schmidt Laboratory
  o Soderberg Optical
  o Sutherlin Optical
  o Twin Cities Optical
  o Walman Optical
  o Hudson Optical
- Direct donation of eye care products from drug companies:
  o Alcon, Inc.
  o Allergan, Inc.
  o Walgreen

Dr. Jim Hess also was instrumental in securing 14,000 eyeglass frames from Hudson Optical to be used as chapter resources.

In his farewell address to VOSH as International President Dr. Hess gave a status report and thanked all of the many volunteers who dedicated themselves to making VOSH better. As President Jim Hess turned his office over to incoming President Phil Freitag, he received a standing ovation from all attendees for an excellent two years of "surging" ahead.

1993-95 Dr. Phil Freitag serves as VOSH/International President

As the new President Dr. Phil Freitag accepted the leadership from Dr. Jim Hess, he began with a few remarks to set the stage of his new presidency.

He discussed the direction VOSH/International would take in the coming two years. He stated that the strength of VOSH/International is in the diversity of opinions of its members and variation of ways to get things done. He suggested simplifying the "Chapter Organization Manual." He suggested the need for a Public Relations Chairperson. He summarized our future direction with an acronym for involvement; People – Offering – Love – Inspiration – Sight – and Help. He challenged every VOSH member to "**POLISH**" our organization like a fine, quality diamond!

Dr. Phil Freitag is from Madison, South Dakota where he had practiced optometry for the past forty years following graduation from Northern Illinois College of Optometry in 1949. He served as president of the South Dakota Optometric Society in 1982. As an active VOSH member Phil had participated in fourteen foreign VOSH missions and had been project director for eight of these missions. He had served as president of VOSH/South Dakota and secretary-treasurer of VOSH/International.

Dr. Freitag always spoke with conviction as he swayed his head in a little side-ways nod. His greatest pleasures were talking about his family, optometry and VOSH. The best advice to anyone who had not met him is, "Don't let him get started talking about any of these subjects!"

His first official *"**Message from the President**" was published in the VOSH/International Newsletter, November 1993.*

"After twenty years of highly successful existence, VOSH/International is well and healthy! This was surely evidence in October at the gala celebration in Chicago marking the 20th anniversary of the founding of our organization. Much credit and praise is certainly due to the tremendous effort of VOSH-Illinois who hosted this event. This was the most spectacular celebration in our history.

VOSH has continued to grow and has become the leader in providing vision care to the needy of the world. An old saying is "Nothing is so good but what it could be better".
We will move forward with this idea – let's make the best even better.

We will try several ideas to make our organization better:
- More frequent and better communication between International and the Chapters
- Easier organization and formation of new chapters
- Increased publicity of VOSH activities in optometric, optician, and optical lab journals
- More emphasis on the value of continuing education credits for participation in missions
- New features in our newsletter such as "Mission Airing," appearing in this issue. In our next issue we will begin to profile people currently active in VOSH. We need to know each other better!

VOSH/International is deeply indebted to many workers and past officers. We need their continued efforts and support! We welcome and solicit any and all suggestions to improve our organization. Thanks for giving me this opportunity to serve as your president."

Much of the VOSH/International business in the mid 1990's involved reviewing chapter reports and mission reports. At one of the earliest board meetings, "standing rules" were adopted for use at the annual general membership meetings. The board decided to waive the requirement that representative show a signed statement from their president in order to vote. Meeting rules also included election procedures and dues being paid in order to vote.

The board also discussed options for securing an executive director for VOSH on a volunteer or low-cost basis possibly from programs such as "RSVP' or "SCORE".

Coloring Books were printed for access and distribution for eye missions. Renowned artist Nancy Drew had donated the artwork for a children's coloring book to be used for children waiting at VOSH clinic sites for eye care.

The 1994 Annual Meeting was in St. Louis and hosted by Past International President Dr. Bud Falkenhain.

In 1995, the Annual Meeting was conducted in Portland, Oregon and hosted by VOSH-Northwest. Friday the board meeting was convened in the morning and in the afternoon a three-hour certified continuing education course was provided by Pennsylvania College of Optometry. The opportunity was offered on Friday evening to join the Northwest optometry students in their annual "Eye Ball" fundraiser. Saturday was the general membership meeting and Sunday morning tours of the optometry school were provided.

During this annual meeting our President Dr. Phil Freitag said farewell with his sincere "THANKS" *(VOSH/International Newsletter)*: "I would like to take this opportunity to thank everyone in VOSH/International for the wonderful cooperation that I received these past two years while serving as your President! I can truthfully say that I was never refused when I asked for your help! This is particularly significant when I do understand how busy all of you really are. Members of VOSH/International are very caring and cooperative individuals!

I would not attempt to single out any particular persons or groups – everyone was most helpful! I could not have had a greater group to work with than the officers and committee persons who served these two years! Our Annual Meeting Committees both in St. Louis and in Portland did such terrific jobs of hosting our organization!

I can truthfully say that I can look back on these two years with great satisfaction feeling that the work of VOSH did continue at an acceptable pace and my memories of these years are all pleasant memories!

Thanks again to all of you for allowing me to serve as your President! Continue to support your new officers and I am confident that VOSH will continue to grow and prosper!"

1995-97 Dr. Michel Listenberger is VOSH/ International President

Dr. Listenberger graduated from Indiana University in 1971 and practiced optometry at the Niles Vision Clinic in Niles, Michigan. Coincidentally he joined VOSH at the same time VOSH/ International formed (October 1979) and he participated in his first VOSH mission to Haiti with co-founder Dr. Walter Marshall of Indiana VOSH in January 1980. His experience included fifteen VOSH missions and ten as trip leader.

As a person and as president, Dr. Listenberger placed greatest value in volunteers above all else because they are the ones on the front-lines delivering the service VOSH provides. During these years his attention was directed to surrounded himself with the best volunteers available with key people like Diane Johnson (editor and supply center), Dr. Nelson Edwards (VOSH domestic mission Detroit), Dr. Gary Blackman (AOA board and VOSH Board), Dr. Ann Slocum-Edmonds (international chapters), Dr. Al Rosenbloom (leading Pacific Rim development) and Dr. Harry Zeltzer, new on the scene but a spark plug of new initiatives and leadership. Many others made valuable contributions.

The theme for Dr. Listenberger's presidency was **"Bringing the World into Focus."** Upon announcement of the theme beach-balls, mapped as miniature worlds were bantered and batted throughout the room in a celebratory frenzy. In his opening remarks after being installed, the following address was given to the attendees of the 1995 annual meeting in Portland:

"As VOSHers we have a unique opportunity to use our expertise in vision analysis and correction to bring the whole world into focus. We have the opportunity to help a child who cannot see their school lessons, to help the early presbyopic seamstress to sew for her family and neighbors and to help employ people who have lost their jobs due to an inability to see effectively. And the world becomes our practice!

More people are "functionally blind" simply because they do not have access to eyeglasses. In some areas eye care is not available and for many they could not afford it anyway. Because of the lack of proper refractive correction, huge portions of the world's population cannot see to function. We can provide them with the vision corrections they need through our volunteer services. We have the ability to change more lives and re-employ more people than any other form of eye care delivery.

Often we hear of major efforts to reduce glaucoma, cataracts and vitamin A deficiency around the world, but these efforts pale in comparison to what we do with a simple eye exam and used eyeglasses. Volunteer Optometric Services to Humanity (VOSH) is often referred to as the "optometrist's volunteer organization." And certainly, opticians, ophthalmologists, optometric technicians, assistants, aids and laypersons are actively involved. What a legacy it is to give someone that "special gift of sight," that is yours to give – Bringing the World into Focus!

The purpose of VOSH/International administration is to provide resources to chapters and members to help them be more efficient and effective in providing vision care to others. State (and National) Chapters are the primary operational unit in that they organize and conduct missions.

This year VOSH hopes to provide:

a) International relations and expansion – co-chairpersons Dr. Ann Slocum-Edmonds and Dr. Darrell Groman
b) Rewrite information guides such as "How to form a chapter" and "How to conduct a mission"
c) Revision of current Constitution and Bylaws – co-chairpersons Dr. Phil Freitag and Dr. Rich Ryan
d) A new revision of our brochure by Kirk Thomas and Dr. Rich Ryan
e) The development of a supply catalogue – Mona Hager
f) VOSH membership lapel pins beginning January 1996."

During this time VOSH took a look at our mission statement. With minor revisions, we recommitted to it. VOSH also reviewed goals and strategies to move forward.

Mission (purpose):

The primary mission of VOSH/International is to facilitate the provision of vision care worldwide to people who can neither afford nor obtain such care. VOSH/International accomplishes this primary goal by service as a coordinating body for affiliated and international chapters. VOSH/International administratively supports the activities of chapters and members in various ways.

Directives (Strategies):

These services include but are not limited to:

1. Serving as a resource for affiliated chapters including those at schools and colleges of optometry
2. Establishing inter-professional ties with other healthcare professions and groups who share similar goals
3. Fostering the development and implementation of programs involving the preservation and enhancement of vision through opportunities for educational programs and research

4. Providing guidance in selecting mission countries, sites, and host organizations abroad and within the United States
5. Publishing a newsletter to communicate the pertinent organizational details of selected mission endeavors; including policy guidelines
6. Assisting in securing, classifying, and distributing both donated glasses and essential examining equipment and vision care supplies

Goals (Outcomes): With these basic concepts to build on, Dr Listenberger, as President, set personal "goals" for the next two years:

1) Expand International Chapters – target Pacific Rim Nations
2) Update materials for Chapter use (How-to guides, brochures, pins, cards)
3) Conduct the first joint-chapter Domestic Mission in Downtown Detroit
4) Recruit the top leaders in the Eyecare Profession to strengthen our future
5) Become the Largest Professional Eye-Care delivery N.G.O. in the World

VOSH was growing and new chapters were being built; many, many mission reports were coming in and new initiatives were generated. During this time the first International chapter from Canada, VOSH-British Columbia with Dr. Marina Roma-March as president was welcomed into VOSH.

VOSH/International created an alliance with the "Friendship Ambassadors Foundation" who adopted VOSH as a service organization and agreed to assist chapters in making mission plans. They provided lower travel costs and helped trip leaders cut through inter-governmental "red tape."

The 1996 Annual Meeting was in Indianapolis, Indiana. On Friday there was an "issues forum" and then a tour the Indiana University Optometry School Indianapolis eye clinic. The evening was for hospitality and an Executive Committee meeting. On Saturday was the Board and Annual meeting capped by a dinner theater that evening, "Crazy for You."

By Fall 1996 the following "member benefits" and initiatives were created and in use:

- Membership Lapel Pins and a Membership Card were offered
- A new VOSH Brochure for information and recruitment was made available
- Revised and distributed new modules for chapter use including "Forming a New Chapter", "Sample Chapter Bylaws", and "How to conduct a Mission"
- Supply items were created for sale using our VOSH Logo
- Revised and standardized eye exam for use on VOSH missions (toward a movement to start collecting data on "outcomes")
- Ann Slocum-Edmonds generated a plan to build VOSH chapters and student chapters in other countries
- An American Optometric Association board member was appointed and welcomed as an Ad Hoc member of the VOSH Board and included on our Executive Committee.
- The process of collecting emails to communicate quickly through this cutting edge technology was began!
- The VOSH/International "WEB" page was launched. Secretary-Treasurer worked on correcting some "bugs" in the system.

Dr. Al Rosenbloom was taking a very active role as a Vice President of VOSH/International. He took a lead in one of the VOSH/International goals to establish a presence and form VOSH chapters in the Pacific Rim nations. The board supported Dr. Al

Rosenbloom to represent VOSH/International at a meeting of the **Asian Pacific Optometric Congress** in April, 1997 in Seoul, Korea. This was funded with a 50% matching grant from an anonymous source.

Dr. Rosenbloom was able to meet with many optometrists who were interested in VOSH. Of these he put together a list of the top ten asian/pacific optometrists and their contact information who he thought would be the best prospects for VOSH chapters.

State Chapters were invited to contact the prospects and offer to do joint eye care missions with them to teach them the VOSH system much the same that early builders like Franklin Harms and Walt Marshall would do.

Unfortunately this was one of the disappointments of this administration that chapters were never persuaded to go that far and invest that much into Pacific Rim VOSH chapters. It turns out that the volunteer mindset is different than it is in North America. Even though this did not achieve success, Dr. Al Rosenbloom was highly regarded for his ground-breaking efforts.

The 1997 VOSH Annual Meeting was in Detroit, Michigan hosted by Dr. Nelson Edwards. It was a full weekend of meetings and celebration.

VOSH/International conducts first joint chapter Domestic Mission -1997

Dr. Carol Hunt, VOSH-Michigan member, organized and conducted the first joint chapter Domestic Mission for the homeless of downtown Detroit. This was conducted at the Detroit Rescue Mission where 200 patients were seen and 100 pairs of glasses were dispensed. Eighteen optometrists, two students and many volunteers helped make this a huge success!

The full story of this event is told in the "Domestic Missions" chapter of this publication.

By the end of 1997 the following had occurred:

1) Expanded International Chapters – target Pacific Rim Nations: VOSH added VOSH-British Columbia, Canada, President Marina Roma-March and did very well establishing contacts with optometry schools abroad
   a. The Pacific Rim expansion was not achieved. Although Dr. Al Rosenbloom made a brilliant try for a very lofty goal, it did not produce results
2) Updated materials for Chapter use (How-to guides, brochures, pins, cards): This was all completed in the first six-nine months
3) Conducted the first joint-chapter Domestic Mission in Downtown Detroit: This happened with huge success
4) Recruited the top leaders in the Eyecare Profession to strengthen the future of VOSH: We did welcome Dr. Al Rosenbloom, Dr. Harry Zelter, John Gehrig and Charles Covington among others that went on to add great value to the VOSH legacy
5) Became the largest professional eye-care delivery NGO in the world

In a farewell address, Dr. Listenberger thanked the leadership of VOSH for their initiative in accepting and taking on projects with enthusiasm. Recognition and appreciations was also given to all the many VOSH members who ventured out around the world making people's lives better through better vision.

1997 Annual Report of VOSH/International

Chapters: 24 state chapters; 12 student chapters with a new international chapter in TWECS – Third World Eye Care Society, British Columbia, Canada, and an affiliate in England (VAO)

Members: 1700 members in state and national chapters

Activity: Foreign missions were primarily in the Western Hemisphere. Also served were Ukraine, Vietnam, India, Uganda and Kenya. Domestic missions conducted in Detroit, Manhattan, Seattle, Spokane, and Houston. Several VOSH chapters have permanent eye clinics in other countries.

Patients Served: 83,000 patients received eye exams with about the same number of glasses being supplied. Over 700 chapter volunteers went on 53 eye care missions.
Most trips from 7 to 9 days.

Financial Report: Income was $21,223.32 (including $6,805 carried from previous year). Expenses were $6,518 leaving assets of $14,705. Most of the income was from member and chapter dues.

1997-99 Dr. Phil Hottel becomes VOSH/International President

Taking office as the next president Dr. Hottel addressed the delegates at the 1997 Annual Meeting in his talk called *"Changing of the Guard" (Reprinted in the VOSH Newsletter).*

"If I were asked to outline my plans for the next two years, there are a couple of sayings that come to mind. The first is the medical guideline, "do no harm". The second is a literary gem, "if it ain't broke, don't fix it." VOSH has experienced steady growth in the number of members overall, the strength of chapters, and the number of missions accomplished for as many years as I have been involved. We plan to expend a lot of effort to try to revitalize chapters who may be struggling and to help newly formed chapters develop into strong ones.

Did you ever wonder what purpose is served by VOSH/International? Consider this anecdote that shows how we are able to exchange information much better within an organizational structure. I recently received a phone call from an ophthalmology resident who would like to go on a VOSH mission to perform eye surgery, and had been advised that I might be of help. Since I needed to contact the other six members of our Executive

Committee about other matters anyway, I asked each one if they knew of any group going at the desired time. I was given the name of two different contacts, and I passed the information along to help the young doctor find what he was looking for.

On behalf of the Executive Committee of VOSH/International, we wish all of you a wonderful and prosperous new year."

Mid-way into Dr. Hottel's first year, VOSH was doing very well and remained active at eye care trade shows, having Dr. Nelson Edwards display at SECO (Atlanta), Dr. Harry Zeltzer display at NECO and Dr. Phil Hottel display at the American Optometric Association annual meeting.

The main focus remained strong in communicating to chapters including mission planning, mission reports and administrative support.

Charlie Covington had been at work on the VOSH Web site until three new Web volunteers came forward. *They published this note in the VOSH/International Newsletter:*

"**VOSH on the WEB**": An enterprising group of VOSHers are working on a Internet Web Site. The site can be used to disseminate information about VOSH in general, offer a "want ad" page, list upcoming trips, and help to recruit new members. Each state will have a section to list upcoming trips, or anything you would like others to know about your chapter. The site will also offer ideas on how to get loans for equipment, where to get glasses, and a myriad of other information."

The Web Site project team consisted of Bob Plass, Walt Mayo, OD, and Dale Cole, OD.

In March, 1998 Dr. Phil Hottel addressed the VOSH members with the following article in the VOSH/International Newsletter.
A Quarter Century of Growth

"VOSH has undergone many changes in its first twenty-five years. The obvious is our growth in numbers of chapters, members and missions. It hasn't always been easy, and even though we share a common goal of providing some level of eye care to needy people throughout the world, there have been some conflicting ideas as to how this should be accomplished. Let us consider some of the questions and ideas that have come up for discussion.

The name Volunteer Optometric Services to Humanity would, by definition, imply that there are optometrists involved in the organization at least in sufficient numbers to impact how the services are rendered. There have been people who expressed the belief that the wording should be changed to "Ophthalmic Services" to be more inclusive of opticians and ophthalmologists, and thus, more apt to draw support from those groups.

A related issue is what does it take to become a VOSH chapter? Should there be a minimum number of members? How many or what percentage of the members or officers should be optometrists, or does that even matter?

The practice of student groups of a dozen or more going on missions with two or three faculty members as the only licensed practitioners has been questioned by some long-term members of VOSH. Some feel it is a more meaningful experience to have a more nearly equal balance in numbers between students and licensees. Do you think it makes a difference?

Another issue came up recently when a chapter wanted to include people from another state in their group, but they were already listed as a member of another state's chapter. How definite a line should be drawn between chapters? Who defines the chapter limits? What's your opinion? Your opinions and comments on these, or any other issues you'd like to bring up for discussion, would be appreciated. Send them to me or to our editor, Joyce Crawley via mail or email."

In October of 1998 VOSH had one of our best annual meeting venues ever – Hollywood Beach, Florida – and we were right on the beach! It afforded a beautiful view of white sands and palm trees swaying as the waves were breaking on the oceanfront. After the day's business, we dined in Oceanside restaurants and heard the waves slapping the boats and the wharf.

On Friday VOSHers had an opportunity to tour the School of Optometry at NOVA Southeastern University. NOVA faculty advisor, Dr. Cliff Stephens and the SVOSH students arranged our transportation and gave us a tour of their optometry school. We were impressed by the beautiful grounds and buildings.

Saturday morning was spent in organizational business and the afternoon consisted of a variety of breakout sessions and discussion topics including Rotary/Lions Grants, computer aided dispensing, VOSH Web Site, liability on VOSH missions and third-world vision care.

In November of 1999 the Annual Meeting took place in Boston on the campus of the New England College of Optometry.

On late Friday afternoon our hosts led by Dr. Harry Zeltzer, faculty and students provided tours of the historic building overlooking the Charles River and the Massachusetts Institute of Technology. To maintain the historic marvels of the building, rooms were often located in interesting places. After the tours a very nice reception for attendees was offered in the atrium. One recent but very impressive display included many posters of individual VOSH chapters, topics of interest and tables display for optometric vendors.

As in any VOSH year many things happened with administration, public relations, VOSH booths, meetings, chapters, and missions. Dr. Hottel completed his term with success as he thanked the many VOSHers that helped along the way.

1999-2001 Dr. Jeff Marshall next generation VOSH/ International President

On a personal note from, Dr. Michel Listenberger,

VOSH was first introduced to me by Dr. Jeff Marshall as a fellow classmate at Indiana University Optometry School in 1971. After Jeff returned from his first VOSH mission in 1976 we talked about the experience. I joined VOSH in 1979 and went on my first VOSH trip to Haiti with Jeff's father, Dr. Walter Marshall, one of VOSH's founders along with Dr. Franklin Harms. The rest is history!

Dr. Jeff Marshall recalls his first involvement with VOSH, and particularly with VOSH-Indiana, run by his father Walter (co-founder of VOSH/International). For a while after graduation Jeff busied himself building his practice in Indianapolis, Indiana.

Eventually, after not seeing interest in VOSH by his son Jeff, his father Walter Marshall confronted him. "Jeff," he said, "You've got to go on a VOSH mission! It doesn't look good for you, my own son, to be indifferent about VOSH when I'm out motivating optometrists all around the Midwest to get involved in VOSH!"

So, the young Dr. Jeff Marshall reluctantly agreed to go on a VOSH trip, but he told his mother, "I'll do this one time. And if you think I'm going again, you're out of your mind!"

Well, with that, Dr. Jeff Marshall's history in VOSH begins. He had to "swallow those words." As of 2016, Dr. Jeff Marshall has been on 60 VOSH missions. His life is changed and history is written.

The History of VOSH/International continues with the following article reprinted from the VOSH/International Newsletter, Spring, 2000:

Dr. Jeff Marshall aims to make a difference

"Anyone who's ever received an email from Dr. Jeff Marshall knows that he always ends his correspondence with the slogan: "To Care To Share To Make a Difference."
Certainly, in his ongoing commitment to VOSH and now with his recent election to a two-year term as president of VOSH/International, Dr. Marshall is making a difference.

The Indiana optometrist's history with VOSH dates back to 1973 when his father, the late Dr. Walter Marshall, took part in a trip to Honduras with Kansas VOSH. The elder Dr. Marshall was so impressed with the program that he returned home and started VOSH-Indiana. Early trips were in conjunction with the Christian Medical Society. In 1976 when Dr. Marshall initiated a VOSH mission to the Dominican Republic, he enlisted his son's help...

...Along with leading missions, Dr. Marshall spends some time each day on VOSH-Indiana or VOSH/International projects.

Dr. Marshall's goals for his two-year role as president of VOSH/International include increasing membership and receiving greater recognition both within the optometric community and by the general public.

'The revamped newsletter and our dynamic new website are important tools in achieving these goals,' says Dr. Marshall. 'We need to let people know who we are and what we do.'

'We (VOSH) are the greatest public relations tool our profession has. Optometrists take the gift of good vision to less fortunate people of the world on every mission.'"

*Dr. Jeff Marshall addresses VOSH members with the article "**From the President's Desk**" in the same issue of VOSH/ International Newsletter, Spring 2000:*

"From its early beginnings in Kansas to the forming of the second chapter in Indiana by my late father, Dr. Walter Marshall, to the addition last year of a chapter in Honduras, VOSH/ International has had as its goal to serve as a coordinator of the activities of many state chapters.

As the new president of VOSH/International, I have set two major goals: to improve communication between chapters and within the general membership.

To accomplish these goals, efforts are already underway to overhaul the VOSH/International Newsletter and a new website is up and running.

I have a third goal: to increase awareness of VOSH/
International, within the American Optometric Association. VOSH
activities have long been a great public relations vehicle for the
profession of optometry. It is time to let the profession know
more about us.

In order to meet the above goals, I need the help
of each chapter. Despite your busy schedules, please send
information about your doings and your upcoming trips to the
VOSH/International Vice-president for your region and to our
webmaster.

Both are but an e-mail away."

Of primary concern at this time was the VOSH Website.
Progress was being made. Chuck Covington, the son of Charles
Covington (VOSH-Florida) was doing well as new webmaster.

The Website included information about the organization,
a bulletin board of upcoming trips and links to VOSH Chapter
websites. Also included are links to other related groups such as
the Lions Clubs. As time continued, more photos were expected
to be added to the site.

During his tenure Dr. Marshall reached out to spread the
word about VOSH. He first appeared at the American Optometric
Association Convention giving a talk with PowerPoint slides.
Showing many pictures he talked about what VOSH meant to
optometrists, volunteers and patients being helped. He imparted
a personal connection of how VOSH drew its members to reach
out to those in need.

Soon after, Dr. Marshall made a similar presentation about
VOSH to Lions Clubs International at their International Relations
Seminar in Indianapolis, Indiana. A large crowd was in attendance.
In response, Lions International recognized the efforts of VOSH/
International in combining forces, to bring better sight to the
world.

One of Dr. Marshall's favorites in VOSH was Ruth Berkling.
Over many years she was his major connection and host in his

frequent and regular trips to Honduras, usually taking fifty or more VOSHers along on his trip. Following is a story of this "hero host".

The Hills of Honduras are alive with the sound of Ruth Berkling, *by Zabelle D'Amico Published in the VOSH/International Newsletter, Fall/Winter 2000*

"Her story reads like a current-day script for "The Sound of Music," but in Ruth Berkling's case, personal tragedy deepened her commitment to a life of service to the people of Honduras.

Even as a child Ruth wanted to help people in other countries. After finishing nursing studies in 1962, she set out on her life journey, traveling initially to southern Germany to work in a clinic. It was there that Ruth met Arnold Berkling, a German businessman who lived in San Pedro Sula, Honduras.

Arnold had returned home in the aftermath of a bad car accident in which he lost his wife and was severely injured. His two young sons, ages three and four, remained with friends in Honduras. Arnold convinced Ruth to return to Central America with him in order to care for his children.

Ruth arrived in Honduras with a working contract as a governess in 1963. Two years later Honduras became her permanent home because she married her boss. The couple celebrated the birth of a daughter in 1972.

Since Arnold Berkling had been a longtime Lions Club member, Ruth found herself happily enmeshed in activities for the poor and sick of this beautiful country right from the beginning. Then during Easter Week, 1978, she and her husband were called upon to fete a group of VOSH-Indiana optometrists who were conducting a clinic in El Progreso, a small nearby town. As time for their stay drew to an end, the Berklings asked the VOSH-Indiana team to come back again. They returned that same October and have been returning at least once, sometimes twice a year, ever since. The team continues to see between 3,000 and 4,000 patients on each mission. Clinic venues change each time in order to help needy people from different areas.

Ruth's role as in-country liaison has been vital to the ongoing success of the program, although after so many years of working closely with Dr. Jeff Marshall (he coordinates the trips from the states), many of the details no longer need to be discussed. What is shared is talk about family and close friendships, even kinship, as Dr. Marshall is godfather to Ruth's middle son.

The everyday rhythm of Ruth's life was suddenly and severely impacted when Arnold died in a car accident in 1980. The boys were in college by then, but their daughter was only seven.

Rather than pack up and return home, Ruth remained in her adopted country. She was named Honorary Consul for Germany for eight provinces in 1983, a post which she continues to hold. Nor did Ruth give up her efforts on behalf of the needy in Honduras. She set about forming a charitable foundation, the *Fundacion Para Servicios Medicos Voluntarios* (Foundation for Voluntary Medical Services) and pushed for ophthalmological services starting in 1984. The *Fundacion* now provides 40 to 50 surgeries annually.

And, thanks again to her organization's persistent campaigning, there is now a permanent eye clinic in San Pedro Sula that helps needy people with eye problems throughout the year. The two-story building has approximately 2,200 square feet on each floor, with areas for examining, dispensing, prepping, surgery, post-op, etc. Ruth can be found at the clinic six days a week.

"The longer you work with the poor, the more aware you become of the tremendous needs," says Ruth. So, two years ago, her *Fundacion* started yet another clinic, one for general medicine complete with a drugstore offering basic medications.

"Supposedly public hospitals treat the poor of our country for nothing," says Ruth, "but they never have medicine. It is only available at the very private, expensive drugstores. I can tell you at this moment we are able to supply our patients with diabetes and high blood pressure medicines."

Two years ago, the *Fundacion para Servicios Médicos Voluntarios* was invited to join VOSH/International as VOSH-Honduras. Along with her far too numerous other duties, Ruth Berkling continues to work hard to keep that relationship strong."

Another heartwarming story that deeply affected Dr. Marshall was that of Hector. Hector wandered into a VOSH clinic in San Pedro Sula, Honduras one day with a non-functional blind eye. VOSHer Dr. Chuck Hornberger of Boston, New York examined him. Being touched with Hector's problem and his inability to do anything in Honduras, Dr. Hornberger arranged for Hector to come to his hometown in New York. There he scheduled Hector with an ophthalmologist. Hector was diagnosed with "retinoblastoma" and went through surgical enucleation, removing his eye to save his life. Years later, Hector lives near Tegucigalpa, Honduras with a wife and growing family.

Throughout his two years as president of VOSH/International, Dr. Jeff Marshall busied himself with a large array of presidential work which was quite traditional to what VOSH presidents were expected to do. He planned and conducted board and general membership meetings, he communicated often through the VOSH/International Newsletter while running all aspects of the administration of chapters, officers and committees. He answered calls and initiated calls with constant attention at providing information and resources that chapters needed to be effective in serving the visual needs of others.

The 2000 VOSH Annual Meeting was in Birmingham, Alabama hosted by Dr. Patti Fuhr, president of VOSH-Alabama and her team from the School of Optometry UAB (University of Alabama at Birmingham). It was a weekend of southern hospitality at its best.

The 2001 VOSH annual meeting was in Bradenton, Florida. Dr. Marshall took the lead in organizing this weekend. He scheduled two half-day meeting sessions so that participants had adequate time for relaxed discussion. On Friday evening there was a poolside wine and cheese party. Saturday's social event was at the Roaring 20's Pizza and Pipes where the attendees heard the music from a grand old theater organ.

In retrospect Dr. Marshall remembers being elected President of VOSH/International in Hollywood, Florida and ending his presidency with his last annual meeting in Bradenton, Florida. His mother, Blanch, living nearby, was on hand to see her son being recognized, applauded and given a plaque for his service as International President.

She must have been so proud!

Dr. Marshall was never one to "sweat the small stuff". VOSH had made a smooth transition from one millennium to the next. VOSH was poised to make some changes that would broaden its reach and expand its horizons.

The 2000's were a decade of fear in some ways with the destruction of the Twin Towers (9-11), Weapons of Mass Destruction (Iraq), and Banking Bailout (defaulted houses). On the other hand, VOSH had a huge expansion of opportunities to pursue a variety of interests and relationships – enabled by the coming of camera phones, I-pods and an explosion of social media sites – FaceBook, LinkedIn and Twitter.

VOSHers probably noted the oversized sunglass trend – even spreading to VOSH clinics overseas. VOSHers were likely to have seen the movie "Slumdog Millionaire".

2001-03 Dr. Harry Zeltzer – East gets first VOSH/ International President

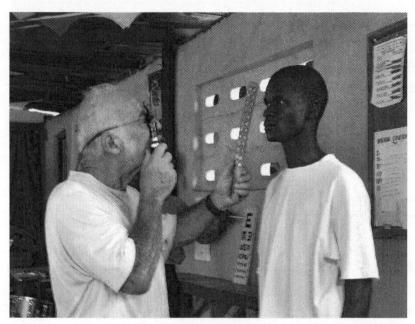

Dr. Harry Zeltzer on an early VOSH mission
(Courtesy of Dr. Dale Cole)

Up until 2001 all VOSH presidents came from the Mid-West. Now for the first time VOSH/International history, a wise man from the East, Boston, Massachusetts (VOSH-ONE), takes charge to lead VOSH as our President.

Dr. Harry Zeltzer had just joined with VOSH/International five years ago but brought a tremendous amount of experience and expertise with him. His dedication and enthusiasm was beyond compare.

The story of Dr. Zeltzer begins with the following *article published in 1999 in the VOSH/International Newsletter:*
Dr. Harry Zeltzer Takes on VOSH Challenges here and abroad
by Zabelle D'Amico
(dedicated Editor of the Newsletter)

Two roads diverged in a wood,
and I took the one less traveled by.
And that has made all the difference.

- *Robert Frost*

"When he retired from active optometry in 1986, Dr. Harry Zeltzer was in good health. He still enjoyed the creative, restless energy that had characterized his 35-year professional career, so he decided it was time to pursue interests he'd been forced to put off for years because of other commitments.

Initially, Dr. Zeltzer tried the back-breaking challenge of year-round commercial fishing using nets and traps. Then he took up growing herbs for a while. Eventually Dr. Zeltzer turned a portion of his skillfully appointed 18th century home into an antique shop. This continues to be a popular stop along busy Route 1 in Ipswich, Massachusetts.

Still, the most important decision Dr. Zeltzer made upon retiring, the one that has changed his life the most, was to sign on for his first VOSH eye care mission.

Since then, despite his myriad of other pursuits, Dr. Zeltzer has initiated or participated in over thirty eye care clinics around the globe, including El Salvador, Mexico, Haiti, Venezuela, Colombia, the Dominican Republic, Albania and the Ukraine. In addition, he has volunteered for month-long stints to serve Navajo reservations in Arizona and frontier nursing program in Kentucky.

Several years ago, following an eye clinic in Mexico, Dr. Zeltzer was invited by the wife of governor of the Yucatan to stay on to serve in some of the more remote villages and towns. She was willing to provide a van and driver. Housing was to be provided by hosts at each stop.

Assisted by his wife Joan, a nurse-midwife, Dr. Zeltzer spent the next three months navigating bumpy, dusty roads to reach pockets of people living in out-or-the-way places. Once there, he'd set up a table and start examining. Joan did much of the dispensing with inventory left over from the just-completed mission.

During their odyssey, the Zeltzers slept in private homes, in a rectory and even in an abandoned building which villagers had spruced up and furnished for the mission, complete with a kitchen and window curtains.

This past February, prior to participating in a weeklong eye clinic in El Salvador, Dr. Zeltzer and his wife spent a week serving in another remote village. 'There's always been an enormous need for eye care everywhere I've served as a VOSHer,' says Dr. Zeltzer, 'but it's especially heartwarming when we are able to reach people in outlying districts, far off the beaten track, where there is virtually no health care available whatsoever.'

Along with the offering his clinical services as a VOSHer, Dr. Zeltzer has been zealous in promoting awareness and participation in VOSH. He spoke with a gentle, almost hesitant tone, but anyone who's been on the receiving end of Dr. Zeltzer's infamous early AM phone calls knows how much he cares and how persistent he is in pursuing growth and change.

Three years ago, Dr. Zeltzer helped found VOSH-NECO, a committee of the New England Council of Optometrists and chapter of VOSH/International, to better serve the six-state New England region. He currently serves as president of the group.

In recognition of his efforts, Dr. Zeltzer was recently elected to a two-year term as vice-president of VOSH/International. Immediately following his appointment, Dr. Zeltzer was assigned the task of bringing the annual meeting to Boston. Now he's on the phone again, working in the background to make it a splendid weekend."

Dr. Zeltzer graduated in 1952 from the Massachusetts College of Optometry. He was in private practice for thirty-five years in Waltham, a suburb of Boston.

He was a bit of an inventor during those days inventing the "X-Chrom" contact lens which is still prescribed today. He also developed a color vision test, a genetic computer and a lens for enhancing hydrospheric vision. With another colleague, Dr. Zeltzer invented the Siezel-Fusor, a device that stimulates binocular vision.

As a Fellow of the American Academy of Optometry, Dr. Zeltzer has lectured and published both in the United States and Canada and also in United Kingdom and Ghana.

Dr. Harry Zeltzer's interest in becoming president was peaked in 1999 at the annual meeting in Boston when he had lunch with outgoing president Dr. Phil Hottel and his wife Thelma. Their casual conversation and reflection got Harry thinking about the possibility of someday serving as president of VOSH/International. Dr. Zeltzer was elected president in 2000 and began serving in fall 2001.

His first challenge and concern was the possible fears of VOSH mission trips going out in the aftermath of "nine-eleven" – the terrorist attack on the Twin Towers and Pentagon. In the first VOSH Newsletter as president, Dr. Zeltzer wrote this message to VOSH members.

"From the President's Desk", *by Dr. Harry Zeltzer, published in the VOSH Newsletter, Fall/Winter, 2001-2002:*

"One of the greatest cities in the world will now be remembered as the site of death and destruction on September 11, 2001. It will also be remembered for the enormous courage and sacrifice of police and firefighters who lost their lives. Personally, I felt what happened also rocked the foundation of our civilization drawing us into a new and dangerous era.

After receiving several calls from members, I realized terrorism also posed a threat to VOSH, mainly for those of us who travel to underdeveloped countries. The ordinary risks of traveling to a Third World country begins to pale in light of that tragedy. Now we must reconsider purpose and risks.

As unpaid volunteers our individual commitment to the Third World eye programs should and can be discharged without explanation. We have a responsibility to examine our purpose as VOSHers versus our duty to loved ones; not an easy task for humanitarians. Compromise and carefully select a mission or serve in other ways. The other reality is an overwhelming need for eye care where it is not available or affordable. That need can only be addressed by VOSH and an un-thwarted determination to correct an imbalance caused by poverty. It is a personal decision for each one of us to make.

For the record, I am happy to report that VOSH is still in business. Missions to Mexico and Lithuania left as scheduled days after the attack. Two or three more missions to Mexico, Venezuela and El Salvador remain scheduled for November and at present there are no missions canceled for next year. Understandably, we have had some individual cancellations but the empty spaces have been refilled. As the new president I am encouraged to move forward and proceed with plans. I hope to increase membership and increase missions using our up-scaled newsletter and new web site. I also wish to bring chapters into closer family by sharing data and building on the sound steps of my predecessor, Dr. Jeff Marshall and fellow officers."

It was likely, at the time, that each VOSH member had a personal story about that day "9-11, 2001". Dr. Zeltzer remembers being a consultant with the Helen Keller Foundation at the time he was seeing this unfold on television. He called the executive director who was about to leave on a ferry heading to the headquarters in Manhattan, which was one block from the twin towers. Needless to say the ferry never left. Within a week the Helen Keller Foundation vintage headquarters less than a mile away crumbled.

"From the President's Desk" turned out to be a recurring theme of Dr. Zeltzer's presidency. As it was, Dr. Zeltzer did spend many hours at his desk at home communicating the message of VOSH/International to all that would listen. His desk and the view from that window overlooking a beautiful countryside, gave him inspiration.

His greatest ongoing challenge, as he expressed in an interview, was to build a strong reason for volunteers to value the membership they held in VOSH International and to extend that value to a chapter's benefits in belonging as well. At the time there were isolated expectations of VOSH/International benefits that exceeded administrative capabilities.

Having a good working relationship with volunteers, he felt a wide diversity of attitudes toward VOSH from "we love this organization" to "what has VOSH done for me lately?"

Dr. Zeltzer took these concerns head-on and went about the business of beefing-up benefits to membership. He began with a focus on enhancing the VOSH Website.

The VOSH Website, at the time, was up and running, but as things continued to change, faced daunting challenges. After working with technical and logistic issues Dr. Zeltzer began to focus on his administrative challenges that would keep him busy for the next few years.

Meeting the challenge took many forms including giving chapters accessibility to VOSH manuals, information, supplies, board actions and VOSH news. And yes, much of this was done through the VOSH Website on Harry's computer.

Building on this website infrastructure, he went about his job of connecting people with VOSH, giving them the availability to leadership and value for the dues they paid to VOSH.

Meeting his challenges, Dr. Zeltzer then created and distributed a comprehensive VOSH Chapter Survey sent at the end of 2001. VOSH/International Questionnaire Results with forty-one percent of VOSH Chapters (11 Chapters) responding to this survey:

- Overall results indicate that VOSH Chapters unanimously support endorsement of the WHO initiative.
- All respondents treat eye infections on missions

- All use recycled eyeglasses for adults and children, but all agree good recycled glasses for children are not readily available.
- Most chapters would like to see VOSH/International find funds to help support Student Chapters.
- The result also showed a large number of individual responses explaining their situation, needs and practices.

The survey turned out to be an excellent source for knowing the needs of VOSH volunteers and chapters' interests.

Dr. Harry Zeltzer's administration was now running strong. In his next message, *"From the President's Desk" published in the VOSH Newsletter, Spring/Summer, 2002,* he writes: "I am pleased to report that VOSH/International is growing (three new Chapters on the way) and that formerly inactive Chapters are regrouping and getting trips underway.

Still, due to the enormous need for eye care in underdeveloped countries, VOSH/International is seeking to increase membership...

...I cannot overstate the importance of our website both within and beyond our organization. Aside from keeping us connected to one another, it is serving as an important database for upcoming missions, people seeking optometrists, clinics, grants, eyeglass recycling centers and more. Check it out frequently: www.VOSH.org.

Your executive board continues to reach out and is in constant contact with Chapters. It is our pleasure to serve as coordinator for the growing number of Chapters and as a proud parent organization.

In other news, VOSH/International recently signed a declaration with the WHO (World Health Organization) and (and gained support from) the AOA (American Optometric

Association) to help eradicate preventable blindness by the year 2020.

Achieving a goal of this magnitude for a non-governmental organization is a difficult task which requires cooperation with other signatories of VISION 2020. Therefore, I propose a closer, but independent relationship with the AOA which will lend its resources and help VOSH reach its fullest potential."

The 2002 VOSH Annual Meeting was in Vancouver, British Columbia, Canada, hosted by Marina Roma-March and TWECS (Third World Eye Care Society), our VOSH-British Columbia Chapter.

The guest speakers for the meeting were, Dr. Scott Brisbon, President of the World Council of Optometry; Dr. Stanley Yamane, Vice President of Americas Professional Affairs, Vistakon; and VOSH/International Past President Mike Listenberger, OD of VOSH-Michigan.

The highlight of this annual meeting was recognition of VOSH receiving a $20,000 grant from Vistakon by Dr. Stanley Yamane.

The October weekend was a success. The beautiful city of Vancouver, BC was, indeed, a wonderful backdrop for the annual meeting!

"From the President's Desk" VOSH Newsletter, spring 2003, Dr. Harry Zeltzer communicates, "Two major organizational changes, one in membership and the other regarding the Annual Meeting, were approved in Vancouver last October. These changes will strengthen VOSH/International and broaden our efforts in providing eye care to needy people all around the globe.

In the past, participation in the Annual Meeting of VOSH/International was unintentionally limited to executive officers and the board of directors, conveying a sense of exclusivity.

To create a closer family of humanitarians within our 32 Chapters, the constitution was amended in Vancouver. Beginning in 2004, each Chapter member will automatically become a member of VOSH/International.

The second major change was to schedule the VOSH/International Annual Meeting to dovetail with the annual American Optometric Association (AOA) Congress that's held in June...

...Our co-meeting with the AOA also opens the door to reaching other humanitarian-minded individuals and hence provides us the opportunity to extend our reach in bringing global eye care to those who are deprived of the service.

This upcoming meeting marks a new era for VOSH/International. The schedule enables us to integrate with the other non-governmental organizations (NGOs) who have similar interests. Possibilities for forming relationships with VOSH/International will be explored by a panel of speakers from several organizations. It is our belief that, working together, we can attain the common goals of Vision 2020..."

VOSH acquires largest donation in its history

In 2002 Vistakon made a major donation to VOSH. (Vistakon is a division of Johnson & Johnson Vision Care, Inc.) They awarded VOSH/International a grant of $20,000, the largest ever received. This was arranged with Dr. Ann Slocum-Edmonds contacting Vistakon through a friendship connection to AOA Public Relations Manager, Pat Cummings, who connected Ann with Dr. Stanley Yamane.

"The grant was announced jointly by VOSH/International Vice-president, Dr. Ann Slocum-Edmonds, who serves as a corporate liaison, together with Dr. Stanley Yamane, Vice President of the Americas Professional Affairs Division for Vistakon." – *VOSH Newsletter, spring-summer 2002.*

VOSH gratefully accepted the generous donation with greatest appreciation.

In 2003 Vistakon followed with a second very generous donation of $20,000 to VOSH/International. Upon presentation of the gift at the VOSH annual meeting in Vancouver, Dr. Yamane said in an excerpt *(VOSH Newsletter, Winter/Spring 2003)*, "One of Vistakon's goals is to develop a lasting partnership with VOSH/International. He challenged the membership to "dream, believe, dare and do."

He noted, "Your VOSH/International leadership has a dream they believe and are daring to do, to help those who are unable to help themselves. They need your support to help them do what seems like an impossible mission. I am confident that you will rise to the challenges before you as we move forward into 2003."

Following these donations from Vistakon, other smaller donations continued to support the VOSH organization, both locally and internationally.

At this same time the VOSH/International Board approved all members of VOSH chapters to be members of VOSH with payment voluntary. *This was explained in the VOSH/International Newsletter, winter/spring 2003:*

"VOSH/International is a 501(c)(3) corporation, meaning that your contributions are tax-deductible.

In changes approved in Vancouver, all members of VOSH Chapters are now automatically members of VOSH/International. A voluntary suggested donation of $10 per person is recommended from each Chapter.

Individual VOSH/International dues remain $30 per year. Chapter dues are $100 per year. We appreciate all donations big or small; because it is through them that we are able to advance our projects to provide eye care to the needy worldwide..."

The 2003 VOSH/International Annual Meeting was in San Diego, California. This year the primary VOSH meeting was on Tuesday, June 17th to accommodate networking with the American Optometric Association. A full day of interesting discussions ensued followed by a VOSH display booth at the AOA exhibition hall.

The goal was met for VOSH members to "leave with fresh ideas and solutions to problems, closer contacts with other volunteers and a deeper awareness of VOSH and its global role in providing eye care to needy people."

To reflect on some of the **highlights** of VOSH/International President Dr. Harry Zeltzer, 2001-03, these excerpts were taken from his files:

"On behalf of the Executive Board I also want to thank Vistakon, a Division of Johnson and Johnson and Dr. Stanley Yamane, Vice President of Professional Affairs for their second generous donation of $20,000. His lecture featured VOSH Organizational Enhancement. Not only representing our sponsor but Stan is also a new member of VOSH...

...Some of our decisions will have historical significance. One exciting idea is to co-meet annually with the AOA in June. The advantage of this arrangement is to gain visibility and an economical saving for those who attend both meetings...

...Proudly, the board of directors approved five new chapters Virginia, Arizona, Africa (Tanzania), India (Delhi) and Varanasi (India). This brings us to thirty two...

...A resolution approved VOSH as a non sectarian and non political organization. This will enable us to have greater opportunity for fund raising and align us with mainstream organizations such as Doctors without Borders...

...Membership will no longer be fragmented. All VOSH members will be members of VOSH/International...

...VOSH/International has created a reliable line of communication with faculty advisors of the 17 student chapters (SVOSH)...

...Our website, frequently critiqued is an extensive source of information. It provides mission dates, chapter photos, a message board, membership applications, contribution forms, scientific papers, newsletters, the results of an identity survey and more...

...Biannual newsletters have been upgraded and distributed to schools of optometry and at professional meetings. Newsletters can also be downloaded on our website. Last October VOSH was featured in the Wall Street Journal as one of the best humanitarian vacations...

...Dr. Zeltzer recognizes Zabelle D'Amico for being a key person in working closely with him to not only communicate, but to produce outstanding newsletters...

...A movement to create a Fellowship of VOSH/ International (FVI) has been approved. Stuart Frank, past vice president of VOSH/International, advisor and president of VOSH/ Northwest is the author...

...A new volunteer post has been created to benefit chapters. John Gehrig, Esq and president of VOSH-Florida will serve as our legal counsel...

...We are moving towards globalized eye care, open to affiliations with other leading non-governmental organizations...

...We also became an affiliate of the World Council of Optometry whose purpose is to improve the quality of optometric education in underdeveloped nations. (Dr. Scott Brisbin, Immediate past president of the WCO attended our VOSH/ International meeting in Vancouver, British Columbia). World Health Organization's program is known as VISION 2020 -The Right to Sight. The goal is to eliminate preventable blindness by the year 2020. Since refractive errors are recognized as one of the leading causes of preventable blindness VOSH will be reaching more of the world's 180 million visually disabled. Last year we treated over 140,000 patients. Next year our projections are greater."

- *Harry I Zeltzer, OD, FAAO*

VOSH/International retools itself for the new millennium

Dr. Zeltzer's legacy was leading VOSH/International to double its capacity toward meeting the overwhelming vision needs stated by Vision 2020. It began with a series of large grants ($20,000 annually from Vistakon) which created a financial 'game-changer'. These grants allowed VOSH/International to greatly expand its outward reach to look globally toward strategic ways of addressing the needs of 180 million who are "functionally visually impaired."

These large donations, coupled with dues easement (board action), represented a primary paradigm shift in the financial funding of VOSH/International. Before 2002 funding was 85% by dues/fees from members/chapters; and after 2003 funding was as much as 70% from grants.

For twenty years VOSH/International generated ten to fifteen thousand dollars annual income. In the new millennium income doubled, becoming thirty-five to forty-five thousand dollars annually.

Much of the "thanks" for this new level of achievement belongs to Dr. Pat Cummings, Vistakon Director of Professional Affairs and past president of the AOA who succeeded Dr. Stanley Yamane upon retirement. Sadly, Dr. Cummings, a huge VOSH ally, died when his private plane went down.

2003-05 Dr. Dale Cole makes history as VOSH/International President

As an author's note, most of the materials for writing this history came from the VOSH archives given to me by Dr. Dale Cole, my predecessor as historian. Dr. Cole also published a history of VOSH in 2004 and has taken many wonderful VOSH photos.

Dr. Dale Cole's predecessor, Dr. Zeltzer, shared the first meeting of Dr. Cole when "he rescued me (Harry) from a run-down hotel in Detroit." Since their first meeting, they have often shared hotel rooms at VOSH meetings. Dr. Zeltzer goes on to tell about Dr. Cole as a person: "The most impressive experience was 'seeing' his calm demeanor in Ghana when his luggage got lost in flight. Dale, being bigger than anyone else on the mission, had to wear Ghanian clothing from the local market. He made quite a hit meeting dignitaries and village chiefs wearing loose gowns with bright colors. We almost lost him and his camera as he blended into the culture."

"Meet your new VOSH/International President: Dale Cole, OD", *reprinted from the VOSH Newsletter Fall/Winter 2003-2004.*

"The new VOSH/International president is deeply rooted in VOSH history. In a sense, you might say he's actually lived it, since his involvement began back in the 1970s when he worked with the founder of VOSH, Fellow Kansas optometrist Dr. Franklin Harms.

During the very year of his first mission, Dr. Cole agreed to serve as co-director of VOSH-Kansas with Dr. Don Kuehn. The two continued to spearhead the VOSH-Kansas Chapter.

Through his years of participation, Dr. Cole has led or taken part in 16 VOSH missions to various sites in Central and South America, Haiti, Africa, Ghana and VietNam.

Dr. Cole has served two terms of the VOSH/International Executive Board. During the past year as president-elect, he was responsible for writing two publications, a "Mission Book," and a "History of VOSH." Already the Mission Book has become an invaluable resource/guide for all VOSHers. His "History of VOSH" represents the first time anyone has attempted to document the origins, growth and developments of this organization. The assignment was a difficult one because, until a few years ago, VOSH remained a grassroots organization.

His VOSH efforts have provided Dale another passion – photography. Initially, he took up a camera simply to take slides on VOSH missions in order to enhance presentations back home. Eventually Dale enlarged a few of his fun shots and began exhibiting them."

"From the President's Desk" Dr. Dale Cole begins his presidential term with a status report as outlined in the following article from the *VOSH/International Newsletter, Fall/Winter 2003-04:*

"As I sat pondering the first few months of my presidency, I asked myself if we are meeting the challenge set forth by fellow VOSH member Dr. Stan Yamane when he announced the second Vistakon donation of $20,000 to VOSH/International in Vancouver last fall. In a keynote address at that Annual Meeting, Dr. Yamane presented the Vistakon Challenge: spread the word about VOSH and meet the opportunities for growth with enthusiasm!

How have we done since that October 2002 meeting? Let's take a look!

Mission Book: VOSH/International has developed a "Mission Book" to aid in preparing and conducting a VOSH mission. The "VOSH Services and Information" section of our website has been updated and individual parts of the book are now available online. The "Mission Book" is also available in hard copy or CD form and is being mailed to each Chapter president.

VOSH History Published: We now have a written history of VOSH that follows the birth of the organization under founder (and fellow Kansan) Dr. Franklin Harms, to the present era of VOSH/International. The history was distributed to all participants at the Vancouver VOSH meeting. It is available to any VOSH member upon request and it is posted on the VOSH website.

VOSH Website: Our website continues to get hits from around the world and is an important link with the world. The number of visits VOSH/International has received is amazing...

...One informative section under the "VOSH Services and Information" heading on the website is entitled "What does VOSH do for you." Check it out. You'll be impressed with what Chapters get for the small contribution made through the state Chapter.

Changes in VOSH/International Membership Structure: Several state Chapters have already benefitted from the constitutional amendment passed in Vancouver in 2002 in which all members of state Chapters automatically become members of VOSH/International...

...Co-ordination of AOS and VOSH/International: During the 2003 VOSH/International Annual Meeting held in San Diego in conjunction with the AOA's Annual Congress, we were graciously welcomed by the AOA President Pat Cummings, OD and President Elect Vic Conners, O.D...

...The AOA invited VOSH/International to participate in the AOA exhibit hall in San Diego. To keep costs down, we shared a booth with VOSH California. VOSH/International had numerous visitors. Several exhibitors around us were amazed at the activity we generated...

...Lions Invite VOSH/International to Denver Meeting: VOSH/International teamed with the AOA in late June when both of our organizations were invited to participate at the world-wide Lions International Meeting... ...Many visitors were hearing about the work of VOSH and the AOA for the first time. A number of potential missions and new Chapters emerged from the discussions.

Forging Relations with Others: Immediate past president Dr. Harry Zeltzer continues to be instrumental in making contact with various health related organizations. Through his efforts, we have bonded with many organizations worldwide...

...Communication with Chapters: Your VOSH/International vice-presidents (Dr. Marina Roma-March and Dr. Larry Hookway, OD) have been assigned to serve as liaison with specific state Chapters and they have additional duties. (keeping communication going)..."

Dr. Dale Cole had a great deal of "pressure" as President of VOSH/International. Since Dale learned VOSH from our Founder Dr. Franklin Harms, he felt he had to do well. Having been trained in the basic principle he continued the model of growth and administration that Dr. Harms had demonstrated. It is noteworthy that even during Dr. Cole's presidency, thirty-some years later, the standard administrative model (except financing) remained the same.

Dr. Dale Cole outlined his administrative goals in the *VOSH Newsletter, Fall/Winter 2003-04:* "**Setting Goals as we move forward"**

"VOSH/International President Dale Cole, OD, has set just two major goals for the two years of his presidency:

1. To expand the VOSH family organization and SVOSH within the USA, Canada and abroad in order to enable VOSH to serve more individuals.
2. To enhance awareness of VOSH/International by educating the public about the work of VOSH/International."

Dr. Cole hopes to achieve these advances through continued growth in eye care missions, through the VOSH International website (www.VOSH.org) and by participation and staffing a VOSH/International booth at meetings of related healthcare organizations.

VOSH/International endorsed the "Vision 2020" document of the WCO (World Council of Optometry) and the WHO (World Health Organization) in 2001.

Dr. Cole believes that, "The goal set by the document, to eliminate preventable blindness by 2020, is attainable and he welcomes the opportunity to face the challenge."

Although "permanent eye clinics" and "sustainable programs" had been part of VOSH outreach for many years, its scope was rather limited. Dr. Dave Krasnow and Dr. Greg Pearl (VOSH-California) had made early inroads into building the foundations of sustainability.

In the early 2000's these sustainability strategies came to the fore-front of VOSH for two reasons. First the income had been boosted dramatically in the last three years ($60,000 by Vistakon) giving VOSH more resources; and secondly the "Declaration to Eradicate Preventable Blindness by the year 2020" (Vision 2020) by the World Health Organization (WHO). Quickly picking up this initiative were the World Council of Optometry (WCO), the American Optometric Association (AOA) and VOSH/ International. These organizations were on the "front-lines" of implementing this initiative. Many other global organizations followed endorsement.

VOSH/International published a number articles, including, "VOSH's Role in Strategies to reduce the Global Burden of Blindness" by Janet Leasher, OD, MPH (2002), "Integrating and Sustaining the Humanitarian effort" in VOSH Newsletter (2003), and "Grassroots Optometry – toward Self-sustainability" by Erik Weissberg, OD, Associate Professor of Optometry, New England College of Optometry, and Heather Zometzer.

Since Dr. Dale Cole initiated action on "sustainability" and "need," he visited several Indian optometric organizational meetings in the Far East. This speech was given at a conference attended by optometrists, medical personnel and workers of the eye/health camps by Dr. Dale Cole, President of VOSH/ International on February 8, 2014.

Presentation in India at a "Preventable Blindness" conference

"I would like to thank BISWA (optometric association), Mr. Malick, Hare Patnaik, and all of you that helped organize this neat meeting today. It is an honor and pleasure to participate in this conference as we go about developing a plan to eradicate preventable blindness by 2020.

Some of you may have never heard or read the actual proclamation entitled 'Declaration to Eradicate Preventable Blindness by the year 2020', presented by the World Council of Optometry and the World Health Organization which was endorsed and signed December 6, 2001 in Philadelphia, Pennsylvania, USA by 23 major organizations from around the world. VOSH/ International was proud to be one of the original endorsees.

Dr. Cole reads the 'VISION 2020 Declaration' published in the 'Sustainability' section of this publication.

After hearing these words, it is obvious that eventually it becomes necessary for those who are responsible for the eye care of people without means and resources, to assemble as one and declare a combined effort to eliminate preventable blindness.

VOSH recognizes the disastrous consequences of blindness as it affects an individual, the family, the nation and the world. Therefore, we applaud the resolution of VISION 2020 to eradicate a prevalent condition with corrective means that are readily available to modern nations of the world.

Demographically, blindness and visual impairment is worldwide. According to WHO (World Health Organization), there are an estimated 180 million visually impaired people worldwide, or approximately 3% of the populations. Of those, 40-50 million are functionally blind – having less than 20/400 in the better eye; 110 million have low vision – having 20/200 to 20/400 in the better-seeing eye.

How are the 'visually impaired' geographically distributed? Nine of 10 visually impaired live in developing nations; sub-Saharan Africa, China, India, and developing Asia (excluding Japan) and nearby islands account for 75% of all the visually impaired in the world. It has been stated that up to 80% of blindness found in developing countries is, in principle, avoidable or curable. Sadly, countless people throughout the world have little or no access to even basic eye care services.

What are the major causes of vision loss worldwide? Cataracts are a very significant cause of vision loss at 43% or 16-20 million people. For most of the developing world, surgery is inaccessible or unaffordable. Thus, delay of care is an important consideration. As the world ages, we will face more age-related degenerative diseases such as cataracts, macular degeneration, diabetic retinopathy, optic neuropathy, etc. These will become the most common causes of blindness.

Glaucoma ranks high among major causes of vision loss, estimated at 15% of the population. Glaucoma presents several challenges – the diagnosis is difficult, the treatment is expensive, labor intensive, and compliance can be questionable, particularly where access to medication is often non-existent. Interestingly, different subtypes of glaucoma may have higher incidence in different ethnic groups. For instance, I found a significantly higher incidence of glaucoma while on a mission to Haiti.

Trachoma ranks at about 11% of the population. It has been endemic in Africa, Eastern Mediterranean, Southeast Asia, 6 Latin American countries and Yemen. There are approximately 18 million children. It is generally caused by Vitamin A deficiency, measles, and neonatal conjunctivitis.

Ametropia, or the need of spectacles due to refractive error, is often overlooked as a major cause of visual impairment. Several research studies have noted that refractive problems are the most common cause of visual impairment. For instance, spectacle correction accounted for 76% of all treatment in rural South Africa clinic, compared with 21% medications and 5% surgery.

Another study revealed that up to half of the children in African institutions for the blind were able to read normal or large print type simply by using spectacles or a stand magnifier.

The simple provision of spectacles may significantly impact the quality of life and economic productivity of millions who have no access to nor can afford, what much of the developed world takes for granted.

Now that we have looked at some of the main issues causing the problem of visual impairment, what can be done by the industrialized countries to move toward the goal of VISION 2020 – elimination of preventable blindness?

1. We must first understand the causes of preventable blindness and where the problems are most prevalent.
2. We must develop a plan to provide eye care, in its many forms, to those in need.

3. We must educate the leaders and the communities within the developing countries as to the problems and how they can contribute to the solution.
4. Worldwide, we must work together as a team to eradicate preventable vision loss.

It is by actions, such as we are taking today, that the issue of preventable blindness can be eliminated. Thank you for your time and sincerely hope that we can work together to make this a better world. Let me leave you with this thought by Kahlil Gibran:

'You give but little when you give of your possessions. It is when you give of yourself that you truly give.'"

When Dr. Dale Cole returned to the states he addressed issues of concern from a divergence of perspectives. This divergence of new and traditional paradigms brought member's concerns.

On one hand, progressive proponents were suggesting that traditional visiting teams providing direct care could not make a significant statistical difference in meeting the enormity of the problem and argued that onsite temporary clinics were not sustainable. On the other hand, the traditionalists valued the humanity of caring and sharing with people in need, the interesting locations that induce volunteers to participate, and the motivation it provides funding support and community visibility. And "yes", they repeat the axiom, "it may not matter to the world – but it matters to them."

In the process of explaining the "new paradigm" and its impact, Dr. Cole answered a lot of member's questions. While doing so he assured them of their value in VOSH, whatever their service persuasion.

The 2004 VOSH/International Annual Meeting was in Orlando, Florida and coincided again with the American Optometric Association and World Council of Optometry, giving attendees expanded options to pursue their interests. The featured speakers for VOSH included Stan Brock representing "Remote Area Medical" serving rural USA; Alfred Rosenbloom, OD, speaking on "Low Vision Practice in a Public Health Setting"; Joshua Silver, PhD, speaking on "Self-Refracting eyeglasses"; Dumas M Simeus of "Providing Medical relief to Haiti"; and H. Hauser Weiler, MD, speaking on "Partnering with VOSH in Honduras". At this meeting VOSH also accepted donations from the President of Spectera for $5,000, and for a third year in a row, a check for $20,000 presented by Dr. Pat Cummings, Vice President of Vistakon.

The 2005 VOSH/International Annual Meeting was near Dallas, Texas and again scheduled in June to connect with a diversity of resources including excellent speakers for VOSH. The feature speakers along with their entitled talk were Robert Norman Bailey, OD on "Ethics of VOSH Eye Care Missions"; Howard 'Skip' Charles on "REIMS, VOSH and expediting the distribution of recycled eyeglasses"; PDG Ike Fitzgerald on "TLERC (eyeglass collection center) and VOSH"; Hare Krishna Patnaik on "VOSH in India"; Jennifer Staple on "Unite for Sight and VOSH"; Satya Verma, OD on "The AOA and VOSH"; and Jerry Vincent, OD on "A Public Health approach to Eye Care in Developing Countries".

Dr. Dale Cole was thanked and applauded at the Texas VOSH meeting for his hard work and dedication to moving VOSH forward into the millennium.

In his last "**From the President's Desk**" *published in the VOSH Newsletter, Spring 2005,* he writes:

"It seems like it was just yesterday when I started my tenure as president and now I am writing my last presidential message. What a two years it's been! We have expanded nationally and internationally and we have become associated with many like-minded organizations...

...During the past two years we have established bonds with S.E.E. (Surgical Eye Expeditions), TLERC (Texas Lions eyeglass Recycling Center), Unite for Sight and our own AOA...

...We are excited about our continuing growth. It will enable us to serve many more countries, thus moving closer to the objective of eliminating preventable blindness by the year 2020.

(We re-enlisted Dr. Harry Zeltzer as the first professional Executive Director of VOSH/International.) In March (2005), Executive Director Harry Zeltzer, OD, and I traveled to Kumasi, Ghana (West Africa) with a VOSH team from Pacific University. We met with students of KNUST (Kwame Nkruma University of Science and Technology) and with representative of Unite for Sight, who was on a mission in the area. While there, Dr. Zeltzer represented VOSH/International as an invited speaker at the WCO (World Council of Optometry) Annual Meeting in Accra, Ghana...

...Mark Cook, OD, president of VOSH-Michigan, spent a month in the tsunami region as a volunteer with Project Hope. Hare Patnaik and I have scheduled the first VOSH tsunami relief mission there...

...The future of VOSH/International is exciting. I am proud to be a part of it. Thanks to all of you for making VOSH/International a leader in the third-world eye care arena."

Dr. Dale Cole lived up to his Franklin Harms heritage as he finished his term by preserving the traditional values of VOSH and introducing some new ones.

2005-07 Dr. Ruth McAndrews is the first woman VOSH/International President

Dr. Ruth McAndrews begins with strengths as a detailed thinker with a clear sense of priorities as to what actions were necessary to make an impact. She was also able to clearly express thoughts and ideas in a way that could connect to others.

Dr. McAndrews went on her first VOSH mission in 1979 with Dr. Walt Marshall, VOSH Indiana, one of the early founders of VOSH International. Dr. McAndrews also had the distinction of being one of three past VOSH International Presidents that graduated Illinois College of Optometry together in 1979, the two others being Dr. Jim Hess and Dr. Wayne Vander Leest.

Dr. McAndrews became another 'game-changer' as she initiated the doubling of VOSH/International's outreach toward global impact by building networking relationships with partner corporations. Eventually her efforts would bring the revenues from $30,000 annually to $60,000 and more – revenues applied to meeting the global needs of the visually impaired. A key part of this growth came from Dr. McAndrews' connections with Optometry Giving Sight (OGS).

This global perspective was continued as the next three presidents, Dr. McAndrews, Dr. Hookway, and Dr. Pearl, united their efforts by working in different arenas (primarily concentrated in Nicaragua) toward sustainability and global outreach.

This account of Ruth McAndrews as a leader was published in the VOSH/International Newsletter, Spring 2005. **It's another historic moment for VOSH/International**.

"When Ruth McAndrews, OD, assumes the helm of VOSH/International in June, she will have the distinction of being the first woman to serve as president of the organization since its inception in the mid 1970's.

A quiet, unassuming woman with a warm, can-do attitude, Dr. McAndrews grew up on a farm in southern Iowa. After receiving a Bachelor of Science degree from the University of Iowa, she attended Illinois College of Optometry (ICO).

Following graduation from ICO, 'Dr. Ruth', as she is more commonly known, returned to Iowa to open her own private practice in Durant, a small town west of Davenport. She has been active in the local Chamber of Commerce and the Tri-County Community Band.

Dr. Ruth served six years on the Iowa Board of Optometry Examiners and was elected Young Optometrist of the Year in 1982. She is a past president of VOSH-Iowa and has served on the VOSH/International board since 2002.

It is interesting to note that Dr. Ruth's initial VOSH experience was to Haiti in 1979, a formative period in VOSH history. Since then, she has participated in over twenty VOSH missions.

Her most memorable pair of VOSH patients included a lady in her mid-70's who was an uncorrected aphakic. The remarkable event was that she had been brought to the clinic by her 23 diopter myopic daughter.

Dr. Ruth and her husband John reside in Davenport. She is an active member of Grace Lutheran Church. The couple enjoys traveling, hiking, bicycle riding, folk dancing and ballroom dancing."

Dr. McAndrews inherited a VOSH organization that had grown in its networking capabilities reaching out around the world. As president she also reached out, keeping communication open and active with a growing number of other Non-Government Organizations (NGO's) who were working together to address the huge challenge of meeting the needs of 640 million people needing eye care.

Her time was spent busy with volunteers, working in the field, and moving VOSH into new methods and delivery modes. In her first address to the VOSH membership she writes her editorial **"From the President's Desk"** by Dr. Ruth McAndrews *published in VOSH/International Newsletter Fall, Winter 2005-2006:*
VOSH/International Board makes organizational changes

"Volunteer Optometric Services to Humanity (VOSH) is now over thirty years old. I remember going to VOSH/International meetings several years ago where the biggest wish was a central data source for information. Where do other Chapters get supplies? Who has found a good host in a particular location? What obstacles or challenges did other mission leaders encounter and how did they manage the situation? While we networked in person and in periodic newsletters, information was scattered and difficult to access.

Today with the VOSH/International website and electronic communication, this dream has become a reality. There have been many occasions where these connections have saved and enhanced missions, but no example is so dramatic as with Hurricane Katrina.

As we go to print, our Public Health Advisor, Dr. Jerry Vincent, is in Thailand preparing a comprehensive plan for optometric assistance for hurricane victims.

Dr. Lloyd Pate of VOSH-Texas and the University of Houston College of Optometry set up a temporary eye clinic in the Houston Astrodome and were able to broadcast their needs. VOSH-Florida and Spectera were able to send frames immediately. We notified Mark Sachs of Restoring Vision, an organization that supplies readers and plano sunglasses for the cost of freight and photos.

VOSH-Virginia sprang into action to enlist volunteers when notified by the VA Department of Health that 1,500 evacuees would be arriving at Fort Prickett in Blackstone, Virginia.

And, when it appeared that victims were to be brought to Camp Edwards in Massachusetts, VOSH-NECO, with the Massachusetts Society of Optometrists, was already offering to provide eye care for the anticipated influx. While that project has been scaled back significantly for the moment, once again, it indicates our ability and willingness to take immediate action.

Similarly, last winter, with the input of Dr. Vincent and our Asian Pacific Advisor Hare Patnaik, we have been able to provide an organized response to the Tsunami region. Dr. Dale Cole led a mission team to that area in late October.

Ultimately, VOSH/International and its Chapters are doing their best to communicate and coordinate with the American Optometric Association, state associations, local optometric societies, and other world-wide humanitarian organizations. Our goal is to be part of the solution in the circumstances.

In the meantime, the need for eye care elsewhere is still overwhelming. In addition to our traditional mission programs, VOSHers are also helping to establish permanent clinics...

...As a follow-up to the visit Drs. Cole and Zeltzer made to Ghana, we are now working with Rotarians and World Medical Relief in Detroit to send more books and examination equipment to the optometry schools in Ghana. Training local providers, improved health care education, and better equipment, results in better ongoing eye care.

All of these efforts require time and money. Consequently, the VOSH/International executive board met with a professional moderator in order to develop a long-range plan. The first step of this plan was implemented by a vote of Chapters in September. We changed the constitution allowing us to expand the size of our working board of directors. Executive Director and Webmaster Dr. Harry Zeltzer, and Secretary-Treasurer Mr. Charles Covington have graciously been doing near-full time positions in perpetuity with no salaries. While VOSH/International has been blessed with generous corporate support, we need to establish additional long-term funding in order to maintain and expand our services. I would challenge anyone to find an organization that has accomplished this much with no paid staff.

Together with your help, we face the challenges ahead."

One of Dr. McAndrews greatest strengths was to invite and draw volunteers into working for the VOSH causes, allowing them to identify and utilize their own, individual interests and abilities. This part of her administration was in full-stride by mid-year.

During her term, Dr. McAndrews oversaw the involvement of VOSH/International in the VERAS (Visión, Education, Rendimiento, Aprendizaje, and Sostenibilidad) project that was conducted under the umbrella of UNESCO. The purpose of the organization was to train local teachers and health promoters in the detection of childhood visual health problems, to diagnose and treat the visual problems detected in school children, and to create a strong network of visual health activists in Central America. Dr. Patti Fuhr took a leadership role in developing this project. VOSH/International became involved mostly in Nicaragua where the next two presidents remained very active with this and other Nicaraguan test projects to explore sustainability solutions.

This is also a time when VOSH began working with KNUST (Kwame, Nkrumah University of Science and Technology) Optometry School in Ghana. This project placed SVOSH optometry students from the Pacific University College of Optometry with students in the KNUST optometry school in Ghana. This co-mission was led by Dr. Dale Cole, John Randall, and Dr. Harry Zeltzer. They also visited and worked with the University of Cape Coast Optometry School students in a similar capacity.

A few years later, with regular contact, and with the generous donation of equipment mentioned below, the optometry school at KNUST became a SVOSH (student VOSH) chapter.

Following future developments, VOSH-Ghana became officially recognized by the government under the leadership of Dr. Adjei, Abena in 2016.

VOSH helps send Ophthalmic Equipment to KNUST Optometry School in Ghana and UCC Optometry School in Nigeria. Collecting donated and new equipment and then sending it to optometry schools was under full-swing in the summer of 2007. This was coordinated and expedited by Dr. Nelson Edwards VOSH-Michigan (also Rotarian) who assisted the Michigan Rotary

Clubs and the World Medical Relief organization in sending a 40-foot container to Ghana. Dr. Zeltzer, Executive Director of VOSH and Mr. Kojo Dom, President of the Detroit Rotary Club were also in Detroit to prepare the manifest for shipment. The value was estimated to be in excess of $300,000 and cost $12,200 to ship.

Contributing donors included Essilor, Luxotica, and the World Council of Optometry. Part of the shipment went on to help the new optometry school at the University of Cape Coast, Department of Optometry (UCC) in Nigeria as well.

These were very busy years for VOSH/International and Dr. Ruth McAndrews.

Fortunately a new Executive Director, Dr. Harry Zeltzer, helped these projects move forward.

Dr. Ruth McAndrews addressed the VOSH membership *in "From the President's Desk" reprinted from the VOSH/International Newsletter, Spring, 2006.*

You can help us create a vision for our future

"The VOSH/International Board is addressing its vision of the future. First of all, in recognition of those visionaries who have led VOSH/International in the past, the honor of Fellowship of VOSH/International will be conferred to past presidents at the combined Annual Meeting and Retreat we're planning to hold in October in Florida.

Building upon this foundation, VOSH/International is taking the Vision 2020 challenge very seriously. The goal is to work together with other organizations to eliminate refractive blindness by the year 2020. To better accomplish this vision, we are restructuring our board and organizing permanent committees with their own objectives and responsibilities.

We need to involve more of you in this process. If you have a skill or area of interest you would like to apply, please let me, or one of the board members know.

Participating in VOSH trips and collecting glasses are important. Still, there are numerous other ways you can contribute to VOSH. Do you, or a supporter, or a relative have skills in communications, promotional development, accounting, or fundraising? Let us hear from you. We need you. As charitable dollars shrink, the challenge to find grantsand other sources of funding becomes even more crucial.

To date VOSH/International has not been especially savvy in asking for funding from major business and private donors to support the many VOSH projects underway and to dreams, we need to continue to develop its content and design.

Other types of donations: In addition to contributing your time and talents, many of you have dusted off unused books and functional equipment for use in optometry schools in Ghana. The shipment has been delayed a second time, but the future recipients are used to waiting and they are excited to know the items will be coming.

Thinking beyond these tangible items, for example, we hope you will also consider donating frequent flyer miles to VOSH/International the next time you get your statements.

Finally, when reviewing your charitable giving, have you considered VOSH/International?"

Following this address VOSH donations increased. In addition to chapter dues for the newsletter and the website, other generous donations came forth. Dr. McAndrews made it a special point to recognize another $20,000 donation from Vistakon. Spectera Vision also renewed its cash pledge of $5,000. In addition, Essilor had generously renewed it cash pledge for air-line tickets for VOSH representatives to attend global conferences of Vision 2020, WCO and for Dr. Vincent to attend the VOSH/International meeting in Florida. Several other personal donations were made to VOSH as well.

In June, 2006, a VOSH Board meeting was conducted separately, but in conjunction with the AOA and WCO. It was in Las Vegas, Nevada. Again, this presented the VOSH board an opportunity to connect with and sustain networking opportunities in vision care on the world stage. A VOSH booth was arranged in the exhibit hall with an excellent location that put nearly five thousand eye care professionals walking nearby. Dr. McAndrews did have an opportunity to speak to the Association of Schools and Colleges of Optometry at their annual meeting.

In 2006 the VOSH Annual Meeting was in Lake Monroe, Florida in October to accommodate the interest in the "destination vacation" concept combining with the VOSH/International meeting. The agenda began with a "Fellow of VOSH/International" orientation and exam session on Friday. Open membership information meetings were conducted both Saturday and Sunday mornings.

The annual meeting location and schedule were appreciated by attendees, allowing the time and opportunity to enjoy the palm trees and gentle breezes of Florida.

Following the annual meeting, Dr. Ruth McAndrews offered a meeting summary in her editorial "*From the President's Desk*" (*VOSH/International Newsletter Fall, 2006*): "**Focus on Fellowship and diversity**"

"Fellowship was truly the theme of our fall retreat for the annual meeting in Sanford, Florida. We wish you all could have been there.

First of all, there was the administration of the first examination for the Fellowship of VOSH/International (FVI). Especially notable was the award to Bob Merriam, a non optometric VOSHer who has participated in over sixty missions. Secondly, we were honored with the attendance of most of the living past presidents of VOSH/International. It was a tremendous opportunity to appreciate the contributions of those who have led us to becoming our current organization.

Diversity of speakers: Dr. Jerry Vincent shared his work and perspective from developing sustainable vision care projects in Thai refugee camps. Dr. Doug Villella, speaking on behalf of VOSH-Pennsylvania discussed his Chapter's development of a hospital in Guatemala. In recognition of this outstanding accomplishment, VOSH/International awarded them the 2006 Humanitarian Award.

As there are always more opportunities than teams, Dr. Nelson Rivera looked at where in Latin America we could provide the results of the VERAS project in Grenada, Nicaragua, one of the poorest countries in Central America. Dr. Ellis Potter, one of the recipients of the FVI award, explored potential collaboration with Rotary International.

Diversity as our greatest asset: Diversity is one of VOSH's greatest assets. One room brought together years of experiences, a variety of philosophies, and a wide range of personalities. When we can focus on a common goal and set aside personal differences in order to listen to each other's lessons and successes, doors are opened for change and progress.

I can't over-emphasize the connections that are created via the website. Mission opportunities are endless. However, through the website, VOSH leaders can not only inspire volunteers from around the world, but they can easily collaborate with other working in the same area to share common problems and solutions.

Need for documentation: We all have our favorite heart-warming VOSH experience that we love to share. However, the reality is that for more recognition, publications, and funding, we need to be collecting specific, consistent data to properly document our results. Dr. Timothy Wingert of UMSL is developing a plan to achieve this goal..."

In 2006 the "**Fellow of VOSH/International**" (FVI) was created. It was designed to encourage members to pursue the knowledge, skills and experience necessary to successfully meet the challenge of preventable blindness around the world. It was also meant to development future leaders who are equipped to meet the challenges of addressing preventable blindness.

The expectation is also that FVI recipients will consult with governmental agencies as well as educational, private, or public institutions. Fellows of VOSH/International will share these objectives with other professionals while they hold this fellowship.

This FVI program was open to anyone who wished to pursue these objectives and to further themselves, their careers and the goals of VOSH/International. The first exam and review sessions for FVI applicants was conducted at the VOSH Annual Meeting in October 2006 in Florida. Dr. Stuart Frank of VOSH-Northwest was recognized for his work in creating, implementing and nurturing the Fellow of VOSH/International (FVI) program. Dr. Ann Slocum-Edmonds and Dr. Larry Hookway have been a major influence in the continuation and application of FVI.

"Dr. Ruth McAndrews, President of VOSH/International and Dr. Harry Zeltzer, Executive Director, Ring the Closing Bell in honor of World Sight Day!"

On October 19, 2007 Dr. McAndrews and Dr. Zeltzer were present for the much heralded ring of the closing bell on Wall Street at the stock exchange. Following the "ringing" they were invited to attend a cocktail and sushi reception, hosted by NASDAQ, overlooking Times Square.

In addition to VOSH/International other invitees were VOSH-New York, VOSH-ONE, the AOA, Vistakon, Essilor, and Alcon. Other associated vision care organizations accepting invitations included the Helen Keller International, International Association for the Prevention of Blindness, International Medical Equipment Collaborative, International Trachoma Initiative, Lavell Fund for the Blind, Lighthouse International, Luxottica Retail, Optometry Giving Sight, Prevent Blindness Tri-state, Salvadoran Association of Rural Health and SCOJO Foundation.

In October of 2007 the VOSH Annual Meeting was in Tampa, Florida. As part of this meeting VOSH celebrated thirty-five years of being VOSH at a "Birthday Bash" on Saturday night.

Dr. Ruth McAndrews presided at her last annual meeting as President of VOSH/International.

This was indeed, a "Mission Accomplished" celebration for a job well done, Dr. Ruth McAndrews. One of Dr. Ruth's greatest contributions to the future of VOSH was the networking connection with Optometrists Giving Sight (OGS) and the Walman Optical grant that brought VOSH to a new level of participation on the global stage.

2007-09 Dr. Larry Hookway leads as VOSH/ International President

When Dr. Hookway walked into a room, he was not someone you could ignore. Although his size towered above, his talents lie in the small detail that generated data and engineered outcomes.

The following is an introduction to President Elect Larry Hookway, OD in the *VOSH/International Newsletter, Summer 2007*:
Meet your incoming VOSH/International President

"When VOSH/International convenes for its annual meeting in Tampa, Florida on October 28th, Larry Hookway, OD, of Willard, Ohio will be named the sixteenth president of VOSH/ International. Just who is this man whose daunting task will be to continue to steer the course of this multi-faceted organization as it continues to partner with other related NGO's to meet the eye care needs of people who have no services available or who cannot afford them?

Dr. Hookway holds a BS in Psychology from Ohio State and he earned his OD from the Illinois College of Optometry (ICO) in 1982.

He had been enjoying the course of his own private practice in Willard, Ohio, for 13 years when he decided to volunteer on a VOSH trip to Honduras in 1996. There was one particular 55-year-old man who worked his way back through the lines to find Dr. Hookway.

The man thanked him over and over. He told Dr. Hookway that he'd made him young again.

A simple pair of glasses had meant so much to him. Needless to say, Dr. Hookway was sold on the VOSH experience.

Since that first VOSH venture, Dr. Hookway has headed up medical teams serving in El Salvador, Venezuela, Tanzania, Ecuador, Argentina, Honduras and Guatemala. In organizing trips, Larry usually works in tandem with Barbara Plaugher, RN, a longtime VOSH, Ohio volunteer. He handles all details concerning equipment and inventory. She's in charge of trip logistics.

For the past 3 years, the self-taught computer geek has singlehandedly input data from his Chapter's eyeglass inventory into the REIMS computer eyeglass selection program, making the task simpler and more efficient for untrained volunteers working in the dispensary on VOSH trips.

Dr. Hookway has felt so strongly about VOSH that he has made it a family affair through the years, inviting his two children to work with him when they turned fifteen...

...Less than a year after his first VOSH trip, Dr. Hookway was appointed to the Board of Directors of his state Chapter, VOSH-Ohio, and he continues as an active Chapter Board member today. He has served as Assistant Director of the Ohio Chapter and he has served two terms as Director (president).

In 2003, just as VOSH/International was focusing on major organizational changes to better meet the challenges of the global eyecare, Larry took on an added leadership role as vice president of VOSH/International. He was named president-elect at the VOSH/International Annual Meeting in October, 2006.

Despite the time he gives to VOSH, Dr. Hookway has also managed to find time to serve on the Board of the Huron River Valley Habitat for Humanity, he's a past president of the Willard Rotary Club, and past Zone Governor of the North Central Ohio

Optometric Association. His spare time is dedicated to Ohio State football and basketball.

Dr. Hookway has been witness to remarkable progress in the VOSH organization during the past eleven years. 'Implementing and maintaining a website has enabled us to communicate inexpensively and in a timely manner with people all over the globe. Then, when the World Health Organization added refractive error blindness to the list of preventable blindness, VOSH/International's leadership began to network with many other NGOs (non-government organizations) providing eyecare around the globe,' explains Dr. Hookway. He gives special kudos to webmaster Harry Zeltzer, OD, for his skill at making connections.

'Working with other like groups has had a huge impact on our organization,' notes Dr. Hookway. 'We're all learning from each other and we're committed to seeking means of working together to do a better job.'

As president, Dr. Hookway will continue these coordinating efforts with the WHO and its Vision 2020 project, the goal of which is to eliminate preventable blindness by the year 2020.

How? 'VOSH/International needs to help provide its chapters information that will help them provide care to the areas of most need,' he says. 'Also, we need to concentrate on making our efforts more sustainable.' Recently, VOSH/International was able to help provide equipment for fledgling optometry schools in Africa and Argentina where there is currently little equipment and few books. The materials will impact the quality of student' training; in turn, they will be better able to serve the eyecare needs of their people, not just for one or two weeks a year, but all year round, for years to come.'

Dr. Hookway is looking forward to meeting the many challenges facing VOSH. 'It has a huge impact on all of us, especially on personal attitude adjustment.' He says. 'You immediately realize how great your life really is, how lucky you are to live in the USA and how fortunate you are to have a skill that allows you to make a real difference in someone's very close friends and the world becomes a better place.'"

As Dr. Hookway began his tenure as VOSH/International President he was preparing the administrative infrastructure for the recently established project that VOSH/International was taking on – the "Presbyopia Study" funded by Optometry Giving Sight.

His greatest shock was when he learned at his first VOSH Board meeting that VOSH was about to partnership with Walman Optical to plan, create and operate a sustainable vision delivery systems in Nicaragua.

Dr. Hookway recognized that the Walman and OGS initiatives doubled VOSH's capacity to reach out globally to those needing vision the worse. This represented the first time the VOSH Board took charge of running large projects themselves; as opposed to (or in addition to) projects primarily being run by chapters!

This was when Dr. Hookway realized that his presidency would be driven by this new paradigm shift. Dr. Hookway also, at this point, connected with the common "global outreach" shared by himself, his predecessor Dr. McAndrews and successor Dr. Pearl.

With these challenges Dr. Hookway's growing expertise in public health actively becoming enhanced with his continuing education. He was progressing though a Masters degree in Public Health, with an emphasis on "Science and Clinical Vision Research" by NOVA Southeastern University College of Optometry – timing meets opportunity.

Walman Optical Grant to VOSH/International: *Reprinted from the VOSH/International Newsletter, Fall 2007*

"Walman Optical of Minneapolis, Minnesota has pledged $70,000 per year for five years to VOSH/International.

Walman Optical is the largest independent ophthalmic company in the United States, with 40 branch offices in 19 states. Walman has been a long-time supporter of VOSH, but this is the first large grant to be awarded.

VOSH/International will utilize this opportunity to go forward with plans to establish a sustainable eye care model in Nicaragua. VOSH/International has completed the process and been approved as an official non-profit entity in Nicaragua. We now want to collaborate with the Ministry of Health, VOSH chapters working in Nicaragua, other NGO's and service groups in the region. Students and researchers are needed for needs assessments, training, and evaluations. Walman will be not only a financial partner, but also a resource for technical advice in the area of lens fabrication and cost recovery components of the plan.

Many thanks to Walman Optical!"

Note: The seeds of this plan were generated by previous president, Dr. Ruth McAndrews, with Dr. Pearl, corroborating with eye care leaders in Nicaragua earlier in 2007.

The "sustainability" plan was originally to simulate the "FUDUM" eye delivery system in El Salvador.

In his first address to the VOSH membership, Dr. Hookway introduced the new direction VOSH/International would take over the next few years *reprinted from the VOSH/International Newsletter, Fall 2007*

"Letter from Larry Hookway, OD, President of VOSH/International"

"A Great Time for VOSH: VOSH celebrated its 35th anniversary at our annual meeting in Tampa. VOSH has evolved into a very exciting organization in those 35 years. I think our founder Franklin Harms, OD., would be very proud of our progress.

Change in Worldview of Importance of Uncorrected Refractive Error: In a press release on October 11, 2006, the World Health Organization announced its updated estimates of visual impairment. For the first time these figures included the 153 million people that have uncorrected refractive error.

Thirteen million children and 45 million working age adults were reported to be affected globally with 90% of those living in low or middle income countries. These figures do not include the issue of presbyopia.

'These results reveal the enormity of the problem,' said Dr. Catherine Le Gales-Camus, WHO Assistant Director-General, Noncommunicable Diseases and Mental Health. 'This common form of visual impairment can no longer be ignored as a target for urgent action.'

VOSH/International Hits New Milestones: In May, the VOSH/International Board of Directors attended a UNESCO (United Nations Education Scientific and Cultural Organization) meeting in El Salvador. The meeting was called by the UNESCO Chair for Visual Health and included people and organizations that could impact visual health delivery in Latin America. Many of the participants recognized VOSH's longtime commitment and experience in providing vision care to developing countries.

Recently, VOSH/International became an official member of the International Agency for the prevention of Blindness (IAPB). For VOSH to be at the table with organizations like the World Council of Optometry, UNESCO, and IAPB shows the respect the world has for our efforts.

During our annual meeting, Dr. Ruth Andrews announced that Walman Optical had awarded VOSH/International a large five-year grant to develop a sustainable model of vision care in Nicaragua. This is exciting and timely. We need to thank Dr. Ruth McAndrews, OD and Greg Pearl, OD for flying to Minneapolis and presenting the grant proposal.

Our Challenge: At our annual meeting Jerry Vincent, OD, MPH, stated, 'That since uncorrected refractive error is now a focus of the WHO, it is up to us, in the next few years to make a difference and show the world that we know how to attack and prevent blindness attributed to uncorrected refractive error. VOSH is up to bat. We need to make the most of our chance. Are we going to strike out?'

VOSH/International's immediate goal is to work with the Minister of Health in Nicaragua and help Nicaragua achieve its Vision 2020 goals. We hope to develop a cooperative effort with the other NGO's (non-government organizations) working in the region. The ultimate goal will be to develop a model of eye care that will eventually provide eye care without outside aid. This goal will not happen overnight and there is a tremendous backlog of people in Nicaragua who have never received eye care. Traditional VOSH missions can help with this backlog of patients and then, in the future, can help with the ongoing care in Nicaragua. We all need to 'think outside the box' and examine how we are providing care and how we can improve our efforts. We have a big job, but VOSH volunteers are special people with great hearts and we can hit that home run."

As a status report, Dr. Hookway followed with his editorial *reprinted from VOSH/International Newsletter, Spring 2008.*
Letter from Larry Hookway, OD, President
"VOSH/International is continually striving to make a life easier for the VOSH Chapters. In recent months we have added some new chapter opportunities. Does your chapter have people that might be interested in adding more missions but the planning of the mission is the stumbling block? VOSH/International now has some easy ways to add mission trips.

- Nicaragua: Sergio Romero is now an employee of VOSH/International and he is the mission coordinator in Nicaragua. If you are planning a trip to Nicaragua or want to add another mission you can contact Sergio and he will set up the clinic sites and make the hotel, meal and busing arrangements for the group. He will also help make sure your paperwork is in order for customs and for the Minister of Health.
- El Salvador: FUDEM has opportunities for small groups. If you contact FUDEM and arrange for a date for your mission, they will make all the arrangements and you

will be included in one of their outreach missions. They manufacture new spectacles for their patients so the group does not have to bring in recycled glasses.

- Other major projects: The VOSH/International Nicaragua committee is working hard to set up a permanent clinic in Matagalpa, Nicaragua. Matagalpa is the second largest city in Nicaragua and is very poor. We will be using funds from a Walman Optical grant to equip a permanent clinic site in the near future. We are currently working with the Minister of Health and the Lion's clubs in Nicaragua to determine the best place to establish the clinic."

Transfer Technology Program (TTP): Many projects were moving forward. In 2007 VOSH TTP sent a forty-foot container to the Ghana School of Optometry in Kumasi. This shipment included equipment and supplies for the school. These donations and outreach programs made a significant difference in the future of optometry all around the world.

Dr. Hookway and the VOSH Board continued their networking effort with other eye care organizations. Board representatives attended the Prevention of Blindness Congress in Buenos Aires, Argentina. Work also continued with Optometry Giving Sight exploring ways the organizations could continue to work together. Also, an effort was made to network with the providers of cataract surgery like the International Eye Foundation (IEF).

As Dr. Hookway said, "It has never been more exciting to be involved with VOSH."

It seems that the "excitement" continued in both VOSH/International Annual Meetings as well. Our President, Dr. Hookway hosted – Anaheim, California and Orlando, Florida – both providing excellent opportunities to have excitement at Disneyland as well!

At his last meeting, 2008 in Orlando, he focused the meeting on "Sustainability". He then looked forward as Dr.

Larry Hookway wrote his last editorial outlining the challenges ahead for VOSH/International. *Excerpts from VOSH/International Newsletter, Fall 2008.*

Challenges:

- "Provide Optometry Giving Sight in your office and to your colleagues. VOSH benefits from the money raised and so do the other groups that are working to eliminate refractive error blindness.
- Make education part of your planning for your short term eye campaigns. Maybe you can train a local person to do screenings or you can help a local optometry school in some way.
- Plan now to come to the 2009 VOSH/International Annual Meeting"

As president, Dr. Larry Hookway attended two conferences of the International Agency for the Prevention of Blindness (IAPB) – a major component in the Vision 2020 solution. Realizing the overwhelming need for correction of refractive error, Dr. Hookway spent much time working on the multi-year Presbyopia Study. Optometry Giving Sight enabled the program with its funding and Pearl Vision sent optometrists to help staff the examination portion of the study – 1872 patients were examined. This study, is wrapping up at this writing (2016) and will soon to be published.

The other major initiative that took Dr. Hookway's time with collaboration with Dr. Pearl was to create a sustainable eye care delivery system in Nicaragua. Dr. Hookway traveled to Nicaragua five times during his presidency working with local governments and administrations to clear necessary certifications and permission procedures. Funded by a five-year Walman Optical grant, this project began as an effort to create something like the FUDEM clinics in El Salvador but instead, through a complex evolution, became Nicaragua's first Optometry School

(UNAN). Even with the twists and turns, the end result was an optometry school – one of the best ways to create long-term sustainability.

VOSH Corps participant Dr. Justin Manning is currently (2016) serving in Managua at the Optometry School.

As Dr. Larry Hookway's presidency began the transition to a new administration, he returned to his home optometry practice in Willard, Ohio and his pursuit of his Masters in Public Health from NOVA School of Optometry. He continued to work on the Presbyopia Study results and publication.

2009-11 Dr. Greg Pearl becomes 'rock-star' VOSH/ International President

Throughout the previous history of VOSH/International there had never been a President from the Western United States beyond South Dakota and Nebraska. VOSH-California had, for many years, been one of the most active chapters. Now VOSH/International had the first president from the west from California.

Like most, Dr. Pearl was hooked by VOSH during his first trip in 1988. He had never seen such demand- such need- such patience. Dr. Pearl felt like a "rock star" surrounded by people who really wanted to be seen.

After twenty years his perspective shifted as he considered that every year he helped maybe a thousand individuals. Did he really change their lives? What about the millions that he didn't help? So, Dr. Greg Pearl placed himself in such a position that he could make a greater impact. In 2006 he and then President Elect Dr. Ruth McAndrews went to Minneapolis, Minnesota to meet with the Walman Optical Philanthropic Board. That relationship resulted in VOSH/International receiving a five-year $70,000 annual grant to create a sustainable program to provide eye care in Nicaragua.

When Dr Pearl went to Nicaragua, he felt the outlying rural countryside would be the best place to set up a base of operation. He rented a house in Esteli, Nicaragua outside of Managua and he hired a Nicaraguan optometrist who had just returned from the states. Having trouble finding an optometrist, they hired a new graduate ophthalmologist moving to Nicaragua. This caused their first setback because after a few months and even before beginning work the new ophthalmologist resigned taking a post elsewhere in the country to learn Lasik surgery. Dr. Pearl then turned to local optometrists that would perform eye exams for $5 each. But, that didn't work well either.

With some disappointment in the outlying country-side, Dr. Pearl moved the base of operations to Managua and hired a local optometrist there. He searched for someone with the passion and personal commitment to make this operation successful. The early strategy was to have eye care campaigns at local churches where they would do screenings, providing reading glasses on site and making custom glasses off-site.

Dr. Pearl and his manager worked hard over the years having their successes and their challenges. Three different managers were hired in an attempt to meet the needs. It was largely a 'cash' business with verbal accounting outcomes. This was not something that would work for sustainable funding and Walman Optical. After fine-tuning their operation they were gradually beginning to become more self-sufficient but they were still losing $3,000 per month. This clinic and project was known as ProVision. *This story's conclusion comes after Dr. Pearl's leadership as President of VOSH/International.*

When Dr. Greg Pearl became President of VOSH/International in 2009 his focus evolved to reaching out to the many VOSH members, VOSH chapter leaders and VOSH missions serving the visually impaired throughout the world and to encourage sustainable thinking.

This formal address by President Greg Pearl, OD, FVI is taken from a VOSH Annual Report, 2010 setting the stage for his administration:

"**Volunteer Optometric Services to Humanity** (VOSH) is a non-political and non-sectarian organization with a proud 39 year history of providing eye examinations and eyeglasses to underserved communities throughout the world. Our founder, Franklin Harms, OD, began VOSH after organizing annual clinic trips to rural villages in northern Mexico with his colleagues from Kansas. Today, VOSH volunteers continue to pay all their own travel expenses to provide the gift of sight to over 100,000 patients annually (70-80 eye care missions). The clinics are primarily throughout Latin America but are also in other developing nations and in the United States.

VOSH/International supports the 50 independent state, regional, student and national VOSH chapters through our website at www.VOSH.org and our annual meeting. We are present in the exhibit hall of every major optometric convention, which provides opportunities for communication and recruitment of new members.

As a signatory to the Vision 2020 initiative of the World Health Organization, VOSH is committed to increasing local optometric service capacity. Our Technology Transfer Program triages badly-needed serviceable ophthalmic equipment to optometric schools in developing nations.

Our ambitious agenda of development projects and our support of our chapters' extraordinary clinic work would not be possible without the generous contributions from the optical industry and our funding partnership with Optometry Giving Sight. We also must thank the tireless dedication of our all-volunteer VOSH/International Board of Directors and staff.

How VOSH/International works:

This is an overview of how VOSH/International administration worked during this period. *This is taken from notes by Dr. Dale Cole 2009-11.*

"VOSH/International is governed by a President and Board of Directors serving fifty-one VOSH Chapters. It also looks forward with networking and planning that can address the future needs of visually impaired people around the world.

The board of directors has telephone conferences several times a year to summarize pre and post missions. Four vice presidents are assigned to different chapters of the organization for the purpose of responding to and conveying issues. Each Vice President has a specific task regarding, fundraising, chapter enlistment, college affiliations, AOA/VOSH enhancement, Lions and Rotary exploration.

The newsletter editor collects data and photos throughout the entire year. After writing, editing, layout and printing, the newsletter is distributed to members throughout the world. The web master keeps an open line with the president of VOSH/International, keeping VOSH.org current.

Chapter leaders can email or call to an open line to make changes and request additions. Members may post notices on the bulletin board.

At the three-day annual meeting information and resources are shared. New officers are elected. Presidents of VOSH chapters are encouraged to attend.

Specifically VOSH/International maintains a data bank, networks with national and international organizations, establishes connections to pharmaceutical and optical companies, encourages research and analysis of Third World eye care, prints a biannual newsletter (sends electronic newsletters), creates and maintains an international Website vosh.org and message board, promotes missions by letting a chapter announce and recruit mission personnel, increases public awareness, communicates information and special requests, provides links to important web sites for travel, health information and other chapters, and provides fundraising opportunities."

In order to implement these programs, Dr. Greg Pearl tried to connect as many Board personnel as possible to oversee each area of operation.

Bylaws update:

In 2011 there was also work done on updating the VOSH/ International Bylaws. After many months they were approved in Boston. Most of the changes were 'housekeeping' amendments to keep up to date with actual practice.

One of the larger Bylaw changes included the evolution over the last ten years from the Board of Directors having chapter representation on the Board (conducted at annual meetings) while the "Executive Committee", consisting of VOSH officers, directed the administration. The Executive Committee had the power to oversee the operation, policies and finances (the president was still the CEO). These changes were positive because the streamlining made decision making easier and it brought more ownership with an expanded board membership.

During Dr. Greg Pearl's administration he also concentrated on other important areas of VOSH business. VOSH/ International along with VOSH-California, took on the project of building an optometry clinic for the Xochicalco School of Optometry in Tijuana, Mexico. This project was made possible by a grant from Optometry Giving Sight. The original grant was $40,000 for construction costs but another $10,000 had to be added for air conditioning. The five-lane clinic opened in November 2010 and is still serving the poorest population of Tijuana. Through its Technology Transfer Program, VOSH has provided equipment for the clinic and new frames for the dispensary. VOSH will be reimbursed with $2.00 per patient examined until the investment is repaid in full.

Follow up note from Dr. Pearl, 2016: VOSH was only getting repaid for 500 patients by 2013 so a new 'memo of understanding' was written for the school to aim toward every senior optometry student to see 1000 patients before their graduation. Admittedly, this may be difficult to achieve with the 'old school south-of-the-border' optometric education consisting of mostly lecture with little clinical experience. Dr. Pearl suggests that some US/Mexico/Latin America clinical faculty changes could move the clinical experience toward the higher volume eye exams targeted to those in need – and VOSH could play a major role in delivery.

The other major initiative that took much of Dr. Pearl's time was the formation and implementation of the **VOSH Corps**. (see chapter on VOSH Corps) The VOSH Board had been struggling with the concept for a few years and the funding continued to be an issue. Optometry Giving Sight eventually stepped in to partner with this program as well. With coordinated focus and effort the VOSH Corps became a reality in 2013. Dr. McPhillips joined forces with Dr. Potter to make this happen.

Early on in the relationship with **Optometry Giving Sight,** the American Optometric Association Foundation approached state VOSH representatives and board members about their allegiances. The American Optometric Association had been a support from the beginning with most of VOSH's marketing and recruiting going through state associations of optometrists. However, with the success that Brien Holden had in building seven to eight new optometry schools in Africa it became clear that the Brien Holden Vision Institute (BHVI) and OGS (Optometry Giving Sight) was also aligned with VOSH in reaching out to the world. VOSHers continued to hold allegiance to each valued partner, relating in different ways.

Dr. Hookway continues with progress on his **Presbyopia Study** in Nicaragua *(VOSH/International Annual Reports 2010-2013):* "VOSH/International in collaboration with the International

Centre for Eyecare Education (ICEE) is conducting a population study of presbyopia in Nicaragua. Past VOSH/International President, Dr. Larry Hookway is directing the project using a protocol developed by the World Health Organization. The outcome will determine both the prevalence of presbyopia in Nicaragua and the impact of uncorrected presbyopia on the productivity of the Nicaraguan people. This project was funded by a grant from Optometry Giving Sight."

ProVision Clinic *(story continues)*

The ProVision Clinic in Nicaragua was still a large part of Dr. Greg Pearl's job overseeing operations while actively working toward sustainability. The outreach team from this clinic traveled to areas of need and examined an average of 250 people per day at these clinics.

"The Pro-Vision Clinic in Managua was founded in July 2009. Led by Program Director, Dr. Alejandra Narvaez, the clinic has a staff of two optometrists, two opticians, a receptionist, and an accountant. They conducted 42 mobile clinics throughout Managua where they performed 10,434 eye exams; dispensing reading glasses, pre-made bifocals, ocular lubricants, and non-prescription sunglasses to the patients. The most difficult cases were referred to the Pro-Vision clinic in Managua where 604 patients were examined and prescribed custom prescriptions.

The Pro-Vision clinic is a registered non-profit tax-exempt entity in Nicaragua and earned $51,837 in income from patient services and glasses. The clinic, staff and supplies expenses were $107,303. Cost recovery has improved from 23% in January 2011 to 72% in December 2011." *(VOSH 2010 Annual Report)*

The efforts put forth were providing much needed eye care to tens of thousands of patients. However, the quest for "financial sustainability" was elusive. Even though efficiency was increased from 23% to 80%, the clinic was still losing $3,000 per month or $6 per patient. The decision was made to close the clinic. Procedures, which Dr. Pearl oversaw, were implemented to pay off debts and store equipment.

The unexpected but favorable outcome of this investment in time, money and relationship building turned out to become the 'seeds' of a new optometry school in Managua, Nicaragua. This school would not only provide for the future vision needs of the people, but would also deliver a constant supply of long-term providers in Nicaragua! This School of Optometry is known as UNAN, Universidad Nacional Autónoma Nicaragua, Managua.

UNAN began their optometry program in 2011 with 34 students. They will graduate in 2016. Eventually, the program plans to train 50 students per year. Under the direction of Dr. Roger Juarez, a 10 lane pre-clinic optometry laboratory is being constructed. Funding for the equipment was provided in collaboration with Optometry Giving Sight.

Thoughts on sustainability:
Dr. Greg Pearl in an interview on February 23, 2016, shared some thoughts about what the ProVision clinic and other experiences taught. He shares the following thoughts:

"Optometry Giving Sight is one of the best relationships VOSH can have. Brien Holden had a vision, did the research, and brought to VOSH the awareness of the plight of the visual needs of hundreds of millions underserved. VOSH was on-the-ground, ready with volunteers to meet these needs.

But this sustainability that meets the needs of millions is not just an architectural plan. It is a living dynamic that is intricately interwoven. El Salvador made FUDEM possible, not to belie the incredible ten-year 'organic gardening (people and culture)' of all the factors necessary to make the plan reality. But El Salvador has twice the economy that Nicaragua has. One plan is not transferable to another country. A person making two dollars a day cannot afford a ten-dollar pair of glasses."

ProVision's investment was intertwined in the economy of the area, coupled with the enhanced value of eye care that Dr. Pearl and Walman brought."

"Optometry Schools", Dr. Pearl suggests, "are perhaps the best places to invest in VOSH clinics. The schools have the administration, optometry students supply the man/woman-power and VOSH can provide the clinical support." And as to new graduates, Dr. Pearl sees two strategies, "Getting new local OD grads to serve in developing areas and to send VOSH personnel to supply, equip and instruct developing schools in underserved areas, does more VOSH toward sustainability."

Dr. Greg Pearl continues to formalize his thoughts on sustainability in a letter to the VOSH Board as Past President.

"I think a truly financially sustainable clinic must be locally managed to eventually succeed without our constant external input or fundraising. I've learned that we can't hire the passion necessary for this work. Local, passionate ownership and management has worked for FUDEM in El Salvador, VAO in Africa and IEF throughout Latin America. The lack of local ownership was also a contributing factor in our failure to succeed in developing a sustainable clinic in Nicaragua.

Continuing to develop non-profit clinics with optometry schools abroad would seem to be a good strategy to achieve financial sustainability while serving the poor by utilizing donated frames and the free labor of the students. However, unless we are willing to invest in supplying VOSH Corps clinic supervisors, I believe that these campus clinics will still be under-utilized by these schools and their underpaid faculty.

To serve the poorest rural populations, the most successful financially sustainable programs are those that ask their middle class patients to pay more for their eyeglasses so to subsidize the provision of eyeglasses for the rural poor of that country, i.e. Aravind, IEF, and FUDEM. I think VOSH chapters can serve a valuable role by materially supporting these clinics and

coordinating our outreach efforts with them whenever possible."
Greg Pearl, OD, FVI

In conclusion, Dr. Pearl worked hard as president uniting with Dr. McAndrews and Dr. Hookway by moving toward global outreach and sustainability. Dr. Pearl was the impetus for the creation of the VOSH Corps and for VOSH's key positioning for long-term sustainability. His primary efforts produced valuable learning experiences as well as great strides toward putting the sustainability puzzle together.

The **2010's** are off to a fast start – a decade yet to be defined. But the 2010's begin with feelings of insecurity and complexity becoming the new "norm." Despite the billions going into Homeland Security, terrorist threats are diversifying and evolving from non-government radical religions organizations (ISIS/ISIL) to home spun shooters from anywhere killing strangers and dominating the news.

In the 2010's we live in a virtual, digital world. We can go anywhere, see anything, and know anything – that is if you can figure out digital complexities. For health care professionals the 2010's brought at least twenty new agencies to oversee our medical records. Smart-phone 'apps' require you to certify that you 'read and agree' with 30-page disclaimers. You may have a hundred password accounts requiring different, complex security rules. The great news for the tech-savvy is the power it puts at your fingertips.

The 2010's bring complexity with a plethora of new words and acronyms creating gobbledygook to the uninformed. "WHO" knows what CRUDEM, FUDEM, ICEE, IEF, FVI, VERAS, REIM, CLOO, ASCO, ALDOO, UNESCO, KNUST, IAPB, RAM, UNAN, IMEC, TTP, and OGS mean? VOSHers, this is your vocabulary test. How many did you get? (See answers in next section "VOSH Programs and Initiatives").

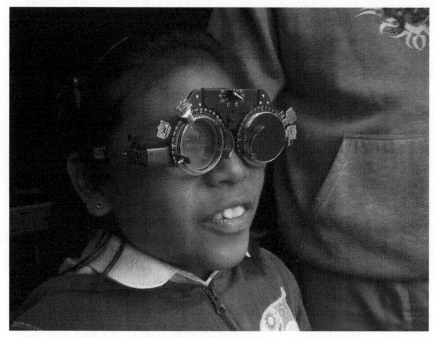

(Courtesy of Jeff Cowan)

(Courtesy of Jeff Cowan)

(Courtesy of Jeff Cowan)

2011-13 Dr. Ellis Potter steers the course as VOSH/ International President

C. Ellis Potter, OD, FAAO, FVI, had established himself in his career and was active in a number of civic service and optometric organizations. It was customary at Kansas Optometric Association meetings to listen to reports of the yearly mission trips. They described exotic locales like "Tegucigalpa" and "Catacamas." Dr. Potter thought, "That sounds interesting. I could go on a trip like that at this time in my career." His first VOSH mission was in 1994. "It was like instant gratification," Dr Potter recalls, when he first stepped on-sight to a clinic bustling with waiting patients – patients waiting for him.

His next mission was to Panama with VOSH and Rotary members. As a Rotarian he was particularly interested in a VOSH mission to Chile. He had heard about Chile from a Rotary "Group

Study Exchange" team just returning from there. His interest was further heightened by discussions with a young Chilean physician on that exchange. So he set out with the objective of finding a VOSH team going to Chile. That turned out to be a daunting task as he searched several different avenues but had no success. He eventually applied for and received a Rotary "Feasibility Study Grant" to go to Chile and seek out the possibility of an eye clinic. He found what he was looking for. Dr. Potter followed by leading eight other VOSH eye care missions to Chile.

Dr. C. Ellis Potter inherited an increasingly fast paced era. A VOSH era of trying a variety of strategies toward sustainability and correcting preventable blindness was rapidly growing. VOSH partnering with NGO's was rapidly expanding as well. It was a challenge to make sense of so many things happening?

Dr. Potter had just the right administrative skill-set and penchant for prioritizing and planning that served VOSH well.

Dr. Potter brought with him to the VOSH Presidency varied experiences in working within organizations. Dr. Potter served as the chairman of the "Primary Care Section" of the "American Academy of Optometry." In addition to local leadership positions he also served state-wide as the Rotary District Governor and served the Kansas Optometric Association as editor of the "Kansas Optometric Journal." As editor he coordinated the January-March, 2004 issue which became a primary source of documentation of the very beginnings of VOSH. Dr. Potter as president-elect oversaw the VOSH Bylaw changes and knew the form and function of VOSH administration. He wasted no time in meticulously putting his action plans to work.

Dr. Potter's strengths were now directed to the presidency of VOSH. He began with authority by insisting that the VOSH Board have a strategic planning meeting in Boston in conjunction with the annual meeting. The purpose was not only to plan the next few years but to bring a continuity of purpose to the board members. Dr. Potter's efforts were directed toward matching the individual strengths and interests with the individual Board and Committee members that led VOSH initiatives. This planning and bonding enabled VOSH/International to continue the actions that were in progress and to continue to grow the organization by moving forward with a unified effort.

New VOSH Logo

VOSH/International had considered redefining its image by refining its logo. The idea made sense when considered along with the creative work Dr. Ruth McAndrews was doing with the VOSH Newsletter. It further took shape when Dr. Potter was talking with Todd Fleischer, Assistant Director of the Kansas Optometric Association. Todd suggested that the Kansas State Journalism Club would be a good resources to create several logo ideas to reflect VOSH identity. They submitted several ideas; the board selected one. The logo enabled identification of either VOSH International or the VOSH Chapter by using either name within the logo design.

Continuing Education Courses: Along with Dr. McPhillips, Dr. Potter developed a COPE approved Continuing Education Course entitled "Eye Care in Developing Nations".

Having to be COPE approved, this became a complex job. Dr. Ellis Potter presented the program at the Annual Meeting in Puerto Rico. Having COPE approved courses at the Annual Meeting was later deemphasized as it was difficult to coordinate and time consuming to produce.

VOSH Corps:

Another primary area of concentration for Dr. Potter, working with Past President Greg Pearl and others, was to develop VOSH Corps. VOSH Corps was to build optometric education worldwide in a long-term effort towards, not only optometry, but towards meeting the vision needs around the world. VOSH Corps also represents a long-term effort that could be sustainable by having optometrists cover the globe.

The first major initiative for VOSH was to put together a system to select and support an optometrist to serve for at least a year in a newly forming international optometry school. Hopefully this would be the beginning of getting other optometrists to also serve.

Patterned after the Peace Corps, the initiative was inspired by the VOSH affiliation with the Brien Holden Vision Institute and supported by Optometry Giving Sight.

These efforts did eventually produce results with the first optometrist, Dr. Justin Manning being sent to serve at Universidad Nacional Autónoma de Nicaragua, Managua (UNAN), optometry school in September, 2015.

In an effort to set a precedence to reach out internationally, Dr. Potter arranged for the first VOSH Annual Meeting to be conducted in Puerto Rico October 10, 2013. The VOSH/International meeting was held in conjunction with the Puerto Rican optometric meeting, allowing VOSH/International members to get to better connected with their Latin American colleagues. VOSH members had the opportunity to tour the Inter-American University School of Optometry and were able to conduct a joint clinic with them in honor of World Sight Day. This truly put an International flavor to Annual Meetings."

Summary of Achievements, 2011-13 *From notes provided by Dr. Potter*

Primary Care Diplomate C. Ellis Potter, OD, FAAO of Iola, Kansas completed a two year term as President of VOSH International at the VOSH International meeting in San Juan, Puerto Rico in October 2013. During that term VOSH International made numerous strides to fulfill the objective and mission statement: to *"facilitate the provision and the sustainability of vision care worldwide for people who can neither afford or obtain such care."*

During that span VOSH/International accomplished the following:

- Developed a 5 year plan to identify goals and objectives
- Developed a new Logo updating and modernizing the VOSH brand
- Produced a Spanish and English VOSH Brochure
- Introduced a new program called VOSH CORPS to recruit teachers and instructors for International Optometry Schools
- Expanded communications with 34 State or Regional Chapters and 69 SVOSH (Student VOSH) chapters
- Recognized 8 new SVOSH chapters (7 International SVOSH Chapters)
- Recognized 5 new state or regional chapters
- Received numerous grants from various organizations to advance the VOSH objectives
- Made numerous presentations at various National and International meetings
- Expanded the TTP (Technology Transfer Program); collecting and reconditioning used ophthalmic equipment and transporting it to needy International clinics, schools and other teaching institutions
- Created the Franklin Harms Society to recognize participants completing 10 mission trips
- Produced a Video detailing VOSH and its achievements
- Reworked and updated the VOSH/International Website; www.vosh.org
- Coordinated and supported VOSH chapter International clinics totaling 80 missions per year that care for over 100,000 patients
- Coordinated 8 domestic clinics in the United States each year.

Dr. Potter's presidency coincided with the 40th Anniversary of the establishment of VOSH International, principally started by a fellow Kansan, Dr. Franklin Harms. During that span 3500 VOSH volunteers have accomplished 3000 clinics attended by over 3 million patients.

Dr. Potter concludes this summary commenting, "So that is what we have been engaged in during the past two years. They are many and varied and help us make progress toward our strategic goals, which we refer to as our five-year plan. In VOSH/International we have accomplished a great deal! With the cooperation, energy and support of the chapters and VOSH Board and Administrative officers, it has been a great year."

As President, Dr. Ellis' detailed planning and extraordinary efforts paid big dividends for VOSH/International.

2013-15 Dr. David McPhillips takes lead as President of VOSH/International

David McPhillips, OD, FVI, FAAO, has a chair-side demeanor that gives confidence and draws attention. These traits, coupled with his ability to delegate the duties of other leaders around him, launches him into the presidency.

One of his first jobs was in hiring a professional Executive Director, Natalie Venezia, Esq., chosen by the Board, and brought an enhanced empowerment to the administration of VOSH/International.

Before Dr. McPhillips became president he got his first start with SOSH (Student Optometric Service to Haiti) while he was still in school at the Pennsylvania College of Optometry. Because he participated both as a Junior and as a Senior, he assumed early team leadership positions. After graduation he realized there was no VOSH-Pennsylvania so one of his first missions as an eye doctor was with Bob and Lila Schwartz to

Honduras. After several years of eye care missions he felt called to form a chapter in his own state, VOSH-Pennsylvania. He joined with a friend and former classmate Dr. Jack Hauler, and together they formed a new VOSH-Pennsylvania.

After going on many VOSH missions to sites in Mexico, Honduras, Guatemala, Cuba and others, VOSH-Pennsylvania members paused to reflect upon the enormity of the need and the limitations of single-trip encounters. They realized that to truly make a global impact meeting eye care needs, they had to build 'sustainability.'

The first foray into sustainability came in the form of creating an independent, self-sustaining eye hospital (Vincent Pescatore Eye Hospital) in the Peten rainforest of Guatemala. VOSH-Pennsylvania helped raise nearly a million dollars and provided equipment along with clinical staff while connecting with two local ophthalmologists to put this eye hospital on its way to reality – and independence. This became a two-tiered operation with literally an entrance for the poor and another for those that could afford eye care – this concept is what made the hospital sustainable – a built-in funding source. Since its creation the rural eye hospital has expanded to four additional full scope satellite eye clinics.

Dr. David McPhillips found his solution to sustainability and he could move forward to other ventures. His original experience was grown from his VOSH roots in Haiti. The following is an account of Dr. McPhillips' pre-presidential Haiti venture back to Haiti in "**Establishing Eye Care in Haiti**," reprinted from the article in the 2011 VOSH Annual Report:

"Once the richest colony in the Caribbean, Haiti is now the poorest country in the western hemisphere, and one of the poorest nations in the world. The earthquake that flattened Port-au-Prince January 12, 2010 ranks among the worst disasters in modern history: Haiti's chronic conditions--extreme poverty, food and water insecurity, lack of economic opportunities, crumbling

133

public health and education systems--left the country even more vulnerable to this acute disaster.

VOSH-Pennsylvania began working in Haiti seven years ago. We were naïve, had very few resources, and were surrounded by great need. The results and progress have been remarkable. VOSH has been instrumental in the support of a full service eye clinic; a social service model clinic to two Haitien ophthalmologists who have been working with VOSH volunteers since the beginning. Partnerships and support from organizations like the International Eye Foundation, Vision for the Poor, Optometry Giving Sight, and others have made this dream a reality.

Calling forth one of our goals of self-empowerment of the people and communities VOSH serves, an entrepreneurial reading glass program has been successfully established. Selected and trained people have been educated to provide reading glasses to people in need in rural areas without access to care. This is also serves as a referral source to the new eye clinic and VOSH teams.

VOSH has also established a partnership with the Hospital Sacre Coeur, the largest private hospital in the North of Haiti. VOSH teams have helped provide quality eye care to the sick and poor in and around this Haitian community with a quarterly presence and also provide education for those who deliver healthcare in this area.

Short-term projects have grown into a long-term commitment and development of a sustainable program. It was once said that "'Someone' would take care of the eye care problems Haitians were facing". VOSH was that someone.

(Courtesy of Dr. Mark Rakoczy)

(Courtesy of Jeff Cowan)

As VOSH/International President, Dr. David McPhillips has taken the next giant step forward to promoting and supporting sustainability by pursuing the involvement of VOSH in the formation of a school **"Establishing Optometry in Haiti"**. This is his address to the members in the 2014 Annual Report:

"Haiti is the poorest country in the Western Hemisphere. Almost 2 million Haitians suffer from uncorrected refractive error simply the need for an eye exam and glasses.

Only 50 ophthalmologists service a country of 10 million, with many of these practicing optometry and not ophthalmology because of income and technology limitations, and a majority practicing in the capital city of Port au Prince only. The profession of Optometry does not exist.

This lack of access to eye health services significantly reduces their ability to break the cycle of poverty through better education and employment. Advocacy has begun, with consultations between stakeholders, Universite d'Etat d'Haiti (UEH), and the Haitian government. The profession of optometry is included for the first time in the National Plan of Haiti.

The Haiti Optometry Program will establish a School of Optometry and Academic Vision Center within the new Faculty of Medicine and Pharmacy building that is currently being constructed at UEH. Work towards the development of a suitable curriculum for the new degree has already commenced, thanks to funding provided by VOSH/International, the Brien Holden Vision Institute, and Optometry Giving Sight. Our goal is to welcome the first students into the new optometry program in October 2016. A conservative estimate is for the school to produce 16 students per year. Upon graduation in 2021, these students will be able to reach a minimum of 24,000 patients in their first professional year."

For the past several years, President McPhillips has been traveling to Haiti to move the development of the new school of optometry in Port au Prince, Haiti forward. He has positive expectations of the optometry school opening in October, 2016. Fundraising efforts continue with great support from Optometry Giving Sight, the Brien Holden Vision Institute, Vision Source, Essilor, and others. Dr. McPhillips has also recently attended the ribbon cutting of a new social eye clinic in Port au Prince, supported by the International Eye Foundation (IEF). VOSH chapters have and will be supporting the clinic through outreach, as they have in northern Haiti.

Dr. David McPhillips announced his VOSH/International theme for 2013, "**Embracing Tradition and Expanding Horizons**." Now it is time for Dr. David McPhillips to turn outward to toward the efforts of its chapters and its members. This is the "Presidential Address" by Dr. McPhillips as it appears in the 2013 VOSH Annual Report:

"I am excited about being the next president of VOSH/International! I'm honored because I'm following in the footsteps of 18 previous presidents; many of whom I have had the pleasure to know and admire, and some whom I did not have the pleasure to meet. They all shared one thing: a dedication to VOSH. I never dreamed after my two trips to Haiti while a student at the Pennsylvania College of Optometry, I would be honored and humbled to be in this position.

I'm excited because I believe the 2014 version of VOSH will be better than ever before, offering more to its members and chapters than at any time in our 43 year history. I believe vision care is a human right, and we as VOSH members are on a mission to transform vision care, one patient at a time.

I'm excited because VOSH/International, in collaboration with the Brien Holden Vision Institute and supported by Optometry Giving Sight, is engaging in a new initiative in building optometric education worldwide called 'VOSH Corps.'

I'm excited because of the many services VOSH/International continues to provide for its chapters: matching potential members with local chapters, providing one voice for the American Optometric Association, Optometry Giving Sight, the World Council of Optometry, Vision 2020, Lions and Rotary International, Surgical Eye Expeditions (SEE), UNESCO, Remote Area Missions (RAM), and others.

I'm excited about the brand new VOSH.org website which will unify chapters through clinic listings, contacts for chapter leaders, recruitment of new members, information, advice, and resources.

I'm excited because VOSH/International has an amazing group of 10 board members and support staff from around the country, all volunteers with a common goal. They are redefining what's possible in vision care, but they need your help.

Paraphrasing what a mission volunteer once said, "I can't take credit for helping the girl see today without taking responsibility for the man's blindness yesterday, so I choose to do neither. Instead, I prefer to simply keep working to improve the system as a whole."

We can do it together!"

For 2014 Dr. David McPhillips' theme is was "**Creating Connections and Building Bridges**." He turns again to the members, chapters, and board to give his annual message. This reprint is taken from the VOSH/International Annual Report 2014:

"For more than 40 years, VOSH/International and its chapters have been the voice of optometry in developing nations. VOSH restores more than vision. It allows individuals to regain independence through sight, to return to work, and to imagine the future. We do this by embracing our traditions while expanding our horizons. VOSH has grown to almost 5,000 members in over 75 state, regional, optometry school and international chapters. VOSH campaigns help over 100,000 patients annually. We have provided free, quality eye care services to those most in need using a variety of delivery systems and clinic models.

As the landscape of healthcare and technology has changed, VOSH has also changed. Globally, there are an estimated 600 million vision impaired (>20/50) who need eyeglasses, 90% of those in the developing world. In an effort to support the World Health Organization's goal of eliminating preventable blindness by the year 2020, VOSH partners with local groups to expand the capacity of their outreach programs. VOSH also partners with many other international organizations pursuing similar goals. These partnerships and these relationships are increasing every year as VOSH chapters expand the provision of sustainable eye health to people worldwide.

Everyone, regardless of their circumstances, has the right to clear, comfortable vision. Everyone has the right to glasses that look and fit comfortably. Local facilities should be supported to provide appropriate low cost or no cost high quality eye care. The vision needs of the planet are enormous, but working together we can provide quality eye care through a multitude of delivery systems thus changing the lives of millions."

Dr. David McPhillips presided at his last VOSH Annual Meeting in New Orleans in 2015. The meeting was productive with information for our chapters and information for running their clinics, both locally and internationally. Thank you was extended to our meeting sponsors National Vision, as their support made our meeting possible. World Sight Day was successful and just happened to coincide with the ten year anniversary of Hurricane Katrina. To commemorate, VOSH, with support from VSP and Optometry Giving Sight conducted a free clinic outreach at the Sanchez Recreation Center. Located in the Lower Ninth Ward, this free clinic conducts free eye exams and provided free glasses that directly benefited the survivors of Hurricane Katrina.

Friday evening attendees met for a cocktail reception honoring the Fellows of VOSH/International. The Saturday morning session highlights included presentations from the World Council of Optometry, American Optometric Society, Remote Medical Access, Optometry Giving Sight, Brien Holden Vision Institute, Vision Impact Institute, Restoring Vision, Mexican Optometric Association and Surgical Eye Expeditions. The afternoon had informative breakout sessions with SEE (Surgical

Eye Expeditions). Also presented was information about working with North American and International student-VOSH chapters, sustainable Clinic Development, and hands-on technology. A highlight of the meeting was a Skype dialogue from Nicaragua with our VOSH Corp placement, Dr. Justin Manning.

Throughout 2013-2015, VOSH has not only maintained and nourished a large number of programs; it has initiated several new ones as well. And, yes, they incorporated efforts to build sustainability. New Programs include:

- VOSH Corps placements in Malawi and Nicaragua
- VOSH Disaster Relief Program designed to facilitate the placement of VOSH volunteers are areas of the more pressing needs following natural disasters.
- A new liaison to developing new VOSH Chapters and service throughout Africa with Dr. Uduak Udom leading the effort. (other liaisons were appointed in India, Mexico and Puerto Rico)
- A new 'Continuing Education Portal" to provide free optometric education to eye care professionals and students in developing nations, as well as quality COPE approved CE credits to our chapter members in North America at a reduced cost. This is in conjunction with the World Council of Optometry.
- The "OD Wire" optometric education site decides to use its proceeds to help fund VOSH/ International along with the Foundation of the American Optometric Association
- A mentoring program matching optometry students in the United States with optometry students in other lands.

- A renewed focus on VOSH Domestic Clinics, chaired by Dr. Victoria Weiss and supported by Remote Area Medical (RAM)
- Mel Muchnik continues to drive the production of VOSH public relations with creative, informative video streams

In reflection, Dr. David McPhillips defines his administration and legacy with the addition of Natalie Venezia, Esq., as VOSH Executive Director. He related that they worked together "daily, tirelessly, planning, coordinating and implementing" change. He goes on to add, "I never could have done this job (as president) without Natalie. She has a kindness, expertise, and passion for VOSH that made everything and anything possible."

Thank you both Natalie and David for an extraordinary year.

2015-17 Dr. Ellen Weiss present and future VOSH/ International President

Dr. Ellen Weiss is leading VOSH in the present as this history is being written and she will lead VOSH beyond this book into the future. Dr. Weiss' first board action as President was to preside over the official endorsement of writing this book on the history of VOSH.

Dr. Ellen Weiss first experienced VOSH as a third-year optometry student at University of Missouri at St. Louis (UMSL) in December, 1991 on an eye care mission to Iguala, Mexico. The next year as a fourth-year optometry student she went to Jamaica with Dr. David McPhillips, mission leader. Dr. Weiss was a veteran VOSHer by the time she graduated and went on to become the president of VOSH-Nebraska which she has been for the last ten years.

While serving on the Board of 'Heart of America' she had several encounters with Dr. Ellis Potter and Dr. Ruth McAndrews who encouraged her to become involved in the International concerns of VOSH. This drew her toward more global issues and further involvement. And as her experience matured, she was encouraged to seek the presidency, which she did.

Dr. Weiss shares her love for optometry with her love to travel. VOSH is a perfect blend of the two. Dr. Ellen Weiss brought strong organizational skills to the leadership of VOSH/International. She is a non-procrastinator and likes to move projects forward toward completion – she "doesn't like to leave things dangling." Dr. Weiss is diplomatic and can motivate and manage people, "especially a wonderful group like the dedicated VOSH Board of Directors." These are truly great attributes because VOSH/International is, at the moment, involved in many projects and initiatives.

Dr. Weiss shares that one of her most insightful preparations for the international presidency was participation in VOSH's Strategic Planning weekend in Seattle, facilitated by Dr. Ellis Potter with notes by Natalie Venezia. During that weekend to supplement the knowledge of VOSH she already had, Dr. Weiss began to understand relationships, priorities, and the individual interests of the various board members. This gave her the perspective she needed to build and direct her administration.

From her beginning as president she identified two **primary goals** quite succinctly. Each of these were identified, both at the beginning of the year with her comments as she took office, in the newsletter's "President's Insight" (January 2016) and again mid-term in her "2016 Annual Report" (January 2017).

The **first** of these primary goals was SVOSH (Student Volunteer Optometric Services to Humanity). This goal reflected a larger vision in VOSH/International to meet its mission of bringing affordable, available eyecare to the world by training and supporting optometry students as well as supporting, initiating and forming new optometry schools in underdeveloped parts of the world.

Her approach is to focus on students and begin by "connecting and strengthening the relationship between Student VOSH Chapters (SVOSH) and VOSH/International resources. This includes connecting with the faculty advisors of each SVOSH chapter; some highly engaged, some repeating, and others new." In order to do this Dr. Weiss appointed Dr. John Spencer to coordinate an organization-wide action plan to have every SVOSH (student) chapter visited in-person by an International board member or committee representative.

Half-way through her two-year term as president, Dr. Weiss reports, "Our SVOSH visits to each of the schools by board or committee members are coming along nicely, and the student enthusiasm is contagious. VOSH was blessed with student interns that helped us in so many ways this past year."

The **second** primary goal for VOSH/International to expand into Mexico. Dr. Weiss detailed this initiative, "Expansion of optometry is on-the-move. A wide-spread optometric credentialing process is underway. Outreach clinics are being developed and equipment is needed (TTP). VOSH will be working with Alvaro Alcala, OD, Asociación Mexicana de Facultades, Escuelas, Colegios y Consejos de Optometría who attended our last VOSH Annual Meeting."

Mid-term Dr. Weiss reports positive progress being made in Mexico. She credits Dr. Marcela Frazier along with Cecilia Denny from Mexico as making a large contribution toward meeting this goal. Marcela and Cecilia are part of the VOSH/SVOSH International Chapters committee of VOSH/International. Dr. Weiss remarks, "I see great potential for VOSH expanding throughout Mexico."

The Importance of SVOSH

"VOSH had a wonderful mixer with optometry students last June during Optometry's AOA meeting, and the enthusiasm and excitement from the interaction has snowballed. We are a volunteer board, and there's so much potential for development, only held back by the time commitment. At this mixer, we had several optometry students come up and ask how they could be more involved with the VOSH organization. From that initial encounter, we have had students helping us update our website, post pertinent information on our social media pages, organize our photos, send out email blasts, and help in so many other useful ways. As president, I have prioritized our outreach to SVOSH students. The VOSH board has developed an informational powerpoint presentation and committed to a board or committee member visiting each of the optometry schools to meet with the SVOSH chapters and school administration to further educate the students and schools about the opportunities VOSH provides. Looking forward, we plan to continue this involvement with new optometry students yearly. Hopefully this outreach and involvement while students are in school will help us retain them as they graduate and go off in their optometry career."

In June 2016 VOSH/International again hosted a reception for optometry students at the American Optometric Association annual meeting. In November 2016 another reception for optometry students was conducted at the VOSH/International meeting in Anaheim, California. During the year VOSH/International also hosted a student video contest with winners being posted on the VOSH/International Facebook page.

Since taking office as VOSH/International President, Dr. Weiss has also spent a lot of time working with TTP (Technology Transfer Program) and Dr. David Stacy. The expansion of domestic VOSH members working with Remote Area Medical (RAM) has also been a positive move forward. There are more and more donations and more and more requests. Dr. Weiss has also been concentrating on filling the VOSH Corps placements.

Dr. Weiss also oversees all of the programs continuing from her predecessor, Dr. David McPhillips. She comments, "This includes a partnership with on-line "OD Wire" which is a portal for optometric education. VOSH/International and the Foundation of the American Optometric Association (AOA) share the non-profit proceeds to further their work.

VOSH is embarking on a long-term growth initiative across the continent of Africa. They have recently commissioned Dr. Uduak Udom (WCO president) to coordinate and inspire this VOSH growth. Details will be addressed in a June 2016 board strategic planning meeting in Boston."

In January 2017 Dr. Weiss updates the progress actively working with optometry schools and VOSH chapters in Africa by saying, "Our newly formed VOSH chapters in Ghana, ably led by Dr. Abena Ntim, held two outreach missions. Dr. Ntim and VOSH-Ghana, in conjunction with Rotary Club of Accra West, organized a free eye screening and education for the people of Kitase and the surrounding community on March 19, 2016. VOSH and the Rotarians, 24 optometry students from KNUST School of Optometry and local dignitaries worked together on this historical event."

Dr. Ellen Weiss continues encouraging participation by new and current members at optometric conferences across the country in her "President's Insight," February 2016 entitled, **Making Connections:**

"Attending an optometry continuing education meeting any time soon? VOSH exhibits yearly at the Heart of America Congress, SECO, Vision Source, AOA, Vision Expo West, Academy and various other meetings. If you're in the exhibit hall, we'd love to have you stop by and say hello. We're always looking for volunteers to staff the various exhibit halls, so please shoot me an email if this interests you. Why does VOSH exhibit? One reason is visibility. Our web page is user friendly and full of great information, but there's a personal connection when we can visit one on one as we swap stories. It's always nice when people stop by and comment how they went on a trip as a student, and their life is now to the point where they want to again become involved. VOSH visibility is also important to other vendors. Companies know what VOSH is about, and we've built great connections and resources in the exhibit halls visiting with the other vendors. Another reason to exhibit is to increase membership. It's an effective recruitment tool for local chapters to work the booth space when a meeting is in their region. What will you find at our VOSH booth? We have a variety of one page flyers that allow people to gather information and read about what is relevant to them. These may include local chapter information, clinic opportunities, and information on our TTP program, VOSH Corps, and annual meeting. So the next time you're at a meeting, take a few minutes to stop by a visit."

During 2016 Dr. Weiss represented VOSH by attending the American Partner's Forum for Our Children's Vision as part of the Vision Expo West meeting. She reports, "The purpose of this meeting was to bring VOSH, Essilor Vision Foundation, Vision Impact Institute, Eyelliance, VSP, Optometry Giving Sight, World Council of Optometry, Charity Vision, Special Olympics and others together to join forces and address the lack of eye care for children in the United States. While there, Greg Pearl and I met with Kim Schuy, president of Essilor Vision Foundation-Americas and Sam Hahn from Kids Vision for Life to brainstorm more about domestic missions and resources regarding US school kids. From this meeting, VOSH has created a calendar on our website highlighting the domestic missions and contact people, to better coordinate timing, personnel and supplies."

Also during 2016 Dr. Weiss attended the International Association for the Prevention of Blindness (IAPB) meeting in Durban, South Africa. She used this opportunity to network with a number of other speakers, organizations and attendees. She also displayed and presented a poster of the VOSH/International Technology Transfer Program (TTP) and how basic needed optometric equipment in developing countries made such a big difference to delivery of eyecare around the world.

The 2016 VOSH/International Annual Meeting was held in Anaheim, California. President Weiss reflects, "We had a great line of speakers at our annual meeting this year, and panel presentations on our TTP (Technology Transfer Program) and VOSH Corps. In addition to our award winners, I had the pleasure of presenting Michel Listenberger, OD, FVI who is the VOSH historian, a Presidential Circle Award for his book "Bringing The World Into Focus. The Story of VOSH. Volunteer Optometric Services To Humanity". Prior to the meeting, I presented at the International Optometric Educators SIG (Special Interest Group) luncheon."

She shares some words about her leadership, "My job as president is to guide, provide feedback, and delegate. We all have different strengths and weaknesses, but together we're a wonderful organization. I greatly admire our volunteer board and the time and effort they put into making VOSH the great organization that it is."

Dr. Weiss is right on track to bringing VOSH/International to a great future. Her success toward connecting with students and student VOSH chapters will bring the promise of furthering our outreach mission delivering eyecare in Mexico, Africa, and around the world.

2017-19 Dr. Tracy Matchinski elected future VOSH/ International President

The room was filled with eighty one visionaries, bound in a common cause from around the world, when the introduction and installation of the new President Elect of VOSH/International Dr. Tracy Matchinski drew their attention. As the session broke for lunch, many gathered around her to congratulate and connect with her. She politely, while in control addressed each individual with respect, giving them her undivided attention. Seeking an interview myself I waited patiently until the room cleared and we began a conversation that showed who Tracy was as a professional, as a leader and as an individual.

Dr. Matchinski's roots in optometry began as a 1995 graduate of the Illinois College of Optometry in Chicago. From there she did her residency at the Pennsylvania College of Optometry (now Salus University). It was a low vision residency at the Feinbloom Center of with mentors Drs. Sarah Appel and Richard Brilliant. Upon completion of Dr. Matchinski's residency she continued her specialty in Low Vision at the Chicago Lighthouse for the Blind. There she worked closely with Dr. Al Rosenberg a renowned expert in Low Vision who also was also active at that time as Vice President of VOSH/International reaching to Pacific Rim Nations introducing them to volunteer eye care. Dr. Matchinski's interest in both grew rapidly as she attributes her mentorship by Dr. Al Rosenbloom to making her the kind of person she is today.

This mentoring relationship continued as she later became a faculty member at Illinois College of Optometry along with Dr. Al Rosenbloom. She feels that her abilities as a Faculty member expand her role as an educator as well as helping her to be most relevant to helping students on dedicated visions mission. She found herself in the role of connecting with as many as twenty students on each of her sixteen eyecare missions. This experience molded her leadership acumen of working from the trenches of productivity, that which goes to the heart of motivation.

In reflection, Dr. Matchinski believes, "Everyone has a skill, often different from others. An educator's (or leader's) job is to connect them to the right jobs and watch them build these skills." In Tracy's experience she has found that "People want to do good but often don't know how to go about it. VOSH is a vehicle."

As Dr. Matchinski looks to the future of VOSH, her vision is on the cooperation between VOSH and the people it serves. That is to locally connect with available eyecare and healthcare professionals, connect with local community leaders and connect with local school systems. In addition connecting with local translators can open possibilities. She sees that education and information for all people will help embrace the value of eyecare, including diabetic prevention and preventive care counseling.

She also sees her role as President with a public health component of expanding eyecare initiatives. This includes a dedication toward eliminating functional blindness and impairment through Vision 20/20 partnering with World Health Organization and others.

One of the greatest strategies of meeting Vision 20/20 goals is to connect students with students – optometry students at home with new optometry students in new schools located in areas where the need is greatest.

Dr. Tracy Matchinski completes her perspective by saying, "VOSH resides at the heart of optometry. It is truly the service component of our profession."

Our future awaits!

Author's Note

We have all traveled through the history of Volunteer Optometric Services to Humanity (VOSH) International. From the inspiration of our Founder, Dr. Franklin Harms, to highly accomplished presidents today, millions of lives have been touched. Those who come to us receive the gift of sight; those who volunteer receive the gift of serving.

When asking VOSH/International Presidents about why they were inspired to serve a lifetime of VOSH, in one form or another, they all responded that it was the emotional feeling of immersing themselves in the experience. To explain this inspiration in words was difficult, but it is a feeling, familiar to most readers.

Beginning with Dr. Harms our best recruiting tool has always been to bring someone along with you to a mission. Give them the opportunity to 'feel' the passion for themselves.

So why do VOSHers volunteer so completely?

You make a living by what you get, You
make a Life by what you Give!
- *Winston Churchill*

(Courtesy of Dr. Dennis Hoss)

(Courtesy of Dr. Dale Cole)

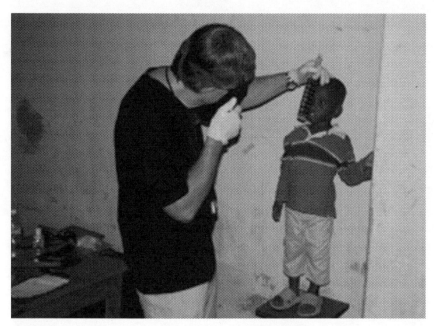

(Courtesy of Dr. Jeff Forrey)

(Courtesy of Dr. Dale Cole)

(Courtesy of Dr. Dale Cole)

VOSH
Programs and Initiatives

Over the decades VOSH has created many innovative programs and initiatives. This section is an overview of some of the highlights of tradition and some of those that continue today. These Programs and Initiatives represent the structure by which strategies are implemented.

As we transition from the richness of the past to the potential of the future, let us take a moment to reflect upon change and see it through the eyes of Programs and Initiatives. What are the current priorities of the officers, directors and VOSH/International as a whole. Where are we now and where are we going?

With reflective observation VOSH/International Executive Director Natalie Venezia, Esq., FVI comments, "As health needs and technology changed, VOSH recognized and supports the need for sustainable solutions to increase the optometric capacity in the poorest countries by supporting vision clinics and optometry schools in underdeveloped areas. As a result, in the last few years, VOSH has developed and collaborated on important programs and initiatives focused on effective eye care delivery and empowering local ODs to continue to provide quality eye care to their local communities. Here are a few of the most notable programs which have shown measurable results:

- VOSH's Technology Transfer Program accepts, refurbishes and ships donated optometric equipment and glasses to clinics and schools in developing countries where it can lead a new purpose of supporting clinical education and provide care to those with limited financial means.

- The VOSH Corps Program supports optometric education worldwide as it recruits and supports North American optometrists to teach optometry for 1-2 years in new and emerging optometry schools in the world's poorest countries, including Uganda, Malawi, Vietnam and Nicaragua. In November 2016, the optometry school at the Autonomous University of Nicaragua (UNAN), Managua graduated its first class of 20 optometry students who now have the potential to examine 80,000 patients annually and over a million patients by 2020 to meet the VISION 2020 millennial goals for Nicaragua. (VOSH was a key partner in developing UNAN along with Optometry Giving Sight. See video entitled " VOSH Building Eye Care Capacity in the Developing World" submitted herewith. https://vimeo.com/183017972)
- VOSH actively supports the establishment of sustainable clinics in Haiti, Guatemala, El Salvador, Nicaragua, Mexico and other developing countries, promoting and supporting local ODs and students providing sustainable eye care.
- The Student-VOSH Mentoring Program, which promotes future optometric humanitarianism, partners Student-VOSH chapters in developed countries with Student-VOSH chapters in developing countries. Optometry students globally are the future of humanitarian eye care and is a primary focus of VOSH, even more so today as technology and social media bring us into each other's work space."

Acronyms

Programs and organizations come with Acronyms. Following are some of the more common abbreviations used by VOSH (Volunteer Optometric Services to Humanity) and its affiliates:

- ALDO – Latin American Association of Optometrists and Opticians
- ASAPROSAR – Asociación Salvadoreña Pro Salud Rural

- ASCO Association of Schools and Colleges of Optometry
- CRUDEM – Eye Foundation in Milot, Haiti
- FUDEM – Foundation for the Development of Women (El Salvador)
- IAPB – International Agency for the Prevention of Blindness
- ICEE – International Center for Eyecare Education
- IMEC – International Medical Equipment Collaborative
- KNUST – Kwame Nkrumah University of Science and Technology in Ghana
- OGS – Optometry Giving Sight
- RAM – Remote Area Medical
- REIMS– Richmond Eye Inventory Software for categorizing glasses
- TTP Technology Transfer Program
- UNAM – Universidad Nacional Autonoma de Mexico

The VOSH Executive Director

For years the VOSH Board had discussed the need and the addition of an executive director to decrease the workload of the presidency.

The advent of Vision 2020 in the early 2000's necessitated a change. In the early 2000's, with the help of Dr. Zeltzer and others, VOSH/International revenues doubled due to to a sizable grant from Vistakon. And in 2005, with the help of Dr. McAndrews and others, VOSH/International revenues doubled again! This gave VOSH/International the financing to quadruple its outreach programs.

The changes were the 'tipping point.' Having an executive director was no longer a dream; it became a necessity.

It didn't take long for Dr. Zeltzer to agree to serve in this position. The VOSH Board passed the motion and the announcement was officially made in the *VOSH/International Newsletter, Fall/Winter 2004-05.*

Dr. Zeltzer Named Executive Director

"Harry Zeltzer, OD, DOS, FAAO, who has worn innumerable hats in various leadership positions for VOSH/ International for the past several years, now has a new title: Executive Director. He will be offering his continued services to VOSH/International as a volunteer.

'As the organization grows and interacts on a global level, it is important to have a knowledgeable person, one versed in the affairs of the organization, to turn to for advice and to represent VOSH/International at conferences and meetings as deemed necessary,' noted President Dale Cole. 'Further I can't tell you how many times Dr. Zeltzer bailed me out in situations where I could not personally follow through this past year.'

At the VOSH/International Annual Meeting in Orlando, the membership established the new position of Executive Director and Harry Zeltzer, immediate past president of VOSH/ International accepted that position, serving non-gratis. This has already been a very beneficial decision:

o   Dr. Zeltzer represented us in Oxford, England to further international relations. While there he established the possibility of VOSH distributing self-refracting eyeglasses developed by Josh Silver, PhD of England (Dr. Silver was a speaker at the recent Orlando VOSH/International annual meeting, explaining and demonstrating the glasses.)

o   Dr. Zeltzer met with Dr. Ajeet Bhardja, president of VOSH-India, laying the groundwork for collaboration of chapters in India

o   Dr. Zeltzer visited Midland, Texas and served as a consultant to the Texas Lions Recycling Center

(TLERC). During discussion, a possible Texas VOSH chapter through TLERC was initiated."

In 2005, Dr. Harry Zeltzer was added to the VOSH/International payroll and began to collect a modest stipend. This action followed a VOSH Board strategic planning session facilitated by Tom Thompson and shortly after, the VOSH Board approved and began his salary.

In 2012, Dr. Zeltzer retired from the Executive Director position, and the VOSH Board employed a new Executive Director. Then VOSH/International President, Dr. David McPhillips approached Natalie Venezia, Esq. to accept the position. She recalls,

"When Dave McPhillips asked me to serve as Executive Director, I was flattered and excited. I think David thought that I had the skills to be ED but also had the advantage of having been a constant factor for so many years. Like Harry, I could help with providing an historical perspective to VOSH issues. At that point, I had been involved with VOSH for about 20 years, as a lay volunteer helping with acuities, then started planning missions, became a director on the board, moved to Board Secretary, then Managing Director, and now as Executive Director. In learning the job of ED, I had the privilege of being mentored by the charming and brilliant Dr. Harry Zeltzer."

Natalie Venezia, Esq. transitions into the role of Executive Director. Having established herself in the work and administration of VOSH, she began administering the office of VOSH/International. *(Source: VOSH Website)*

"Community service and volunteerism have always played an important role in Ms. Venezia's personal and professional life. Since retiring from a San Diego law firm, Natalie has led or participated in 18 VOSH missions with VOSH-Illinois and VOSH-California. Besides VOSH, she has also led several missions for Operation Rainbow, a non-profit organization providing free reconstructive surgery for children with cleft abnormalities. In 2007 Natalie began serving as the VOSH/International Board Administrator. She was instrumental in consolidating the efforts of a geographically separated, all volunteer board. Electronic communications became streamlined and accessible. The website was re-designed and made more user-friendly. Her organizational skills and attention to detail have been invaluable. This past year, Ms. Venezia became the VOSH/International Executive Director. Natalie is continually an inspiration to the entire Board of VOSH/International, owing much of what it has accomplished to her tireless efforts and dedication."

When asked to describe her role and daily life after three years on the job, Executive Director Natalie relates, "Governance and administration in VOSH is complex: There is no real office (it is "virtual"). There is no staff. There is a very limited budget and definitely no frills. The VOSH Board is truly a "working board" (and they work tirelessly and passionately) and are scattered around the United States, Canada and Australia, the Board advisors and liaisons are located in North America, South America, Mexico and Central America, Africa, India and Australia. The 75 VOSH chapters are located around the world and the patients that we serve are in almost every country in the world.

While the board of directors ensures that VOSH, as a diverse organization, stays aligned with its mission and provides oversight and guidance to the chapters, its partners and associated parties, the executive director is involved day-to-day details and operations of VOSH, working to execute the Board's policies, programs, and initiatives. In reality though, because VOSH is a volunteer organization, the role of Executive Director is one of "chief coordinator," "chief communicator," and constantly looking to raise funds to improve programs and chapter benefits, really the role of a jack of all trades. In a typical week, I respond to inquiries on all levels and through all modes (phone, Skype, email, texts, Facebook, website inquiries) on a myriad of subjects: chapters looking for mission resources or collaborations, organizations inviting a VOSH mission to their town to provide services, issues related to the AOA, the AAO, the IAPB, OGS, BHVI, requests and ideas from board members, from donors, from those organizations looking for donated optometric equipment. I work with the President, Vice President and Treasurer on policy and financial matters. I plan the annual meetings and the mid-year meetings. I review applications of new chapters. I write grants and seek fund raising sources. I work with others to redesign the VOSH website. I oversee social media and communications. I work with VOSH's legal counsel on agreements, MOUs (Memorandums of Understanding), and other matters. I have revised the VOSH Constitution and Bylaws. I coordinate the interns who have recently become a wonderful addition to VOSH Board. On any given day I speak with people from Africa, India, Mexico, Canada, the USA, and other places. I am working off the Board's 5-year plan to achieve the vision the board has set out. The role of the VOSH Executive Director is a varied and ever changing role, challenging but with a consistent effort towards supporting the board to accomplish the mission of VOSH.

I love my job! I have the pleasure of working with some of the finest humanitarians in the world people who care passionately about providing critical quality eye care, who have set the highest standards for themselves, who strive to develop eye care clinics and sustainability in developing countries, and people who respect and like one another and most admirably, people who have sacrificed their time and personal lives to make a difference in the lives of others." – Natalie Venezia, Esq., Executive Director, VOSH/International.

Perhaps the most significant change that vastly enhanced VOSH/International capability and professionalism was the addition of the position of VOSH/International Executive Director.

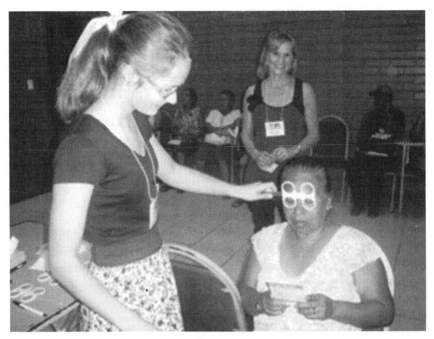

(Courtesy of Dr. James Vaught)

Foreign Missions – traditional model

This is a classic example of the basic model of VOSH foreign missions taught by founders Dr. Franklin Harms, Dr. Russ Dorland and Dr. Walter Marshall and repeated during many trips, even today.

This information was authored by Dr. Ray Mienheartt, VOSH-Indiana and published in the Journal of the American Optometric Association, Volume 49, Number 2, February 1978.

VOSH-Indiana

VOSH-Indiana made its first mission in November 1974 and nine others since. These include four to the Dominican Republic, two to Haiti, three to Honduras and one to the Navajo Indians in Arizona and New Mexico. Regular membership in VOSH is limited to Indiana optometrists, associate membership are available to out-of-state O.D.s other professionals and lay people. The organization under Indiana law, has a twelve-man board of directors and has qualified for a non-profit mailing permit. It is financially solvent, relying primarily on dues and contributions for funding. It has its own printing shop. The general public is asked only for old eyeglasses which are then recycled by optometry students at Indiana University, Illinois College of Optometry and optometric assistants in offices throughout the state. The Lions Club and the Jaycees have each made the collecting of old glasses their state project and contribute many thousands of pairs each year. After the glasses are collected, each pair is carefully examined for cracks, breaks or scratches. Each selected pair is then neutralized, put in a plastic bag and labeled according to power, single vision or multifocal and whether for a man, woman or child. Only good, durable glasses are taken on a mission and only about one pair out of each twenty collected is suitable for our use. The glasses are then put into one of the twelve specially designed and built wooden crates. The twelve crates can hold up to 20,000 pairs of neutralized and catalogued glasses. A typical mission will use up to 5,000 pairs of glasses per week. Experience has taught us that plus lenses are prescribed about 98% of the time. Whenever a myope is found, it is often in the -10.00 to -15.00 diopter range. Nearly every optometrist returns home with a prescription of high minus that he has fabricated in his lab and then mails the Rx to a missionary or peace corps worker who sees that the patient receives it.

Although a missionary in every sense of the word, VOSH-Indiana personnel prefer to be called "visionaries" to differentiate themselves from church missionaries.

The visionaries pay all their own expenses, take their own equipment and donate their services under usually very trying conditions. Usually the living and working facilities are rather primitive, the food isn't too good and we must be extremely careful of the local water. Whenever possible, we travel with an

Indianapolis flying club, AmbassadAIR, in their own Boeing 707. This not only permits much cheaper air fare, but also greatly simplifies the logistics involved in transporting more than a ton of medical material and our own equipment which includes the VOSH-Indiana library of glasses.

When visionaries return home, they are always in great demand to speak at clubs, church groups, service clubs, etc. The question always comes up, "Do you receive subsidies from our government, a foreign government or a Church?" The answer is an emphatic "no". We are not offered, we do not receive nor do we want any subsidy.

A typical VOSH-Indiana mission usually consists of 25-30 persons – the Haiti missions have more than 50 people. An ideal mission consists of about 40% OD's, 10% M.D.'s (ophthalmologists preferred) and the remainder lay persons. Everyone works hard on a mission. Lay persons are needed for traffic control, "pickers" to select the proper Rx after the examination and as interpreters. We usually have a ground host such as Medical Group Missions, the local Rotary Club or a religious order to make ground arrangements for the working area, living and eating facilities and interpreters. VOSH-Indiana missions have been set up in hospitals (one hospital kitchen staff had a pet pig, another had a cat with kittens), a former dictator's mansion, schools, mud huts, a leper colony and a provincial capitol building with armed guards surrounding the area.

The ground host sends out the word when we will be there. The first day of a mission usually consists of patients from the immediate area. Most of these people have been promised things before that never materialized – they want to be certain before they travel great distances. When the word goes out that we are there and are examining and dispensing glasses, they start to arrive. They come on foot, burros and anything that has wheels. It's nothing unusual for an interpreter to tell a doctor, "This person lives 50 miles away and walked here to see you." Crowd control is always a big thing. Riots and near-riots have broken out when it is time for us to leave and many hundreds of people are still waiting and more arriving.

The patients are lined up and brought to registration table where their name, age, occupation and whether or not they are literate are written on a VOSH-Indiana prescription blank. They pay a registration fee of about 25 cents which the ground host keeps to help defray the expenses of hiring interpreters and other personnel. VOSH-Indiana requires that the ground hosts sign a statement that no one will be turned away if they cannot afford the registration fee. These people are poor but proud. By paying a fee, they feel they are not receiving charity. Next, they go to the screening area where an optometrist using a penlight and ophthalmoscope and with the aid of an interpreter, decides whether the patient should go for surgery (if available), for medication, for complete refraction, be examined only for reading lenses, or sent home because he either doesn't need help or is beyond help. The screening doctor also records such things as "blind" in OD, cataract, suspected glaucoma," or any other pertinent information that might save the examining doctor some time.

Glaucoma is so rampant in this part of the world, the examiner often spots steamy corneas, and shallow anterior chambers before the patient gets within ten feet of him. Trachoma is very common. The patient proceeds to the examining area where distant acuity is determined. He is then scoped using a trial frame and lenses. If the patient is literate (and few are) a reading card is used and they are given plus to best near acuity. If illiterate, a rice bowl complete with bugs and sand is often used. It is rewarding to see a smile come on a woman's face as you add plus and she starts to see the sand and bugs and knows she will now be able to do a better job cleaning rice and be able to sew again. Presbyopia seems to affect these people at age 30 and disrupts their way of life for they have to make all of their clothes.

The patient then takes his record to the dispensing area where the "pickers" select the proper (or as near as possible) lens correction out of the men, women or children's boxes. We dispense all the plano sunglasses we can get. When you work out in the hot, wet, cane or banana fields in terribly bright sun, sunglasses are worth their weight in gold.

The optical laboratories donate hundreds of obsolete sunglasses to us. After moving onto the fitting area where the frames are adjusted, screws tightened, etc. the patient goes to select a case for his new glasses. This department is often manned by a teen-aged visionary.

Up to this point the patient has had no say as to the choosing of the frame or lenses, (they all want gold or rhinestones), when they are permitted to choose the case, they often spend over an hour to get just the right case.

VOSH-Indiana goes only to the poorest of the poor areas to take care of those who have no visual care available and couldn't afford it if it were available. Most of the natives earn less than $2 per day and they don't have work every day. We have had on several occasions, wealthy people call us from as far as 100 miles away, offering to pay us to examine them and their families and they will send the prescription to the state to be filled – visual care isn't always available even when you have money. For the most part, the natives seem happy and have accepted their lot in life. They raise large families in thatched or mud huts, live mostly on rice and know from the time they are little children that they will never rise above the social and economic level of their parents. The missionaries tell us it is common for a 9 or 10 year-old girl to have a baby. The infant mortality rate is about 50% at birth and of those who survive birth, about 50% die before the age of five. In this part of the world, if you live to be an adult, you are tough and have good resistance to disease or you don't make it. Rarely do we see a retarded or deformed child – they are permitted to die when infants. Obesity is practically unheard of but the hospitals are full of children dying of malnutrition – they are bloated and their hair turns red. Many visionaries have left the hospitals sick and crying at the sights they saw. Extremely short of even the most basic medicines and equipment, they are very excited when we bring in medicine and supplies. On one mission we were able to bring 750 pounds of medicine donated by a pharmaceutical company to a physician that was on the mission. Another time we took other OTC drugs. We see many cases where an eye has been scratched and due to the fact they haven't even the most basic medical care, infection has set in and the eye is destroyed.

When the visionaries return home, they don't put these experiences behind them and forget these people. Many have returned on their vacations and one such group took a boy recovering from burns to town and bought him several complete outfits after making arrangements for him to go to school for the first time in his life. A young Dominican man had taught himself to speak English by a correspondence course he had somehow acquired.

He came to our first mission Dominica and volunteered to be an interpreter – thanks to some Indiana visionaries and their financial help, he is now in his third year at the University of Santo Domingo and will be able to return to help his people. Dr. and Mrs. Tom Butler of Taylorville, Illinois were so impressed with a young interpreter they met while on the last Honduran mission, they made arrangements and brought him to their home and he is now in his 3rd year of high school in Taylorville. Friendships have developed between VOSH-Indiana members and the citizens of various countries and letters and packages flow back and forth.

A professional journalist was sent by his newspaper chair to write about one of our Honduran missions. The report was in many newspapers complete with pictures. Many letters were received concerning the articles including one from a Honduran who as a girl in Honduras was denied visual care for lack of funds. Without exception, as soon as a mission is completed, the ground host, peace corps personnel and missionaries ask, "When will you return?"

The day after a mission returns home, the enormous task of setting up another one starts. Transportation must be arranged, the library must be rebuilt, members must be notified, the long, slow process of contacting the ground hosts and those members interested in participating begins. Next comes the collecting of airfare, registration fees, living expenses, etc. All this work entails about 6 months work before a mission ever leaves Indianapolis.

On the last several missions, VOSH-Indiana has subsidized and permitted 4th year optometry student from Indiana University and the Illinois College of Optometry to participate on the missions. These young people work hard and have experiences that will influence their lives and practice as long as they live. They see poverty, terrible living conditions, disease and many other things they have been protected from their entire lives.

Letters from returning students testify as to the impact the mission has had on them.

VOSH-Indiana is proud to be able to bring this experience to these young people (as many as 13 have participated on one mission). A continuing education seminar is being planned with all profits going solely for student participation on missions...

...Whenever visionaries get together, they always talk about the sights they have seen, mutual acquaintances, the dirty, stinking marketplaces with half-rotten meat hanging in the sun, the funny and pathetic things they have seen.

VOSH-Indiana has come a long way since it was organized by its present chairman, Walter Marshall, OD of Indianapolis following his return from Honduras on a 1974 mission led by VOSH/Interstate director, Franklin Harms, OD

A VOSH-Indiana mission is one of the most rewarding experiences a person can have. Nearly every mission is given an appreciation party by the ground hosts or the townspeople themselves, and sometimes invited to receptions given by the American Embassy. All visionaries on a mission to Aswa, Dominican Republic were made honorary citizens of the city. Yes,

VOSH-Indiana and its visionaries have matured to a great extent in less than three years which we feel gives us the right to use the slogan: "YOUR CAREER ISN'T COMPLETE 'TIL YOU'VE BEEN ON A VOSH-Indiana MISSION!"

Domestic Missions

Domestic eye care missions are rooted in the needs of those near us. Volunteer school vision screenings were done before it was government mandated. Several optometrists have provided eye care at health clinics on reservations of our Native Americans. In 1971, Dr. David Krasnow, VOSH-California worked in such a clinic as an optometry student through Project Concern. In the late 1970's, Dr. Krasnow became the founder of the first interurban eye care clinic for Native Americans in Los Angeles.

In the early 1990's, VOSH-Northwest was recognized for its domestic volunteer eye care missions. This account was given by Dr. Rich Ryan VOSH-California and later international secretary-treasurer of VOSH/International *in the VOSH/ International Newsletter, June 1993:*
"VOSH-Northwest receives Points of Light Award" from President George Bush.

"The Union Gospel Mission in Spokane, Washington houses a VOSH-Northwest sponsored clinic which serves the homeless of the inland northwest who come to the mission, as well as many impoverished persons of the area. Shortly before President Bush left office, the Union Gospel Mission project was given the 974th (of 1000) of his 'Points of Light' awards."

Dr. Walt Michaelis was the founder of this clinic serving twenty people per week, many receiving pre-owned eyewear. In the Points of Light letter sent by President George Bush, this quote stood out about why we serve VOSH as volunteers:

"We must not allow ourselves to be measured by the sum of our possessions or the size of our bank accounts. The true measure of any individual is found in the way he or she treats others; and the person who regards others with love, respect, and charity holds a priceless treasure in his heart." United States President George Bush

At the same time VOSH-Northwest was also conducting a similar volunteer eye care clinic in Seattle, Washington, jovially called the "**Seattle Millionaires Club**." This was a joint project between the West Seattle Lions Club and VOSH-Northwest. It was also supported by area optical laboratories such as Alpine, Nigro-Walman, Optical Supply and Tura.

Dr. Michael Matsunami founded the clinic in 1991. *In the VOSH/International Newsletter, June 1993* he says, "The primary goal at the clinic and the club is to assist the less fortunate in getting jobs. The clinic has provided more than 300 homeless people with free eye examinations and glasses."

VOSH/International conducts Domestic Mission in Detroit

First VOSH Chapter-wide Domestic Eye Care Mission 1997

Board members sat around a table in a hotel suite in Portland, Oregon brainstorming about how VOSH could reach out to people in new and innovative ways.

Do we really want to have an International Annual meeting in Detroit? "Why not?, offered Dr. Nelson Edwards, then Secretary Treasurer of VOSH/International. The other members all refocused their attention on Nelson as he responded, "Not only does Detroit have easy access to our largest contingent (Midwesterners) but the inner city downtown has some of the greatest needs in the Country! We could do a VOSH-wide Eye Care Project."

Well after many reservations were expressed, the majority of the VOSH/International Board accepted reflecting the adventurous pioneers they were – ready to take on the challenge.

Dr. Nelson Edwards, the host of the Detroit Annual Meeting contacted Dr. Carol Hunt. Carol Hunt, OD, VOSH/International Project Coordinator became the organizer of this first Domestic VOSH/International Mission in downtown Detroit, Michigan. The scope of this project is revealed by this information taken from her report:

"VOSH/International's first domestic project took place at the Detroit Rescue Mission Ministries facility, 138 Stimson, Detroit, Michigan on October 17, 1997 from 9AM to 4PM. A total of 200 patients were examined, 100 glasses were prescribed and 3 referrals were made. Volunteers involved in this project included eighteen optometrists, two Ferris State University College of Optometry students, optometric assistants, student from the Crockett Career Technical Center Optometric Assistant Class, and a number of other supportive volunteers.

A grant in the amount of $3,000 was provided by the Michigan Affiliate of AFVA (American Federation for Vision Awareness). The project was also funded by donations of $3,000 provided by Michigan VOSH and $1,000 provided by MDOS (Metropolitan Detroit Optometric Society).

OICD (Optometric Institute and Clinic of Detroit) shared frames donated to them by Classic and provide the use of a Titmus screener. Henry Ford – 1st Optometry provided mydriatic, mydriatic spectacles, use of an auto-refractor, non contact tonometer, trial lens set, and is willing to assist with lab work at 10% off wholesale costs. Kay Optical of Redford, Michigan has also agreed to provide laboratory services at a 10% discount. Alcon Pharmaceuticals (with the encouragement of Dr. Sheila Duda) provided a generous amount of Soderberg both loaned and auto-refractors for this project. Mike, the owner of Metro Vision in Detroit volunteered to provide the lenses for 50 Rx's at no charge to VOSH. As an optician trained at Michigan's Ferris State University he plans to do the work himself.

Expenses included supplies, forms, copying, Banner from American Sign Company, T-shirts from Arrowest, Detroit, a luncheon, Donation of 10 tables to DRM, Van Rental and Insurance, Laboratory costs including lenses and postage/delivery costs.

A great number of people are to be thanked who helped behind the scenes; particularly the individual shelter contacts: Cynthia Sackett of Wayne County Family Center, Sister Cecilia and Luther Jenkins of COTS (Coalition on Temporary Shelter) and Lois Tosh of the Detroit Rescue mission. Ms. Tosh stepped in when our original contact person, Dr. Theda Bishop became ill and was instrumental in the facility set-up and luncheon. Also many thanks to Jacquelyn Krycian, Optometric Assistant Instructor at Detroit's Crocket Career Technical Center and her students. We hope this was an experience these high school young people will remember and can use in the future."

(*This information was extracted from a number of sources including personal files and documents provided by Dr. Carol Hunt, project chairwoman.*)

Domestic Missions with RAM

VOSH, for many years, has partnered with Remote Area Medical (RAM) and others to reach rural areas that do not have access to eyecare and eye wear. Dr. Vicki Weiss has lead the way and was recognized as Humanitarian of the Year in 2015 in this regard.

Software to Catalogue Glasses

(Courtesy of Dr. James Vaught)

In preparation for early VOSH trips, optometrists, opticians and lay persons gathered together for months before their missions to sort, clean, neutralize, label and categorize according to prescription strengths – minus through plus. These would then be packed into boxes for transporting to the mission site. The volunteers going on the mission would be responsible for preparing these glasses.

Most of the glasses were collected, either in the local optometric offices or stores. Lions Clubs were dedicated to eyes and larger collection programs generated many pairs of used, donated glasses. It was a big deal for a patient to donate their previous prescriptions, giving others a chance to see.

This was a lot of work. As the personal computer became available, the thought occurred, "Why can't we use a computer program to catalogue eyeglasses?"

In the early 1990's several efforts to develop software that would assist with this task were undertaken. Dr. Nelson Edwards of VOSH-Michigan was one of the first to use software developed by a program in the Detroit area.

Programmers on the West Coast were also busy developing eyeglass software as described in the *VOSH/International Newsletter, Fall/Winter 2001-2002:*

"Pioneer in computer cataloguing of glasses"

"If you've ever worked in the dispensary of a VOSH clinic, you've encountered firsthand the frustration of going through box upon box to find the best available prescription for the patient. When volunteer Dennis Gunst experienced the problem, he took on the challenge of writing a computer program to simplify the task. Along the way he's set up a complete glasses recycling center and developed a few other innovations."

After working with his mentor and friend Dr. Neil Mietus, Dennis joined VOSH/International. Neil comments that "Dennis showed us how to measure, mark, edge and mount lenses on the spot in ten minutes."

"While helping out in the clinics, he came to feel strongly that a computer could be a big help in cataloguing prescriptions. In the early 1990's, Dennis Gunst collaborated with Mexican student Martin Figueroa in writing one of the first computer programs to facilitate the task of selecting recycled eyeglasses for patients. The two men wrote a computer program using 'weighted' errors to determine which pair of glasses would provide the closest match for the patient's prescription."

In the late 1990's members from the East Coast created software as well. The **REIMS** (Richmond Eyeglass Inventory Matching System) program was developed by VOSH to provide Chapters and Mission Leaders a computerized software program for sorting and accessing eyeglass libraries. Mr. Howard (Skip) Charles and Dr. Phil Richmond of VOSH-NECO who began work on the program as early as 1997 received the VOSH/International

Humanitarian Award in 2005. This program is still used by many VOSH missions.

This information about REIMS was provided in a document by Dr. Harry Zeltzer: "The program is named REIMS (Richmond Eyeglass Inventory Matching System) for the late Dr. Phil Richmond who was a founder of the New England VOSH chapter. It was developed for the use of Friends of ASAPROSAR (Asociación Salvadoreña Pro-Salud Rural – Salvadoran Association for Rural Health) at the suggestion of their President, Dr. Alan R. Gruber. It was written in FoxPro 2.6 for Windows and runs on all Windows platforms (Windows 7 64 bit version requires some special adaptation.)

Friends of ASAPROSAR began supporting the activities of Dr. Vicky Guzman whose mission was to improve the health of poor Salvadorans in the area of Santa Ana, El Salvador.

Volunteers from the Boston area began visiting Santa Ana in the late 1980's. It was soon discovered that eye care was the most pressing medical problem among the poor of El Salvador. They had no affordable options…

…As word of REIMS spread through VOSH and other humanitarian groups, the program has been adopted by many organizations including the Lions and Rotary Clubs, U.S. Navy and Air Force programs, Mobile Medical Mission Hospital and others. It is being used in Vietnam, South Africa, El Salvador, Nicaragua, Guatemala, St. Vincent, Honduras and Mexico.

The most labor intensive requirement of the use of REIMS is entry of the inventory.

Once the inventory has been entered, REIMS is ready to find the best matches for the Rx's from the refraction stations."

One of the principal contributors to REIMS, not mentioned above was Dr. Robert Zeller, who was a retired gynecologist/obstetrician from Massachusetts who cleans, neutralizes, and labels about 5,000 eyeglasses between eye campaigns while entering each prescription into the computer program.

Technology Transfer Program

The Technology Transfer Program (TTP) is a program whereby VOSH/International collects donated ophthalmic equipment, repairs and refurbishes it, then ships it to needy schools and clinics.

Before the official adoption of the TTP name, many smaller efforts donated equipment and supplies to clinics around the world. Most of these deliveries came as VOSH missions brought equipment to mission sights, often leaving behind key equipment for use by nurses and local eye/medical professionals. In time, VOSH mission sites that were regularly visited began establishing part-time and eventually full-time eye care clinics using the donated equipment and supplies.

Informally VOSH Chapters were responsible for transporting equipment to their work sites. For example, in 1990 Rick Myrick and Ted McCallister drove a bus-load full of equipment and supplies from Kansas and Illinois to their permanent worksite in Guatemala. The bus itself was left in Guatemala to assist future VOSH trips as well.

A major effort in 2007 was made to bring equipment and supplies to Ghana. This was coordinated by VOSH/International and Dr. Nelson Edwards, VOSH-Michigan. The Rotary Clubs in Michigan along with World Medical Relief assisted with this effort. VOSH/International also raised funds from donors, including Essilor and Luxottica and members of WCO, for the $12,200 shipping costs.

Three hundred thousand dollars worth of equipment was collected including phoropters, slit lamps, test books, optical lab equipment and 50,000 pairs of readers from New Eyes for the Needy. The supplies were delivered to KNUST optometry school in Ghana with some also given to the new optometry school in

Cape Coast. Glasses were shared with schools of optometry in Abia and UNIBEN, Nigeria.

Following the 2007 shipment, the name "**Technology Transfer Program (TTP)**" was organized formally as a VOSH system to facilitate future donations, repairs and shipments. Implementation of this program was supported by the Esther Kahn Foundation secured by the efforts of Dr. Harry Zeltzer and Dr. Ellis Potter.

Jeff Forrey, OD was the first chairman of the TTP. Dr. John Randall a visiting professor (sponsored by WCO) applied for Ghana chapter membership. He attended the annual meeting because of the large shipment Ghana was able to receive.

VOSH/International partnered with Optometry Giving Sight to give power and resources to the Technology Transfer Program. With this partnership great strides can be made throughout the world toward sustainability of eye care delivery systems.

Technology Transfer Program
(This report is reprinted from a 2011-12 VOSH/International Newsletter)

"TTP coordinates the collection and reconditioning of used equipment to be distributed in optometry schools around the world where there is a desperate need for examination equipment. Some of the tactics that this strategy enables are as follows:

- o VOSH-Southeast distributed trial lens sets to optometry schools in Peru 2 years ago with 53 of 100 sets being sold @ $150/set
- o TTP provided equipment to new eye clinic @ the Xochicalco School of Optometry in Tijuana, Mexico. VOSH/International helped remodel the clinic with $40,000 of OGS funding

o TTP provided Nicaragua more than 30,000 eyeglass frames, lenses, and several lensometers
o In Peru, TTP provided to several optometry schools, permanent sustainable clinics and Peruvian government and non-government organizations—textbooks, hand instruments and handles, 165 surgical instruments, 1000's of frames and lenses, several auto-refractors, several 104-piece trial lens sets and trial frames
o In Trinidad-Tobago, TTP provided to the new Bachelor of Optometry program @ U. of West Indies significant major teaching and practice tools including edgers, contact lens sets, frames, textbooks, keratometers and lensometers, etc
o Facilities with donated recycled equipment and supplies
  - Pro-Vision Clinic- Managua, Mexico
  - Xochilcalco School of Optometry-Tijuana, Mexico
  - CRUDEM Foundation- Milot, Haiti
  - ASAPROSAR-Santa Anna, El Salvador
  - FUDEM-San Salvador, El Salvador
  - EUROHISPANO-School of Optometry and Science, Lima, Peru
  - National Eye Clinic-Nicaraguan Govt.
  - Argon laser presented to Nicaraguan Government's National Eye Clinic
  - U. Of West Indies in Trinidad School of Optometry
  - The Haiti Eyeglass Project
o VOSH/International Technology Transfer Program (TTP) currently has collected, refurbished and sent more than 60 donated instruments to clinics and hospitals in developing countries that are lacking equipment.

o This program is in collaboration with a warehouse committee of VOSH-Southwest. SOUTHEAST
o Further support from VOSH provides essential infrastructure such as diagnostic equipment, educational materials and training to create sustainable eye care clinics. The Student-VOSH chapter of the Illinois Optometric College is collaborating with VOSH-Illinois, wherein OD's donate their time after graduation to train and educate personnel in clinics established by VOSH using the equipment VOSH has shipped.
o VOSH of New England (VOSH-ONE) INTRODUCED VOSH/International TO THE ESTHER KAJN FOUNDATION WHO IN TURN submitted a grant request to the Esther Kahn Foundation for $25,000 which they received in August 2010. This funding will be used for recycling and shipping of TTP equipment to clinics and optometry schools in developing countries as well as establishing a sustainable clinic."

This invitation appeared on the VOSH Website:
Be a Part of the Solution. Help a clinic or school Envision its future. Donate or request used Optometric Equipment
"The VOSH/INTERNATIONAL Resource Management Team partnering with Optometry Giving Sight welcomes your interest in our Technology Transfer Program (TTP). VOSH, through TTP, collects, restores and ships used optometric equipment, lenses and frames to needy clinics, teaching institutions, hospitals and N.G.O.'s. VOSH/INTERNATIONAL is a 501c3 non-profit organization. Your donation is tax-deductible."

Dr. David Stacy is the current chairman and coordinator of the Technology Transfer Program (TTP). His efforts to secure donations and equipment, insures the success of this program.

Fellow of VOSH/ International – FVI
- *From VOSH Website*

The Fellowship of VOSH/International program was created by Dr. Stuart Frank with assistance of a VOSH committee in 2004 for the purpose of acknowledging the skills and experience necessary for a member of VOSH to advise on the global challenge of preventable blindness; to foster the development of future leaders to meet the challenge of VISION 2020 and to prepare individuals who may be asked to consult with governmental agencies, educational, private, or public institutions, and the media on issues related to the mission and vision of VOSH/International. Fellows of VOSH/International are expected to exemplify those characteristics which are deemed important for achieving the primary mission of VOSH. Among those characteristics deemed important are:

   a. Demonstrate understanding of the world-wide need for eye care, including: demographics; basic epidemiology; major causes and geographic patterns of vision loss worldwide; specific challenges for the prevention and remediation of vision loss; the role of VOSH, WHO, and other non-governmental organizations.
   b. A basic understanding of the philosophical constructs underlying volunteer, charity, and humanitarian programs.

c. A knowledge of and sensitivity to cultural considerations in the delivery of health care to underserved populations.
d. A demonstrated level of commitment to the primary mission of VOSH/International, as set forth by the fellowship committee, through participation in a variety of activities listed below.
e. Knowledge of the history and organization of VOSH.
f. Demonstrated understanding of a VOSH mission, including mission preparation, logistics, the roles of various team members, and philosophy and approach to delivery of care during a mission.
g. Membership in good standing of VOSH/International. However, a non-member may be awarded the title of Honorary Fellow of VOSH/International in exceptional cases.
h. Successful completion of an oral interview to be given at the annual meeting of VOSH/International.
i. A completed application for fellowship.

The first examinations and inductions for Fellow of VOSH/International were completed in 2006, in conjunction with the VOSH/International Annual Meeting at the Palms Island Resort and Marina, Lake Monroe, Florida. As of 2015 there are 29 Fellows of VOSH/International.

The Fellow of VOSH/International (FVI) program is currently chaired by Dr. Ann Slocum-Edmonds and Dr. Larry Hookway. *This information is taken from the VOSH website.*

Franklin Harms Society

VOSH participants have volunteered thousands of hours of service providing vision care to those in need. To honor those dedicated individuals, VOSH/International has created The Franklin Harms Society, named after its founder, Franklin Harms. This honor recognizes those optometrists and other volunteers who have served in 10 or more VOSH clinics. Fifty-eight individuals have now qualified for this recognition.

- *2014 VOSH/International Annual Report*

The requirements for this will be:

-To have participated in a minimum of 10 mission trips, domestic or foreign.

-To be a current member of VOSH.

-Complete an application listing the missions, date, destination, name of chapter, address and email address.

A Franklin Harms Society member will be:

-Honored with a personalized diploma

-Recognized at the VOSH/International Annual Meeting

-Listed on the website as having received this honor

World Council of Optometry WCO

VOSH became a partner of the World Council of Optometry (WCO) in 2001. The WCO enabled VOSH to make optometric connections around the world.

The World Council of Optometry (WCO) is an international membership organization with a mission to facilitate the enhancement and development of eye and vision care worldwide we do this through education, policy development and humanitarian outreach.

Optometry exists in 90 countries and the WCO is committed to promoting optometry worldwide by providing a network for exchanging ideas and innovation.

WCO serves as a forum for member organizations to respond to public health needs and opportunities around the world. In the changing world of optometry, WCO acts as a unifying voice, encouraging the launch of international projects and services that meet the needs of patients, optometrists and the ophthalmic industry.

In countries where optometry is well established, WCO is working towards improving optometric services or expanding the scope of practice. Where it is not well established WCO supports the development of optometry in countries that need assistance.

Endorsement of WCO by VOSH was signed in December 2001. This action pledged VOSH support for the Right-to-Sight and Vision 2020 of the World Health Organization. Dr. Zeltzer, as VOSH/International Executive Director and Dr. Anthony Di Stefano, Executive Director of WCO signed the agreement working together for the next few years.

Dr. Zeltzer represented VOSH at the World Council of Optometry (WCO) General Delegates Meeting in April 2005 in Accra, Ghana. This was held in conjunction with the Ghana Optometrists Association and African Council of Optometry meetings. The program focused on *VISION 2020: the Right to Sight.* Experts at this meeting discussed the potential of several multidisciplinary models to eradicate preventable blindness. An emphasis was placed upon correcting refractive error and low vision. At this conference Dr. Zeltzer presented a talk on **"Integrating Volunteerism into Long-Term, Sustainable Projects."** D.D.D. Sheni, Bsc, Msc, PhD, FAAO, FOA, FNCO, President of WCO presided.

In May 2006 Dr. Zeltzer attended the WCO meeting in Milan, Italy. Three hundred people registered from 40 countries with most of the attendees representing education, industry and non-government organizations.

The VOSH/International affiliation with WCO continues today. The connection brought VOSH closer toward developing strategies to advance new international chapters, working with UNESCO and VERAS.

VOSH Reserves Disaster Relief

The VOSH Reserves Disaster Relief program was developed to help in the recovery process for those that have been affected by natural disasters worldwide. A VOSH team responded to the devastation of Typhoon Haiyan in the Philippines in 2014 by examining 8000 patients and providing needed eye care and eyeglasses that had been lost. This was a great help to these people on their road to recovery. In February 2016 a VOSH team traveled to Nepal to help those affected by the recent devastating earthquake.

VOSH members are invited to join the "VOSH Reserves Disaster Relief" team. There is no commitment to participate. You will be part of a list of experienced VOSHers who will be contacted when organizations ask VOSH for eye care assistance following natural disasters. Details of each trip will be provided and it is your choice to then participate.

Reprinted from VOSH/International website 2016

VOSH Corps

Originally VOSH Corps was organized in 2010 under the direction and advocacy of Dr. Greg Pearl, president of VOSH/International at that time.

VOSH Corps introduced *(Reprinted from VOSH/International Website 2016)*

"VOSH/International, in collaboration with the Brien Holden Vision Institute Public Health Division and supported by Optometry Giving Sight, announces a new initiative in building optometric education worldwide. We invite North American ODs to serve in emerging optometric institutions as faculty and program development assistants. This is a fantastic opportunity for those just entering the profession; those who are transitioning to retirement; or those looking for a new adventure. VOSH/International will review applications with final selection and placement by the Brien Holden Vision Institute.

We are seeking optometrists with an interest in the academia required for recently established optometry programs aimed at addressing the human resource needs of eye care delivery in developing countries. The successful candidate will be required to assume the position for a minimum duration of one year (reviewable) and relocate within a reasonable time once a position becomes available. VOSH/International will review applications with final selection and placement by the Brien Holden Vision Institute."

VOSH/International makes its First VOSH Corps placement *(VOSH website 2016)*

"VOSH/International is pleased to announce that it is making its first placement in the newly established VOSH Corps program. Dr. Justin Manning has been selected to serve one or more years in Nicaragua on the faculty of the optometry school at UNAN-Managua, Universidad Nacional Autónoma de Nicaragua.

The goal of VOSH Corps is to build optometric education worldwide. VOSH Corps is a collaboration with the Brien Holden Vision Institute and is supported by Optometry Giving Sight. Modeled after the Peace Corps program, graduates from North American optometry schools are recruited to serve in emerging optometric institutions around the world as faculty and program development assistants.

Dr. Justin Manning is a graduate of The Ohio State University College of Optometry and has completed a residency at The Veterans Affairs Puget Sound Healthcare System American Lake Division in Tacoma, WA. He will begin his tenure at UNAN in September 2015.

When asked about his reasons for applying to VOSH Corps and his future plans, Dr. Manning said, "During my first Student VOSH trip (to Nicaragua of all places), I thought to myself, if there was any way I could make a living doing this, I would do it in a heartbeat. That sentiment only grew following my second SVOSH trip to Bolivia. Since those two trips, the dream to move abroad developed and when the opportunity to return to Nicaragua presented itself, I knew it was where we were meant to be. I had the opportunity to go to Managua in March to volunteer a week with the Brien Holden Vision Institute Eye Health Mentor Program. Meeting the students, I was blown away by their love of optometry, passion for bringing eye care to the people of Nicaragua, and deep desire to change their country. I can't wait to get to UNAN and join the students in that passion and drive, working with them to develop their clinical skills. It really is an honor and privilege to be able to serve in such a meaningful capacity."

Optometry Giving Sight

Optometry Giving Sight is the only global fundraising initiative that specifically targets the prevention of blindness and impaired vision due to uncorrected refractive error – simply the need for an eye exam and a pair of glasses. More than 600 million people around the world are blind or vision impaired because they do not have access to the vision care they need. Your donations allow Optometry Giving Sight to fund the solution by supporting programs that:

- Train – local eye care professionals and;
- Establish – vision centers for sustainability to;
- Deliver – eye care and low cost glasses."

Optometry Giving Sight and VOSH are a good match. VOSH has the people power on the-ground, professional viability and the local connections, while Optometry Giving Sight has the marketing evidence-based research and fund raising capacity to complement each organization.

Optometry Giving Sight provides grants for sustainable eye care programs aimed to treat refractive causes of avoidable blindness and visual impairment. Both VOSH Chapters and International may partition for partnering sustainable grants. *(from VOSH website)*

VOSH/International Partnership with Optometry Giving Sight

The following summary was provided to the VOSH Board and this publication by Clive Miller, the Chief Executive Officer of Optometry Giving Sight. Clive has worked in the not for profit sector for twenty-nine years and is a member of the VOSH/International Board of Directors.

In 2008, VOSH/International and Optometry Giving Sight established a partnership to help VOSH/International and its members to play a leading role in the development and implementation of sustainable eye and vision care projects in Latin America. The 5 year "memorandum of understanding" (M.O.U.) was renewed in 2013.

As of this 2017 publication, Optometry Giving Sight has allocated or disbursed more than $600,000 to the following VOSH projects:

- **2009** – Purchase of trial lenses and hand instruments by VOSH-Florida for students at Schools of Optometry in Peru

- **2009** – Establishment of a Vision Center, Xochicalco University, Mexico providing clinical training for students and access to affordable local services for people in need in the adjoining barrios.
- **2010** – Mid Level Ophthalmic Training Course coupled with a Primary Eye Care Program in Nangahar Province, Afghanistan.
- **2010** A Population Study and Outreach/Referral Screening Program, with results published at the American Academy of Optometry meeting in October 2012 by lead investigator, Dr. Larry Hookway. The data for the quality of life and spectacle usage surveys was collected by trained local workers. Community health nurses screened and dispensed readers and ready-made equal sphere bifocals to an estimated 2,000 people.
- **2011** – Ongoing support for the Technology Transfer Program whereby used equipment is shipped to schools and practices in Latin America.
- **2011** – Equipment was purchased to establish the first teaching laboratory at the Autonomous University of Nicaragua (UNAN). The laboratory was inaugurated on July 26, 2012 and has 3 full lanes and 10 practice refraction lanes, and has greatly assisted the 50 students who graduate from the program each year. Additional equipment was provided in 2013.
- **2012** – The Vision Entrepreneurs pilot project in Haiti was implemented by VOSH-Pennsylvania to deliver prescription eyewear and sunglasses to poor people in remote parts of Haiti. 24 local people received training to help sell reading glasses and sunglasses to those in need. Program was ongoing in 2013 and 2014.
- **2012** – Funds were donated to provide equipment for a vision center at La Plata School of Optometry and Optics in Argentina as part of their "Visual Health for

All" program, which also promotes the important role of Optometry and Optometrists in primary eye health.

- **2013**. VOSH/International and Optometry Giving Sight allocated funds to support a documentary film on the life of Dr. Tom Little, who was killed while on an eye care mission in Afghanistan. The film was released in 2015.
- **2013** – Funds were allocated to a new project, VOSH CORPS, which was launched in June 2013, in association with the Brien Holden Vision Institute, which will enable new graduates to do their residency at a School of Optometry in an underserved community in Africa or Latin America.
- **2014.** Funds were allocated over 5 years to help support the development of an optometry program at the University of Haiti.
- **2015.** Funds were donated to support the Technology Transfer Program (TTP), Student VOSH (SVOSH) Mentorship program, and Student Outreach.

Optometry Giving Sight was also pleased to nominate Dr. Greg Pearl as an Eye Health Hero at the 9th General Assembly of the International Agency for the Prevention of Blindness in Hyderabad, India in September 2012."

Sustainability and Attainability

In the 2000's VOSH was serving the needs of about 100,000 patients annually by providing on-site professional eyecare and glasses. But, if 285 million people were visually impaired, and 39 million people were blind, (statistics from early 2000's) the current VOSH model was not a global solution. VOSH/International refocused attention on the "Vision 2020" challenge to be part of the solution serving the 285 million.

The historic model of VOSH missions taught by Dr. Harms worked very well for thirty years. It connected people at home in the United States with people in remote areas of the world needing eye care. It generated relationships, caring and even peace among diverse peoples. It educated communities to understand the value good vision could bring; people understood future replacement was a worthy endeavor. Providing eye care hands-on changed lives, realized by the gaze in the eyes, the moment that gift was given. VOSH connected communities at home with communities around the world. By 2016 this VOSH model was still working and had served over two million people since inception. This was still only a small part of the 285 million visually impaired people still in need.

"Sustainability" describes the strategy to expand eye care missions by building self-supporting clinics, or delivery models that would become self-supporting. That would mean independent financing and local eye care delivery personnel.

But this objective becomes a matter of "attainability" as well, considering the scope of global need and available resources. It requires new paradigms of delivering eye care.

VOSH set its sights on being pioneers of new programs and initiatives for sustainability and attainability. Let us consider a brief history.

FUDEM Clinic El Salvador (Foundation for the Development of Women)

One of the most "sustainable" and successful clinical systems in VOSH history has been one initiated by David Krasnow, OD, MPH, MBA of VOSH-California. It was assisted by VOSH-California members and even today VOSH trips are invited to provide outreach care in selected remote areas of El Salvador.

Dr. Krasnow's interest began as a student at Southern California College of Optometry in 1971 while working with Native Americans through Project Concern. In the late 1970's he founded the first interurban eye clinic for Native Americans in the inner city of Los Angeles. His first foray with VOSH was in Costa Rica in 1986. His connections began with the Consulate General of Costa Rica who was a patient in his Beverly Hills office. This led Dr. Krasnow to become connected to the Minister of Health and then the Foreign Ministry. The contacts opened the door for several clinics to be conducted in Costa Rica over the next few years.

In 1989, his government connections led him to meet the First Lady of President Alfredo Cristiani of El Salvador, Margarita, which in turn led him to Lic. Claudia Quinonez Sol.

It was common in El Salvador and many Latin countries that the first ladies were active in charitable/medical work. Working with Dr. Krasnow, Claudia became the founder of FUDEM which was a woman's program. They created eye care in El Salvador, not available from government.

Following are a few excerpts from an article written by David Krasnow, OD, MPH, MBA entitled, **"The Evolution of an Eye Clinic in El Salvador"**

"It is always interesting to look at a program retrospectively. In 1989, I was approached by the founder of a non-profit organization in El Salvador to assist in the development of an eye care program in that country. The initial meeting with Lic. Claudia Quinonez Sol ran for several hours. The content covered potential numbers of patients to be seen on a daily or weekly basis, types of pathologies expected, methodologies for referrals of medical or surgical cases, and dispensing of glasses. We discussed how I would teach as many as 15 lay people, with no prior medical or optical experience, and how to work with their projected patient population."

El Salvador at this time was just rebounding from a ten-year civil war. As its first transitional democracy, Dr. Cristiani became the president of El Salvador. There was still some unrest in the countryside. Rebuilding the country's infrastructure was underway but slow. This made for administrative complexity including an unpolished system of clearances, certifications and licensing. Fortunately, with North American support and returning influential families, order was being restored and people were returning to their homes and lifestyles.

Dr. Krasnow continues his account, "My underlying premise centered on the creation of a long-term sustainable model that would eventually put me out of business. After a meeting with President Cristiani and the Ministers of Health, Interior and Security, a program was launched 89 days after the initial conversation. The initial programs that occurred 2 or 3 times a year looked similar to the typical VOSH program, but they were managed by FUDEM, a local women's organization learning on the "fly." We decided that we needed some type of permanent space. Our first "clinic" was created in 1992. Slowly, with the assistance of 3 part-time local ophthalmologists, our protocols developed. Our first Optometrist, Dr. Cuchilla, still works at FUDEM. One key advisor, Dr. Chepe Lopez Beltran became Minister of Health. Some of the original FUDEM volunteers still play a valuable role at FUDEM, 24 years later.

What evolved from those humble beginnings was a business model, changed many times, along with a long-term strategy to create local capacity to serve the huge underserved population. Traditionally, 85% of the rural and 65% of the urban population has no access to vision care services. Our goal then and now is to provide an increasing scope of high quality services to the people most in need. We needed examining equipment, chairs and stands and everything else that clinics require. We obtained lots of used equipment. I donated 5 lanes (of equipment) to FUDEM. We eventually migrated to larger and larger facilities and added staff, while constantly assessing processes and outcomes. A major goal was developing our own lab to fabricate glasses. Used glasses were not an option. Poor quality and barely 20% utilization after dispensing provided the impetus for a FUDEM lab. In the interim, we shifted from recycled glasses to using local labs. They were very slow, very expensive and not sustainable.

In 2002 we migrated to a house of about 4500 sq. ft., housing about 35-40 staff. A seminal change took place when Lic. Nina Palomo became the new President of the foundation. She knew that we had to expand and grow into the Standard of Care for the country. She negotiated a move to our current location that covers a city block. We migrated to a state-of-the art clinic with all new equipment and our own lab to fabricate glasses for all of our patients. We developed a new 5-year plan, created updated processes for exams, patient referrals and lab fabrication. We outfitted an operating room that gradually expanded to 3 modern operating rooms. Outcomes analysis and quality controls were instituted along with a pharmacy. This complicated evolution was master minded by Mrs. Palomo. We needed licenses and permits and community buy-in. We needed approval of the government, but not government support. Of course, we spend countless hours designing the layout of the clinic, management office, optical shop, surgery center and lab. This was a collaborative iterative process.

The ongoing growth ultimately included 6 clinics, a low vision program, contact lens center, several optical boutiques, a pediatric program, a diabetic screening program, retina specialists, pediatric surgeon, glaucoma surgeon, OCT, YAG surgery, a dental program, and an extensive community outreach with 6 mobile clinical programs running 5 days a week.

What operates quietly behind the scenes is both an active Board of Directors, and clinical chiefs responsible for ongoing operations. In addition, processes are in place to constantly record a plethora of data in the clinic and the lab. Those data points are constantly scrutinized and analyzed to determine what changes are needed and to evaluate the quality of care on a weekly and monthly basis.

Built into the systems are measurements of every type of pathology, its frequency of occurrence, the numbers and types of glasses dispensed, and a measure of each individual doctors and lab personnel's productivity."

Dr. Krasnow concludes, "A vision that I articulated in an outline, on a legal pad, in the winter of 1989 has grown to be one of the finest models for vision care in the world. Thank you FUDEM for helping my dream come true."

FUDEM went on to be independent and self-sustaining. Currently in 2016 FUDEM is seeing 330,000 eye care patients and fabricating 180,000 pairs of glasses per year. FUDEM has six permanent clinics and many rural out-reach programs all over El Salvador. They employ 400 employees including 54 ophthalmologists and optometrists. FUDEM is a 'fee-for-service,' based on need run by a ten-woman Board of Directors. Dr. Krasnow remains a 'board consultant.'

So, it appears that El Salvador, thanks to FUDEM, is about as close to "sustainability and attainability" of the meeting the needs of preventable blindness and impairment as is possible. But consider that this project took Dr. Krasnow ten years getting off the ground and required ongoing support by the top influential women of El Salvador.

Another significant factor in success was using a 'business model' including 'management by measurable outcomes' – plenty of them. This is what truly opens a non-profit to the corporate world.

Could this model transfer to use in other Latin American countries? As Dr. Krasnow remarked, "If you see the way one Latin American country does things, you've seen the way one Latin American country does things." They are, indeed, all quite different, making the Vision 2020 eye care solution unique, wherever you go.

A Call for Action

One of the most profound effects of "Vision 2020" was that it generated a dialogue throughout the eye care industry about ways to meet this unmet need – 285 million visually impaired. Vision 2020 redefined the first twenty years of this new millennium in global eye care.

As VOSH grew and evolved over the years, several serious attempts had been made to quantify (measure) mission outcomes. Prior to 2000 attempts were made to collect all patient information by asking every VOSH mission to use a standard, basic exam form. An accounting of the forms would be sent to VOSH/International for compiling data. (Names would remain confidential.) The awareness that Vision 2020 brought was to raise-the-stakes in data collection and validation of vision outcomes.

Janet Leasher, OD, MPH, FAAO, a VOSH-Northwest and VOSH-Honduras member was becoming a spokesperson for the awareness of global blindness and vision impairment. In 2001 she addressed the membership at the VOSH Annual Meeting in Florida.

Dr. Leasher comments, "Although we've known this for years, only recently has its importance been recognized enough to create target strategies to eliminate the problem. And, it has only been within the last decade that we've had statistical tools to justify the global burden of disease. Therefore, not only the impact of blindness on people's personal lives, but the impact of their disability on society and the economy can be measured."

In 2002 Dr. Leasher received a grant from VOSH/International for a study in Honduras to quantify acuity of a community before, compared to after, a VOSH mission is conducted. Receiving the award, she shared this viewpoint in the *VOSH/International Newsletter, Spring/Summer 2002* on **"VOSH's Role in Strategies to Reduce the Global Burden of Blindness** by Dr. Janet Leasher.

Excepts begin with the Causes of Blindness: "Eighty percent of the world's blind live in the developing world. The leading causes of blindness have been identified as follows: Cataract; Trachoma; Glaucoma; Onchocerciasis or River Blindness; other causes are diabetic retinopathy, macular degeneration, hansen's disease (leprosy); childhood blindness, with measles and vitamin A deficiency being the leading causes; and particularly of interest to VOSH, blindness due to uncorrected refractive error or low vision."...

..."The status of the world's blind will not get better unless we look beyond the box that we have created around VOSH. Ocular health of the impoverished people in the developing world will not get better unless we look at social justice, human rights and all the determinants of health."...

..."A Formal Evaluation of VOSH Role: This is a moment in time to ask ourselves who are we really? Where is our destiny pulling us?

We need to evaluate our program, as if we were a bilateral governmental funding organization such as USAID. How effective are we in accomplishing the goals of our mission? Do the recipients of our care really need it? Do they appreciate it? Do the recycled glasses that we give out really make a difference in their lives? How are we influencing their awareness of the importance of vision care? How well are we educating them as prevention and protection of their vision? Are our messages culturally relevant?...

..."A Need to Establish Partnerships: I believe the time is right for VOSH to develop partnerships with other groups that are providing eye care. Whether or not we just coordinate our trips to the same country with other groups, like we've started to offer through the 'Upcoming Trips' list or partner with other organizations." (WHO, WCO and others)...

..."If we collaborate with local doctors, with Ministries of Health in the countries where we work, if we link with optometry educational programs which already exist, if we offer to provide Continuing Ed to local doctors while we're there, if we provide them the data we collect through our missions, we will be taking a step forward."

Dr. Dale Cole, as VOSH/International President becomes one of our more vocal leaders about opening our minds to see other alternatives of vision care to meeting the overwhelming needs around the world. During his administration, VOSH Newsletters were packed with articles and ideas about how to achieve "sustainability." In a feature Newsletter article Dr. Cole states, "Training local individuals would have some merit. It certainly won't replace the work we now do but it can certainly work in tandem with our present system."

Educate and Train Locally

A great many eye care educators weighed in on the "sustainability" challenge over the next few years. University professors saw education as a key factor.

Erik Weissberg, OD, Associate Professor of Optometry at New England College of Optometry and co-author Heather Zornetzer urged in an article entitled "**Grassroots Optometry – Toward self-sustainability**" published in the *VOSH/International Newsletter, Fall/Winter 2004-05* wrote, "While traditional VOSH missions are important, we also recognize that the majority of the people we are treating do not require our expert help and rather can be treated by local workers with some simple training and the appropriate tools.

This concept has been tried before, but often required equipment that either gets lost, stolen or malfunctions under less ideal conditions. Our proposal focuses on the transfer of knowledge with simple tools to accomplish the goal of training 'grassroots optometrists.'

'Grassroots optometrists' will serve as the base of what will be a pyramid approach to providing vision care in the region. Our immediate goal is to create a team of local workers trained to treat presbyopia, educate the community and simultaneously screen for more complex conditions. With community health care workers treating presbyopia, a large portion of the vision care needs could be addressed....

... Those needing more complicated eye care would be funneled toward the appropriate facilities." The article continues on describing how they tested the "grassroots optometry" model over a three-year period.

Jerry Vincent, OD, MPH, Blindness Prevention Consultant at the University of Houston College of Optometry wrote the article **"Rethinking the Clinical Mission; we need to train the locals"** *published in the VOSH/International Newsletter, Fall/Winter 2005-06* begins by making the case that it is not feasible for professionals working with nonprofit organizations who provide around one million exams a year to increase their output to serve 500 million people. He suggests that we train local people to refract. Dr. Vincent says, "An optometrist who trains 2-5 health workers each year to independently do simple refractions will be responsible for a significantly higher output compared to the optometrist who sees all patients. The resource base of VOSH could be used to extend refractive correction to a much greater number of people if missions were training oriented rather than clinically oriented."

He goes on to mention a number of countries working with named NGO's doing this currently. He notes that, "WHO (World Health Organization) has encouraged the training of non-ophthalmologists in basic cataract surgery and lid surgery for Trichiasis. Expect WHO to endorse the training of local health workers to do refractions."

Patti Fuhr, OD, VOSH-Alabama and Clinical Faculty at University of Alabama Optometry School wrote the article **"VOSH Participates in Pilot Screening Project in three Countries"** *published in the VOSH/International Newsletter, Spring 2006':*

"In early fall the UNESCO Chair in Visual Health and Development initiated a one-year pilot vision screening project. The project is now underway in Guatemala, El Salvador and Nicaragua.

General goals of the project are to train local teachers and health promoters in the detection of childhood visual health problems, to diagnose and treat the visual problems detected in schoolchildren and to create a strong network of visual health activists in Central America.

Acronym for the project is VERAS, which stands for Visión, Educación, Rendimiento, Aprendizaje, and Sostenibilidad. The word VERAS means 'You will See!'"...

..."An initial planning session was held in El Salvador in September, 2005. Training sessions were held in Managua, Nicaragua, in January 2006. The first in-field implementation of screening and examination of children occurred in March 2006, in Granada, Nicaragua."

Thirty teachers and ancillary personnel learned the protocol and screened over 1,000 children in a 3-day period. "Volunteers from VOSH-Florida and VOSH-Alabama examined all children who failed the screening and matched numbers of who passed the screening."

Nicaragua and El Salvador: VOSH Proving Grounds for Sustainability

These two countries became proving grounds for VOSH/International utilizing four different strategies toward finding solutions to the "sustainability" and attainability of meeting vision care needs globally.

- Build and/or support international optometry schools – VOSH Corps
- Create a financially sustainable eye clinic in El Salvador FUDEM initiated by Dr. Krasnow with IEF (International Eye Foundation) support
- Train local workers to provide eye care – Dr. Weissberg, Dr. Fuhr (VERAS) in Nicaragua
- ProVision clinic in Nicaragua by Dr. Greg Pearl with presbyopia study by Dr. Hookway

2016 – What did we learn? – Where do we go from here?

In 2016 we are four years away from 2020. Although we have made huge progress, it's still small compared to the challenge.

In an effort to meet the challenge of "**Sustainability and Attainability,**" VOSH has placed a huge emphasis on the overwhelming unmet needs of the blind and visually impaired. In the process VOSH has developed and implemented a number of programs that address those needs, such as VOSH Corps, the Technology Transfer Program, and our partnering with new optometry schools in developing nations.

With "sustainability" dialogue, we must be sensitive to a schism evolving between those providing eye care by traditionally conducting annual mission trips, and those belying their efforts as inconsequential and dependent. As Dr. Coles suggests, both components are part of the puzzle and could be reciprocally powerful. Let's 'sustain' the one hundred thousand patients we do serve while we 'attain' solutions for a 100 million we don't serve.

So what has history taught us about "Sustainability and Attainability?"

- A wide diversity of Governments and Non-Government Organizations (N.G.O.'s) must network with a cohesive global strategy
- There are not enough certified eye care professionals to deliver the care – other systems must be utilized
- We know that 90% of people over 50 years-old need glasses for near
- We know 80% of the visual impairments are avoidable (glasses)
- We know that 'identifying' (accessing) the visually impaired population is difficult
- 90% of the world's visually impaired people live in developing countries and are very difficult to find and access

- Education and training is probably a big part of the solution
- Blindness and visual impairment relates to failing at school, in jobs, with health, and personal lives. This contributes to personal and public poverty.
- Every country is different in its resources, infrastructure and culture

Admittedly, there is no one, simple answer to global sustainability and attainability. But what role can VOSH play in sustainability and attainability? VOSH has strengths, weaknesses, opportunities and threats. It seems that forty years of history and fifteen years of living with this challenge have taught us something.

Could VOSH keep expanding its outreach by focusing on what we do best? The above issues could be applied to growing optometry, itself, into all developing nations where the need exists – taking the solution local. The complexities of countries, governments, economics, certification and a dozen other things will be worked out by the cadre of eye care providers on site – the marketplace.

Conversations with Dr. Greg Pearl, Dr. David Krasnow and Dr. David McPhillips lead to a possible VOSH focus – build and support new optometry schools in developing nations. We are uniquely qualified to position ourselves with this strategy in the solution.

VOSH already has the tools of VOSH Corps and TTP to build on as well as the partners such as Optometry Giving Sight. Our greatest assets are our members! Could they serve as clinical faculty, equipment/supply sources, and conduct rural co-missions by partnering with specific developing schools, VOSH Chapters and SVOSH-International?

VOSH/International could develop and resource the strategic infrastructure, including a business model of escalating resources tied to performance outcomes (such as equipment for student patient exams).

Supporting sustainability today toward attainability tomorrow.

Student VOSH (SVOSH)

Student Chapters of VOSH are not really an initiative or program of VOSH. They are VOSH! In fact a student organization called SOSH (Student Optometric Services to Haiti) predates VOSH to 1968.

SVOSH (Student Volunteer Optometric Services to Humanity) are an integral part of the VOSH Mission. In fact they hold the key to the future of VOSH reaching around the world. They not only are active in their most formative career years, but students can connect with students in other lands, administratively, purposefully and ideologically.

New optometry students and new optometry schools are perhaps the greatest resource to achieving the 20/20 (World Health Organization and World Council of Optometry) vision!

More eyecare professionals in developing countries most effectively enhances our ability to truly meet these voluminous needs of the functionally blind and vision impaired around the globe.

Where optometry students go; there goes the future of optometry.

VOSH Stories

The Footprints of Visionaries

As we read these stories and essays, it is as if we are following in the footprints made by those who walked before us. These footprints tell us about the fun, the adventure, the joy, the tears, the hopes and the passions of VOSHers.

"Real heroes don't wear capes. Real heroes don't stand on stages in the spotlight. Real heroes don't wear their names on the back of jerseys. Instead, real heroes are ordinary people who give their lives to causes bigger than themselves."
-David Bruns, President, Optimist International

We begin this section with an overview of the history of SOSH (Student Optometric Services to Haiti) to Haiti founded in 1968. Later Student VOSH became known as SVOSH.

SOSH – 1968

"Student Optometric Service to Haiti" by Dr. Paul Hayes is reprinted from the Journal of the American Optometric Association, Volume 49, Number 2, February 1978.

The Student Optometric Services to Haiti (SOSH) was founded in 1968 by Dr. Algernon Phillips, then a fourth year student at the Pennsylvania College of Optometry.

Since its founding, SOSH has provided free vision care to approximately 30,000 Haitians.

The program is entirely under the direction of the students of the Pennsylvania College of Optometry and is funded by private contributions, foundation, religious organizations, service clubs, industry and individuals.

Sharing a common land mass with the Dominican Republic, Haiti is the poorest and most densely populated country in the Western Hemisphere. Because of Haiti's relative poverty, proper eye care is almost nonexistent. As a result visual problems and ocular pathologies are frequently seen.

In recognition of this tremendous need, a SOSH team has traveled to Cap Haitien, Haiti, in January of each year . . . The group's effort has been to provide complete visual examinations including ophthalmoscopy, tonometry, biomicroscopy, sphygmomanometry, and fundus photography when indicated. Free eyeglasses are dispensed to every individual requiring corrective lenses. Also, every pathology is carefully documented and treated or referred for surgical evaluation. Since 1969, SOSH has seen about 30,000 patients, dispensed 15,000 eyeglasses and treated over 1,000 potentially sight-threatening pathologies.

The logistic problems

Preparing for each SOSH trip is a year-long effort. Each intern is assigned several projects of special importance, including fundraising, public speaking, obtaining equipment and supplies and fabricating needed prescriptions. SOSH is unique compared to other volunteer optometric service groups in that all of the work is accomplished by the students.

Each successful project is directly proportional to the amount of student effort. The aspect of team-work is the hub of every SOSH project.

The task of fundraising is a primary concern. The largest source of funds is from various religious organizations. The next largest source of funds comes from the Pennsylvania College of Optometry community, i.e., the Alumni Association and the Student Council. Also contributing are several foundations, private businesses and individuals.

Preparing eyeglasses for prescription in Haiti is a job that includes the collection of old eyeglasses as well as the fabrication of new ones. Thousands of old eyeglasses are donated by individuals, groups, and service clubs. These are screened for quality, washed, and individually neutralized to determine their power before adding to our stockpile. If any lens powers are in short supply or any special prescriptions are needed, the SOSH members fabricate enough spectacles to make up the deficit. POC and several optical companies generously provide all of the equipment necessary to examine the patients.

The trek to Haiti

Leaving in mid-January, each SOSH team spends approximately two weeks in Cap Haitien. Traveling by air to Cap Haitien insures the quickest and most convenient method of transporting all the equipment. The main clinic is set up at the Justinien Hospital and approximately two hundred patients are examined daily. A screening team travels to various schools and about four hundred children are examined daily. About twenty percent of these children are referred to the main clinic for further testing.

Each patient visiting the clinic is issued an exam registration card by the hospital staff. While at the clinic they receive a complete vision analysis. This consists of determination of visual acuity, external examination, ophthalmoscopy, and refraction.

Blood pressure and tonometry is taken on each patient over thirty-five years of age. When a refractive correction is indicated, spectacles are prescribed and dispensed free of charge.

For the past two projects, a team of ophthalmologists has arrived during the second week of the SOSH visit. Working as an eye care unity, the optometrists refer all pathologies that require treatment and surgical intervention. With this team approach, the Haitians are guaranteed total eye health care.

The team customarily receives a warm greeting by the mayor of Cap Haitien, the public health officials, and the commander of the north Military Department. The acceptance of the project is perhaps the best measured by the response of the Haitians. When walking through the town, one must always carry a penlight so as to "examine" the eyes of the always eager Haitians. Each morning a long line of patients awaits the interns when they arrive for work. The line continues to grow with patients who have walked miles to have their eyes examined. Each year, the SOSH team continues to find warm and friendly Haitians who graciously accept the work that is done for them.

Meeting the need

The SOSH program has grown steadily each year. This year's team has been enlarged to twenty-two interns, making SOSH '78 the largest effort to date. Plans for further expansion of the program include possible arrangements to send students twice a year instead of only once. Sending a smaller team to Haiti, perhaps in August, in addition to the regular January trip would be a step towards continued care and allow for necessary follow-up procedures.

The SOSH '78 trip will mark the tenth anniversary of student eye care to Haiti. Truly a service organization, the theme of the Student Optometric Service to Haiti continues to be one of unselfish commitment to give others an opportunity to help themselves.

Seeing Through Different Eyes
"VOSH-Kansas to Guatemala", VOSH/International Newsletter, March 1995 VOSH Archives – author unknown

A Catholic convent in San Andres Itzapa, Guatemala – that was the setting of the home away from home for ten days in March for a VOSH team from the United States. It was a setting of beauty – surrounded by mountains that were covered with a blanket of plush green foliage, volcanoes crowned with sparkling white snow, cobble stoned streets lined with brilliantly colored blooming vines and domed by blue sky. It was an atmosphere of adventuresome adjustment as the team let go of luxuries taken for granted in the United States but hard to come by in Central America. We were in Guatemala to serve the people in the best way we knew how, by providing eye care. Everything else was to be put on hold."...

...."After an interesting first night's sleep at the convent, (we were awakened at 3 AM by Guatemalan roosters who can't tell time), we were fed a wonderful breakfast that school bus to Parramos where we would be the villager's guests at Mass and they, in turn, would be our first patients in the clinic.

On entering the church at Parramos, our eyes feasted on an amazing sea of color made up of this Guatemalan parishes' Indian women dressed in their Sunday best and filling the center of the church. It was breathtaking. The men lined the perimeter of the church. We were seated in the front of crude wooden benches reserved for their American guests. Fr. John Vesey preached a moving sermon on "Seeing with New Eyes". He talked about the physical sight the doctors could give them and the change of attitude the Mayan people could cultivate themselves – to bring about peace within their homes and between tribes that had been in conflict for centuries. In looking back on this Guatemalan VOSH trip, we realized that we saw the events that took place through new and different eyes also. The following are the team's observations that took place during our time with the Guatemalan people.

Through the Eyes of Hospitality
"At the end of the mass in Parramos, the people showed their hospitality with a beautiful act of personal sacrifice. The people came to the front of the church carrying vegetables, fruits, beans, rice, etc. – enough to fill two huge baskets that were sitting

at the alter. They presented the food to our team to sustain us throughout a week of work. These were people who could barely feed their own families, yet they laid an abundance of food at the feet of we, wealthy, well-fed Americans." – Bev Cole

In Patzicia at the end of the week, we were given beautiful opening and closing ceremonies to bless and thank us for our work and to pledge the people's prayers for us.

"I thought the welcome and closing at Patzicia was very moving. Maybe it was because it was the last day or because of all the people trying to get in that couldn't. Over all, the love shown us was beyond measure or words." Barbary Gray Madre Marina was the nun who served as Hostess at the convent. She was a rare and beautiful human being.

Don's farewell to Madre Marina – "We came as strangers, but you treated us as angels" – summed up the hospitality we experienced. – Jill Edmands

Through the Eyes of Family

Our VOSH team experienced "family" in so many ways – as literal family, team family and global family. Many expressed their feeling about this closeness.

"The highlight of the trip was to have my twenty year old granddaughter accompanying us and for her to experience this diverse culture. This experience will go with her for a long time and has been a tremendous bonding for both of us." – Norm Abrahams.

"I was pleased and moved by the interactions between team and hosts – all worked hard to accomplish a common goal of giving vision to those who couldn't see." – Don Kuehn

"The work of translating gave me the humbling opportunity to articulate the doctor's gentle spirit and then to turn around and translate the beautiful and loquacious blessings that the people prayed for those who came to serve them. The gentle touch of these people was an reenactment of Jesus' washing the feet of disciples." – Sister Mary McGlone

Alba, one of our Guatemalan interpreters came home from the United States to interpret for us. She had a deep concern for her native people.

"I was truly touched and moved by Alba's enthusiasm, her love and her concern for her people." – Dale Cole

"The experience of seeing the parents of children whose vision was nearly non-existent was humbling to me. You could see that if they could, they would give their own eyes so their children could see. The children, of course, are so unfortunate because of their lack of eyesight, but very fortunate to have such loving parents." – Robert Ashton

Through the Eyes of Gratitude

Many experiences of successfully serving the Guatemalan people left their mark on the team.

"After I finished fitting a pair of glasses and placed them on one woman's weathered face, her eyes sparkled and she hugged me and thanked me in Spanish. I had given her a pair of glasses I would have refused to wear if someone would have given them to me." – Dana Graber

"I wonder at the quiet politeness of the people as they come to my station. You find their visual problems, which sometimes are many and complicated. When I have finished and they are to go on, they express their thanks as though they are saying "thank you for witnessing my need." – Lowell Goodwin

"Sometime in the fall of '94 a local Wakeeney family brought glasses for the VOSH trip. I had the inspiration to save out two pair of cataract glasses to be packed with my instruments. The first pair was dispensed without incident. The second pair was dispensed by Eldon and I later in the week. We were all rewarded when an elderly man smiled broadly while reading letters on the wall chart at a distance he hadn't seen in years." Bill Benkleman

"My most touching experience occurred when I fit an old man with glasses and gave him a reading card. He put it down and took out his Bible and started to read. I called over an interpreter who started to cry. He was reading the story of the blind man being healed." -Scott Kuehn

"My highlight was an 85 year old lady brought in by her very caring daughter. The patient had an advanced cataract in one eye that couldn't be corrected. However, with a very strong lens we were able to significantly improve sight in the other eye. Her face lit up with the most beautiful smile I've ever seen." Dave Crum

"It was worth the trip many times over to see the children's eyes light up when they were fitted with very strong Rx's." Charlie Haupt "Several things made the trip special. One was the smile on a little five-year-old Indian girl's face that had probably never seen anything clear, when lenses were put on her that allowed her to see." Eldon Gray

"Even though I knew how many patients the doctors planned to help, I was awed by the magnitude of what was accomplished." Mary Scimeca

"On the day we were packed up to leave, a woman came up to me on the street wearing her new glasses and a huge smile. She blessed me and asked me how to clean her glasses, and blessed me again." Cathy Nalivaiko

San Andres Itzapa, Chimaltenango, Tecpan and Patzicia. Shopping in Antigua and touring the Mayan Indian ruins at Tikal gave us the opportunity to bring home some colorful Guatemalan art and history. When our time ran out, the statistics showed that we had seen 2000 patients, prescribed for all but 200, and referred 68 for surgery to be done by a medical team that was to follow us. We had learned that the poor nutrition, the surgery to be done by a medical team that was to follow us. We had also learned that the poor nutrition, the smoke from unventilated cooking fires and the unprotected exposure of the yes to strong sunlight caused an uncanny number of cataracts and pterygiums in both the young and the old. But in the midst of all of this poverty, we had learned to see through "new eyes." Dee Fitzgibbons summed it up when she said, "This world is just not fair sometimes, but I recognize they have gifts we don't – the way they accept and the way they react to each other. It's God's way."

Blind and Can't go to School
by Eldon Gray, OD of Kinsley, KS
Reprinted from "VOSH", Kansas Optometric Journal, January-March 2004

In the outback of Honduras at Agua Caliente, a mother brought her 12-year-old son to the "clinic" and through the interpreter said her son had been unable to attend school for three years because his teachers said he was "blind" and couldn't come to school anymore.

Examination revealed (that) he was a 20-diopter myope. This was put in a trial frame and we took him outside. He said through his tears, "I can see trees and that house over there."

Needless to say, his mother and I were also looking through tears. We were able to get him some glasses. I don't know the outcome of his situation, but I do know VOSH probably had a huge impact on this young boy's life and the lives of his family.

A Christmas Gift
VOSH-Ohio in India, Nov. 14, 1989 – Jan. 4, 1990
Reprinted from VOSH/International Newsletter, April, 1990

VOSH-Ohio has completed two successful mission projects in India. Their mission team two led by Dr. Darrell Groman consisting of eleven persons, arrived in Agra, India just as VOSH-Ohio's mission team one led by Dr. Maggie Corbin of Alabama and her group of six, were leaving. Maggie recorded 523 patients seen in seven days even though their twelve crates,

(6,000 pairs) of eyeglasses, were held in London for five days. Darrell's team two examined 1183 patients in nine days.

The patients were very pleased to have been seen by the VOSH teams. They would arrive very early in the cold mornings, as early as 2 AM, to wait in line. Each person was charged one Rupee (6 cents). The hospital staff scheduled the numbers of persons who would be seen each day. The rest would be asked to return the next day. It is always discouraging to know that many are turned away from the clinic, as we cannot see everyone who needs vision care. As everywhere else, the lines of the underserved are endless.

All of the patients were seen at the Shanti Mangalick Hospital on Fatehabad Road in Agra. The electricity would frequently go off during the day for periods as long as half-an-hour and the salt pan in the dispensary never seemed to heat up well. Dr. Groman's group was perhaps the first VOSH mission team to see patients on Christmas Day. Both teams would have benefitted from having more interpreters. Unfortunately, the Lions of Agra were not present to help as translators, as requested.

When the project was completed, Dr. Groman tried to send the unused eyeglasses home, but the crates were lost en-route. The food was also a challenge. "There were many spicy rice dishes with a lot of curry," reported Darrell. "This is probably the only time I lost 15 pounds instead of gaining during the Christmas season."

We each had our special moments and enjoyed our VOSH experiences in India. In spite of some "Delhi belly" and a few other obstacles, we are glad we went . . . and wished you could have joined us!"

India is a land of diversity and unique cultures. We saw the magnificence of the Taj Mahal in Agra, a city of much poverty. There were animals, as well as people, everywhere: camels, donkeys, pigs, goats, horses, dogs, monkeys and the ever-present sacred cow. One wonders how Mother Cow can lounge so peacefully in the midst of the traffic of India . . . but she does so with an expression of nonchalance. Most of the Indians are rather stern-faced, so an occasional smile by a happy patient in the clinic seemed to brighten everyone's day.

The entire team worked very hard and looked forward to a few days of rest and recuperation. They had an opportunity to travel to Kathmandu to see the Himalayas of Nepal. SVOSH students visited family in Gujarat and New Delhi. Several enjoyed the city of Daipur where they visited Amber Fort for an elephant ride. They stayed in a crumbling old palace that had no running water and were entertained by the local snake-charmers.

During a train trip Dr. Groman became separated from the group. "The trains don't always run on schedule and one train was cancelled, then the next was over two hours late," he said. He finally managed to catch up with the rest of the group.

Good Morning Vietnam!

By Dr. Bill Lenon, Santa Clara, CA
Reprinted from the article "VOSH-California: Mission Vietnam"
in the VOSH/International Newsletter, September 1991

This was a great trip! During this March 1991, our group of seven volunteers examined and treated over 1,000 patients in five clinic days at various community clinics in and around Hanoi, the capital of Vietnam. We started out meeting with the directors at the Institute of Ophthalmology. Even after reading our initial proposal, they were a little skeptical as to how our group would be able to examine that many people and provide them with proper eyeglasses on the spot.

The first day our group was closely supervised by the Institute, who had arranged for us to see the most difficult refractive patients staying at the hospital. When I was asked how many patients we'd be able to see on our first afternoon, I said about 100. The Institute director scoffed and schedule 20. Within the first 45 minutes the director quickly rounded up another 75 patients.

We brought a Nidek AR 1600 Auto-refractor, generously donated by Marco Ophthalmic Instruments in Jacksonville, Florida. This allowed Lan Bui to refract the patients in less than a minute. The doctors then checked the patients. . . . . *they were escorted to a fitting room with 4,000 pairs of glasses.*

Most of the people had never worn glasses. The majority were hyperopic, but we had a surprising number of extremely myopic patients. On the last day I saw a lady who was -28.0 OU and I remembered seeing a pair of -26.00 when I was sorting the glasses. It was nice to have something so close for her. Those patients needing surgery were referred to the Ophthalmology Institute in Hanoi. Three ophthalmologists and three nurses from the Institute helped us each day. The doctors were relatively unfamiliar with refractions. They generally just performed a fairly rudimentary trial lens refraction when needed. Cataract patients do not receive implants or eyeglasses after surgery due to the cost. Most glaucoma patients are treated surgically since one month's medication costs more than the surgery.

It was fun working in the little communities in the environs of Hanoi. Few westerners would have reason to visit these places and the people were very gracious. One afternoon, after a short lunch break, Don Seiler and I were taking a little walk around the village. Two different women came out and thanked us for helping their people and presented us with freshly picked bouquets of flowers. We were also invited into homes for tea and snacks. I think everyone on the trip had some wonderful experiences that will be remembered forever.

We had a nice farewell reception at the 202 Restaurant in Hanoi. Our hosts all rode their bicycles and we all rented our "xich los" (ric sha-type vehicles). Everyone ate so much we probably all would have done better to walk home that night! I was constantly amazed at how much food the Vietnamese could eat and yet you rarely see anyone overweight.

Dr. Seiler won the "shopper's shopper" award. I don't know how he got all that stuff home. Vietnam is a shopper's paradise for the unusual such as marble carvings, musical instruments, rugs, clothing, etc. It's also a great place to eat on the cheap. They have all these little hole-in-the-wall restaurants with kindergarten-size chairs and tables where the main dish is about 15 cents and it fills you up! Vietnamese cuisine is great. If you're really daring you can try roast puppy, bat blood, snake, whole fried sparrows, etc. Most of us ate more traditional dishes, but Lindsey was pretty daring.

Nebraska Sees "Life in Guatemala"

Report from "Nebraska-VOSH, Guatemala," VOSH/ International Newsletter, January 1999

A trip to Panajachel, Guatemala was led by Dr. Gary Pederson, President of the Grand Island Lions Club and a 17-year VOSH member, Dr. and Mrs. Charles Gray, Dr. Ellen Weiss, Dr. Jerry King and Dr. and Mrs. Doug Johnson. The Mayan Indian people were forming lines when they arrived and more came after word of the clinic spread.

The people are farmers and housewives. It is common for girls of 13 to marry. Their husbands encourage them to have children so that there will be someone to care for them in their old age, and the women have as many as 12 children. Only half will survive to age five. Men live a little longer than the women, who are required to spend long hours working around the home, often getting up at 4:00 AM to prepare tortillas, carry wood, care for the children and wash clothes in the stream. The average lifespan is about fifty.

Children are expected to attend school for six years, although most finish less than three.

Communication is difficult, because none of the patients speak English, and very few speak Spanish. Quichet is spoken, one of 22 dialects in this mountainous region. For this reason, villagers are often unable to communicate with others in nearby villages.

More than 700 patients were examined on this trip, including many who had never had eye care.

The Eye Ball A fundraiser
by VOSH-British Columbia
*Title edited from the VOSH/International
Newsletter, Spring/Summer 2001*

TWECS (Third World Eye Care Society), a VOSH Chapter based in British Columbia, initiated an Eye Ball five years ago in a comfortable site with a maximum capacity of 150 people. The event sold out.

Since that time, the Eye Ball has become an annual event, earning a total of $78,000 for the British Columbia Chapter.

In its first year, organizers had just 28 items for a silent auction, solicited through telephone marketing alone.

Live entertainment was provided by "Malpractice," an 11-member band of medical doctors. They were a hit, as were featured cultural dances from the Philippines, site of the VOSH Chapter's then most recent eye care project.

For the second Eye Ball, singer Elton John donated a pair of his concert prescription sunglasses which sold for $2,000.

The fundraiser has consistently grown. This past year the group held their fifth Eye Ball at a larger ballroom with seating for 300. The event sold out again. Tickets were $85 per person, the actual cost of putting on the event.

Monies raised, all $19,000, came solely from the sale of over 100 auction items. The event received considerable newspaper coverage the day after the party.

The Eye Ball is now a major annual event where the three O's (optometry, ophthalmology and opticianry) come together for a greater cause.

Funds have been used to purchase major project equipment and general supplies.

Balderdash

by Diana Carriger, OD, Topeka, KS
"Reflections on VOSH," Kansas Optometric Journal, January-March 2004

For those of you who didn't play enough "Balderdash" at the New Year's Eve party, you can pick the definition you think fits.

Vosh: A food made from turnips in South Africa
Vosh: A Russian word meaning good-bye and good riddance.
Vosh: A life-changing experience.
Vosh: A mild expletive.

I pick number three. Although I had traveled around the world as a teenager, the trips I've made for VOSH to Honduras (four times), Bolivia and Thailand stand out as the most meaningful journeys ever. The joy of helping others with skills and equipment that to us seem commonplace and even out-dated, but which to the recipients are just short of magic, is always new and exciting. The changes that VOSH has made in my life include a recurrent gratitude for hot running water, for fresh vegetables and fruits that we can eat raw, for reliable electric service, for paved roads, for central heating and/or air conditioning, for friends I've shared great times with.

The patients we see "out there" are so alike yet so different from our patients back home. I examined a woman with a two week old baby in Honduras who had traveled two days to get to the clinic. She walked for one day and rode a bus for another! Then she had to take the same amount of time to get back home. There was the teenage girl with a prescription of -12.00 (sphere) who had never had glasses. The lady who came in with Iritis, holding a washcloth up to her eye in pain; and left with a smile, medicine bottles and sunglasses.

In Bolivia, three-fourths of the patients had over six diopters of cylinder! We kept asking each other, "Are you retting what I'm retting?" These were all children under 17.

We decided that this was a combination of genetics (a native Indian population) and the fact that they were living and working at 14,000 feet altitude and squinting all day. We had oxygen tanks in case of altitude sickness and we were advised to take Diamox prophylactically. Since my IOP runs around 7 mm Hg normally, I wondered if my eyes would implode! My fingers started tingling so badly that I quit the stuff anyway. VOSH is hard to define. It is a mix of exhaustion, joy, new experiences, camaraderie, physical discomforts, pride of achievement, and the realization that people are the same all over the world.

I was Blind, But Now I See
by Wm. S. Benkelman, OD, WaKeeney, KS
*"VOSH Happenings," Kansas Optometric
Journal, January-March 2004*

Drs. Dave Crum, Norman Abrahams, Dale Cole, Eldon Gray and I were roommates (segregated from our wives) in a Guatemalan convent. We arose in the morning after a night of dogs barking, fireworks and possible gunfire. I told the fellas that I wouldn't need to make my bed. "Why?" ... because it was barely slept in!

Three VOSH Happenings that touched me during that week were: A man needed glasses to read his Bible. After being fitted he opened his Bible to John 9:25 and read "... though I was blind, now I see." During an evening storm the electricity went off leaving us in darkness. We discovered that about 11 people had travelled a long distance and could not return ... so we did the exams by candlelight.

The third memory is of a man who had no glasses since his cataract surgery. Eldon examined him, checked with the dispensary and determined there were no glasses available. I had carried a pair of aphakic glasses along with my instruments and asked Eldon to see if they would work. When his patient put the glasses on he immediately began pointing to the tumbling E's with his hand and smiling broadly. Tears flowed freely as we shared in this poignant moment.

Go Buc's Sunglasses
Thirty years and still going!
By Greg Kane, OD, Palatka, Florida
Published in VOSH-Florida Newsletter, August 2008

In February of 2008, my old buddy Jerry Potts and I went on a mission to Chinandega in Nicaragua with Suzy Bamberg's group. Jerry is a retired optician, and I am a twenty-six year optometrist. We live in northeast Florida. In 1977 we were both struggling young opticians in St. Petersburg, Florida working for the same optical chain, and in need of extra money. So we bought an optical lens engraver and started our own little mail order lens engraving company. We did very well, but for extra cash, we also engraved lenses at the local flea market on Saturdays and Sundays. There we sold sunglasses with engraved initials and rhinestone work. The old frame salesman we bought the sunglasses from, (Woody from Lowry Optical) would trade us X number of nice sunglasses, and in return we would engrave logos for him at no charge. As it turned out, the poor hapless Tampa Bay Buccaneers were hot in 1978-79 and we all did a bang up business selling those sunglasses in the area with "GO BUCS" on one lens and the Buccaneers logo on the other lens in orange and white. I went to optometry school in 1979 and we sold the business and went on with our lives.

Turn the clock forward to 2008. Now we're here in Chinandega. I'm doing eye exams; he's fitting glasses and running the auto-refractor. I take a patient over to his area and tell Jerry to fit this old guy up with a nice pair of sunglasses to combat his cataracts and photophobia. I go on to the next patient. Ten minutes later Jerry comes over to the exam station beaming, and yelling, "Look at this dude!!!" Smiling ear-to-ear he's got a pair of those "GO BUCS" sunglasses in his hands, and says "Remember these?"

From 1978 to 2008, imagine, these shades turn up in a box of old sunglasses in Nicaragua thirty years later! Together we have a good chuckle, slap each other on the back, re-live the old times, and share the sheer quirk of fate this demonstrates with our fellow mission mates. Needless to say, I kept those sunglasses as an icon of our optical longevity, and we gave the old dude a newer model of sunglasses. You know, when I think about all the eyes I have examined over the twenty-some year span of my optical life, this VOSH event kind of summarizes it all. I started out a young perspiring optician. Then became an OD, built my practice, raised my family, and now that I am in the twilight of my career, I finally have time to do VOSH mission work and travel, help others in poor circumstances, and see the world. And damn if it isn't the completion of a full circle. VOSH is a great way to help our fellow man. You owe it to yourself and your fellow man to find a mission. And while you're at it, take some friends! We all need the experience.

Expedition to Africa

By Mike Lightner, VOSH-Michigan *(a first-time VOSHer)*
Reprinted from VOSH/International Newsletter, March 1997
With editing by Dr. Michel Listenberger, OD, FVI

Africa, the dark continent, land of adventure and romance, the domain of the wildebeest, zebra and lion. How could anyone resist the opportunity to go on a VOSH mission to the land of your childhood dreams? My wife, Penny, an optician in Niles, couldn't resist, nor could I, though I make my living in the computer industry. Tracey Walker, an ophthalmic assistant in Grand Rapids and fellow rookie VOSHer, also couldn't resist, and in fact, has dreamed for years of studying primates in Africa. We joined veteran VOSHers Terry Foster of Milford, Dr. Michel Listenberger of Niles and the expedition leader, Dr. Nelson Edwards of Fowlerville, to create a small but capable and highly flexible VOSH team. We were accompanied by cinematographer Jim Jabara, who, along with his able sidekick, Kip, the Masai, made many of the arrangements for the expedition and without whom we would have been as lost in the Serengeti as Dorothy was in the Land of Oz. Jim's wife, Josephine and their two young sons, Justin and Jordan, also accompanied the VOSH team.

Dr. Edwards had cautioned that because it was our first venture in this region it would be an "exploratory" trip and that we could expect almost anything. The itinerary was as solid as a soap bubble and the only thing certain was change.

We left Detroit December 29 and flew to Amsterdam, where during a twelve hour layover, we took a mini-tour of this beautiful city's canals and shops. Then on to Nairobi, Kenya on another direct eight hour flight. After a quick lunch with one of our Kenya sponsors, Dr. Alice Mutungi, we were off on a small plane to a dirt landing strip in the Masai area of the Great Rift Valley, then via Land Rover and truck to the Mara River Tented Camp. After 36 hours of travel we could finally rest or so we thought.

It was New Year's Eve and our hosts the Maasai were throwing a party! Who could resist a Masai celebration next to a river full of hippo's with bush babies (monkeys) chatting in the surrounding trees? The native music was pounding under the open-air thatched roof. As tired as we were, our bodies were bobbing with the beat. The Masai opened up to invite us into their dance – consisting of holding your arms straight to your side and jumping straight up and down, repeatedly. We were having fun, but out of breath. Tracy thought it would only be hospitable for us to reciprocate by teaching them a dance of our culture – wouldn't you know it; we taught them the Macarena! It was a hoot! Happy New Year 1997!

As we straggled back to our tents we were accompanied by armed Masai guards to protect us from the marauding hippopotamuses that would be coming out of the river during the night. We knew this was a New Year's Eve we would never forget.

The next day we got to work, conducting the first of eleven clinics in fourteen days all over southern Kenya. Getting through customs with 3,000 pairs of glasses and the optical testing equipment at Nairobi had not been a problem. Conducting clinics in Masai villages, however, proved to be somewhat more difficult since it would require prior approval from each Masai Governing Council. To effectively serve the native population in the Masai Mara area, we resorted to conducting clinics on the grounds of Tented Camps. These are privately owned lodging facilities which serve the tourist industry both inside and outside the Masai Mara Game Reserve. Our clinics in the Tented Camps served the Masai workers and their families and would draw Masai from surrounding villages. We were very well received and our services were greatly appreciated.

On January 5, our team split up, with Drs. Edwards and Listenberger, Penny, Tracy and Terry flying in a small bush plane north to Kisumu, where they were met by the local sponsor and host, Mr. Silvanus Malaho. They then took a truck overland to the village of Shidunga.

They stayed the first night with families in the area – a unique experience. Our hosts were so grateful for our presence as we all split up as we were being hosted in separate homes. One of our female members Penny ended up as guest of an elderly man who gave his small house to her for the night. To keep her safe, he locked her inside so she would not be bothered by neighbors wondering in during the night. She was grateful, but 'freaking-out.' It was dark, dirt floors and thatched roof. As she lay sleeplessly in her bed she wondered – are there rats? Are there snakes? Are there bugs? Wait! Their toilet facilities are outside! I've got to pee! Well she made it to the morning with little sleep but good spirits, what a 'trooper'. Boy did she tease us when we rejoined and found out how easy our home stays were. We deserved all the teasing she could dish out.

The team spent the next three days conducting clinics for almost four hundred people in Shikunga, Malava and Bungoma. At the end of the second day, all the people of Malava gathered in the village center to thank the VOSH team with rhythmic clapping and speeches. The team was very moved by this display of gratitude and promised to try to return next year.

On January 8, the northern segment of the team again boarded a small plane and flew to the remote Loita Hills. It was so remote that flying in we couldn't see any landing strip, wait, there it is, that little line of dust on top of a hill in the middle of nowhere. We landed; we unloaded and we waited to meet the other half of the team. We waited for 20 minutes. Although we could see about ten miles in all directions, we saw no sign of human life. The pilot had another fare so he had to leave us, turning the plane, taking off and disappearing into the horizon.

About five minutes later we saw one, then another, then several humans walking into sight from below the crest of the hill. They were tall and thin wearing red toga-like sheets carrying a spear in one hand and a club in the other. They stopped, surrounding us while staying about 40 yards away. Not knowing their language, we forced a smile, gestured and just stood there desperately looking for our Land Rover pick-up – nothing! One of our team commented, don't you just feel like 'Indiana Jones' at a moment like this – that took the edge off – well kind of. Alas there it was a little plume of dust rising from the valley below, not even on a road, just across country – that must be them. Our hopes were confirmed fifteen minutes later when the other half of our team pulled up and said, 'sorry we're late.' Yeah right, easy for you to say. But we were so glad to see them we embraced with renewed hope.

Having remained behind in the Mara, the land rover team had safaried overland 170 kilometers with the luggage and supplies to this joyful reunion with the rest of the team at the village of Ilkerin. On a hillside above the village we constructed a campsite with three 3-person pup tents which we purchased the day before. We spent the next two days and three nights up close and personal with the African wilderness. At night, we were protected by a Masai warrior who would sit by the fire with his spear (and club) and watch over our camp. He kept the campfire burning to keep the animals away and would not sleep until we emerged from our tents in the morning.

Sitting on logs away from the fire, there was no ambient light at a mile high. Looking up at the sky we saw interesting cloud formations. Wait those are not clouds; those are stars. It was most inspirational. Speculating, it occurred to us that when the signs of the zodiac were identified, it wasn't by connecting dots. It was as if they 'saw' these signs like we would see animals in clouds.

While in Ilkerin, we visited the home of our local host, Kip, and his family, and conducted a clinic in Ilkerin for the Masai people of his village.

After breaking camp at Ilkerin and saying goodbye to Kip and his village, we safaried back to camp. During our journeys across the Serengeti we drove a 12-year old Land Rover.

The rough terrain took its toll on the Rover. It kept stalling. We had to carry water to fill the boiling over radiator at every stop; and we had to push it to engage the engine to start it.

Well, this old rover was part of the fun of the journey – except for one time.

This time we stopped to observe a female lion who appeared about to give birth.

But after a few minutes Tracy said she really had to pee, but then the land rover refused to start! After a bit the female lion walked about twenty-five yards away and sat down, keeping her attention on a couple of hyenas who were circling. This was our chance! We jumped out and push-started the Land Rover! Up hill!!

Tracy had to go so bad that when we pulled into camp she jumped out immediately and went running full speed for the restroom but she slipped and took a fall and badly skinned up her knee.

We arrived back at the camp in the Masai Mara area and conducted one last clinic at the Fig Tree Camp compound nearby. Then it was a flight back to Nairobi where we conducted two more clinics before finally getting a well deserved day of rest and shopping.

During our trip, the doctors noted the majority of prescriptions written were low minus and were somewhat surprised they did not see more problems associated with increased ultraviolet radiation at high altitude (generally elevations of 5,500 to 7,500 feet). Many patients did complain of itchy or aching eyes and we were amazed that hardly any of them wore a hat (let alone sunglasses) to shade their eyes from the almost continuous sunlight. In total, we conducted eleven clinics in ten different locations and served 1,028 people. The experience of meeting and helping these people is something we will never forget.

The magic of East Africa left its mark on all of us. We were sad to leave that beautiful land with its magnificent wildlife and kind and gracious people. Speaking for my wife and myself, we look forward to returning to Africa someday and we especially look forward to the next VOSH adventure!

As we all began the long flight home, something had changed in each of our hearts, though indescribable, it seemed to give a new meaning to life itself.

Please Give Extra Care to this Old Babushka
By Darrell Groman, OD, Ohio VOSH
Reprinted from VOSH/International Newsletter, August 1993

"Koszonom szepen vegett szemuveg" nevezett anyuka. (Mama said, "Thank you very much for the eyeglasses.")

This was repeated 3,000 times in Hungarian, Ukrainian, or Russian for eight days in border cities of Mukasch and Beregszasz, Ukraine. The location was in the Carpathian Mountains, Transcarpathia. The land has remained the same, only the borders and governments have changed in the last 75 years. In succession: Austro-Hungary, Czechoslavakia, Hungary, Russia, Ukrainian Socialist Republik, The Soviet Union, and now a free Ukraine. This once was the Second World. Hammers and sickles were still evident, some were intact and a few were smashed. On the city square, pedestals remained; Lenin's name and statue had been removed. (In both cities, they say that the statue is kept in a warehouse. For what?) A lot has happened since the people voted for independence only eighteen months before. The nurse has Freedom for $4 a month . . . her salary. The water main on the street was fixed months ago; nobody has had the initiative to fill up the five-foot hole and level it off. There are piles of stone in the middle of the street. We simply drive around the piles and up on the sidewalk. We stayed in private homes. My host mother is a radiologist. She makes $7 a month. She said her tanned skin is not from sunbathing, it is just that her x-ray equipment is thirty years old and it leaks. The locals do not eat meat because it is so expensive. Our hosts served us meat. Water arrives in the faucet three times a day for two hours each: 5 to 7 AM, 1 to 3 PM and 5 to 7 PM. Buckets hold water for the times in between. I was usually the last one to leave the clinic returning home at 7:15 PM. The Europeans say that they can tell who the Americans are because they smell the nicest. After a few days, the strangers who I met on the street wouldn't know that I was an American. The Gypsy kids stuck their hands into my left pocket where I keep my Ukrainian kynohs (coupons) and Hungarian forints; over the eight days I gently removed their hands four or five times. People sit outdoors on benches in front of their homes, people walk, people ride their bikes. The women have an art to it, somehow their dresses do not get tangled up in the spokes.

"Please give extra care to this old Babushka, she is a survivor of the Siege at St. Petersburg." The people pushed and shoved, hoping to be seen by the VOSH-Ohio team. I thought that the glass door/wall dividing them from us was going to shatter, so I told somebody. Within a short time, two local police came to maintain peace and order. We saw 2,800 or so patients "formally" in the clinics. Another 200 or so eyeglasses were passed out through the open window at the dispensary to the people outside. They knew that they had no chance to be seen in the VOSH clinic. Many already had prescriptions written by local practitioners. I was told by more than one person (so it must be true) that if they can get glasses, they wait for two years to get them. The people had strange refractive conditions: high myopes of -9.00 to -13.00 and even -18.00: high astigmats of 4's, 6's, and 8's at any axis. Not like Guatemala where the Indians had high cyl axis 180 degrees or Managua, Nicaragua when the astigmatism patients were all axis 90 degrees! Sometimes the people wore glasses, but it was rare to see bifocals or specs with cylinder. It was difficult to convince the people that bifocal glasses were better than two pairs of eyeglasses. Bill Campbell said that he had found the local optician. She had lens blanks of -3's to +5's, spheres, no cylinder, no bifocals. She took the frame and traced the eyewire on a piece of cardboard. She then cut out the pattern and traced it with a glasses etcher on the lens blank. She then took a lens chipper to chip the lens down to size and smoothed off the edges with a file. She seemed to not have any regard for the optical centers of the lenses. No wonder Fyodorov came up with radial keratotomy! If the Soviet system cannot produce spectacles for the people, then modify the cornea.

Our hosts were the Reformed Church of Transcarpathia and the recently-formed Christian Medical Doctor's Association. Our host, Bishop Gulacsy had served time in the gulags of Siberia for 7.5 years for his Christian beliefs and activities. To hear the congregation sing out during the church service, having been repressed for 48 years, gave me goose bumps. Now there is Religious Freedom. I cannot imagine what life was like in the Soviet Union! I am reminded that I have no right to complain about anything at home...

...Our return to the First World/American culture was buffered by experiencing the Western European culture of Hungary in Debrecen and Budapest. All enjoyed viewing the Danube and Pest from the Buda side.

Rainbows and Revolution

First VOSH-Michigan Mission Haiti, 1986
By Michel Listenberger, OD, FVI

Our VOSH-Michigan's inaugural mission was to San Rafael in the North part of Haiti. We were hosted by a local Baptist Church arranged by Nick Bruckner of Niles coordinating with Reverend Ecclesias Donatien of Haiti. That mission turned into quite an exciting adventure because although the State Department had thought the political unrest would not increase, we ended up in the middle of the Haitian Revolution which led to the overthrow of Jean-Claude (Baby Doc) Duvalier.

After a long, tiring day we arrived at our clinic site. Our eyecare team went to work and others started assisting with the construction projects at the church. All was going well until the second day of our Eye Clinic. While the eye care team was busy, protest marchers and tire fires filled the streets in Cap Haitien about fifteen miles away. Thankfully, two of our team members had been in Cap Haitian to get construction supplies and saw these demonstrations. They rushed back and reported to us that afternoon.

In consultation with people who could know the dangers, we packed up our equipment and supplies. Our plan was to leave at dawn the next day and go to Port-au-Prince where the team would be near the airport and could safely exit the Country.

We made it to Port-au-Prince by driving around boulders and around road blocks, finally arriving in Port au Prince and secured ourselves at a Holiday Inn with walls around our compound enclosure. From that point on we began calling (rarely getting through) and talking with our Charter Airline Company who, finally after three days, said they were sending us down a plane to pick us up. The fires and gunshots in the streets escalated around us as we waited, packed and ready to run. Our fear held some hope, at last.

The greatest worry as the mission leader was the responsibility for twenty volunteers who were on our trip. Decision making is easier if you have good information. In this situation, with lives and political agendas at stake, decision making requires good information. We kept getting conflicting information, we didn't know who to trust – and we were in a strange land. I felt later that it was like we were in the movie with Nick Nolte, "Under Fire" with the situation disintegrating all around us.

Our plane finally came. We were quickly loaded in a pickup truck, men in the back and women crouched down in the front. We took the back streets to the airport driving through clouds of black noxious smoke from burning tires. When the plane landed we were told to grab our luggage and board the plane. We needed to leave as soon as we could. As the plane lifted off the runway, looking out the window, we saw above the black smoke a full rainbow in the sky – someone was watching over us. All were safe.

Snippets from the Newsletters

Various articles appearing in VOSH/International Newsletters

The boy who could not see

A young boy in Honduras was led into the clinic with his eyes closed. His friends said the sun bothered him. Upon examination, it was discovered he was extremely nearsighted— not able to see clearly beyond 5 or 6 inches. With the proper prescription, his eyes opened wide. Looking through lenses of his prescription he began to cry when he looked to the playground and saw, for the first time, trees and buildings and his friends playing. He said he was going back to school to learn to read as they had dismissed him many years ago because they thought he was dumb.

A determined lady

An elderly lady in Honduras walked 8 hours to the clinic, was diagnosed with cataracts, had the surgery that afternoon, slept on a hard bench in the school hallway that night—refusing any pain medication, was examined and fitted with glasses the next morning and walked the 8 hours home wearing the biggest toothless grin you would ever see.

Baby sees for the first time

A 14-month-old baby in Haiti was diagnosed as having had cataract surgery by just having the lens capsules lanced and the lens of the eyes dissolved—leaving her blind. The Baptist missionary host happened to have a hobby as a lapidarist (ground and polished rocks). With his help, the dispensary staff was able to grind down adult cataract lenses to fit into a child's frame. When the glasses were placed on the child, she looked at her hands and then looked into her mother's face and smiled, never having seen her mother clearly before.

Midnight Train to St. Petersburg

By Stan Sagara

Reprinted from VOSH/International Newsletter, December 1995

A sudden movement awakens me. From the clicking of the metal wheels on iron rails I realize that I am in a sleeper car in the dark. Now I remember. I am on the midnight train from Moscow to St. Petersburg. I am here as a part of a team of 25 people from VOSH Northwest, here courtesy of KLM Airlines who donated the 25 tickets as part of "Bridging the World", their celebration of 75 years of service.

Thinking back to the previous week, we had arrived at Schipol Airport in Amsterdam on the 30th of June, 1995 and were met by Natasha Rabchevsky, a representative of our host organization in Russia, Cradle of Hope Adoption Center. She accompanied us to Sheremetyevo Airport in Moscow where we were met by Alexander Melnikov, Inter-region bureau director for the same organization. We were taken by bus to our hotel, a military hotel near the Olympic Stadium, and after sleeping off a bit of our jet lag, we spent the weekend touring Moscow, seeing Red Square and the Kremlin and experiencing Moscow's excellent and beautiful subway system. One of the highpoints of that weekend was a delightful visit to Moscow circus, courtesy of our hosts.

On Sunday, our large group split in two. Seventeen team members moved to the Moscow State University Dormitory where they stayed while working at the City Cardiology Clinic. The other group of eight boarded a bus for a one and a half hour trip to Domodedovo, a small town southeast of Moscow. There they were greeted by the city deputy mayor, Dmitri Gorodetsky, the head of the local Red Cross, and the chief of the Domodedovo Hospital. Over the next five days, 1500 patients were examined in Moscow with 1000 being examined in Domodedovo.

The work experiences of both teams were in many ways similar and in many ways different. Both teams were amazed by the fact that the majority of patients knew their prescriptions and even their P.D.s! The doctors in Moscow were overwhelmed by glaucoma patients being treated quite differently than the standard practices of the USA and by cataract patients being treated with anti-cataract drops. The docs in Domodedovo made a friend for life of the hospital's ophthalmologist by giving him the first topical anesthetic he had seen in six months and by donating a plus cylinder phoropter. At first at both locations, the patients and the sponsors had been a bit unbelieving of our good intentions of providing free eye exams and glasses, but by the end of the week there were big smiles and hubs and kisses passing from person to person. The Russians are great gift givers and both teams were surprised by the number of gifts that they received from their patients, with the group from Domodedovo receiving more cucumbers than they could ever hope to eat. Our Russian hosts also rewarded our hard work. The Moscow group was entertained at a reception in the Russian parliament building. The Domodedovo group was treated to several banquets during their short stay and were welcomed and bid farewell by Professor Vladimir Lukin, former ambassador to the US and chairman of the foreign affairs committee.

And so, on Saturday after a very busy and rewarding week of work, and possibly weakened by the quantity of vodka which we had consumed at the banquets of the previous night, the group found itself on the midnight sleeper train to St. Petersburg, anticipating four days of well deserved R&R. We found ourselves in the hands of a very experienced and delightful guide, Valentin Navarra, who made his city come alive for us with his knowledge of its history and art. We toured beautiful palaces, saw fantastic art collections, and experienced magical ballet in this fairyland city, but our four days came too quickly to an end, and we found ourselves once again traveling back to Seattle via an overnight in Amsterdam.

Home of Dracula Romania 2008

This Story is written by author Barbara Plaugher in her book,
Perseverance: Missions to the World.
It is filled with interesting VOSH stories. Barbara, a VOSH veteran agreed to share this story with us.

When I mentioned to most people that our next mission was to be to Romania, their first response was "Isn't that where Dracula was from?" It's not impossible to forget Count Dracula, the Bram Stoker character inspired by Vlad Tepes, an actual 15th century prince of Wallachia. He is known to history as "The Impaler" for his ruthlessness to his enemies. Although history knows him as the demon in Romanian folklore, in Romania he is considered a national hero who liberated the country from the Turks.

Our gracious host for this mission to Romania was the Rotary of Targoviste. We worked with the Rotary in 2003 and sent in a small team for eye care and were anxious to return to this area again. The vice mayor of that city carefully pointed out to me that Romania is much more than Dracula, even though this image is skillfully exploited by tour operators, who organize visits to Sighishoara, the city of his birth, Bran Castle, known as Dracula's castle, and the capital of his kingdom in Targoviste.

Targoviste was our destination for October 11th, 2008. Arriving in our group were team members from Washington, Texas, Illinois, Missouri, New Jersey, Colorado, Kentucky, and of course Ohio as VOSH-Ohio conducted their 4th mission for this year. What a wonderful time to come to Romania, as the weather was pleasant and the leaves were turning to their fall colors.

We had arrived into Romania after a long overnight flight into Amsterdam and then another flight into Bucharest with a bus ride to Targoviste. Prior to our arrival we had worked with the Ministry of Health to provide correct documentation to enter the country through customs without a hitch. And we did just that, as we found that customs were closed for the day and we walked straight through the airport. What a pleasant surprise!

We started out seeing the city of Targoviste, setting up for clinic, and going full force. After our first day of clinic when we examined over 600 patients, our host took us to a concert at the Music School of Targoviste. We were privileged to sit in the front row. The only problem was that it felt so nice and relaxing with a warm room and beautiful orchestra music. You can only guess what happened next!

Our host provided housing in a dorm at the Valahia University of Targoviste and our clinic was held in a large gymnastic room in the same building. This was an ideal setting to hold a clinic. We set up for our 4 ½ days of work and remained in this setting for our entire days of clinic.

Interpreters from the high school were provided, as English is taught in the schools beginning in the elementary grades. After clinic we were able to visit a local school and provide some books in English and German to the school. Our team donated books, school materials, and clothing for the children in the school and the underprivileged. We also made a visit to a daycare center for handicapped children, where many of these items were donated.

VOSH-Ohio held a mission in Targoviste in 2003, and from that visit a friendship developed between our lead optometrist, and Dumitru Stefan's family. Dumitru again became our contact for this mission. A successful mission always starts with a good contact and this indeed was a successful mission.

Our team members melted together when newcomers to the group soon became old time VOSHers, and we worked like a well-oiled machine as we processed 3,291 patients in our short time of work. There were six policemen who did an excellent job assisting with crowd control. The real challenge to the team came on Wednesday, as we were approaching 800 patients for the day. I walked out doors to see how the patient flow was going and saw that there were approximately 50 more people outside the fence. Then I found out that some of these people had stood there since 12 midnight, and it was now 4 PM. I was overwhelmed! Needless to say, we brought them into the clinic. It is so difficult to turn people away, even though the team may be to the point of exhaustion. We managed to see all the patients of the day and didn't lose the team either to exhaustion or to a walk out.

We had over 100 referrals, mostly cataracts. These were to be seen in a local hospital ophthalmology clinic, as worked out through the Rotary. Our one problem that occurred during this clinic was the lack of glasses in certain prescriptions. We had 277 scripts that we were unable to fill. The Rotary contacted a young local optometrist, who was willing to work with our group and fit these glasses, if we could mail them to him. After we returned home, some members of the team pulled these scripts from the

Pandora Eyeglass Sorting Center, and mailed the glasses to the Rotary. We had contact with our hosts, and received information that they were able to get the glasses to the proper patients. This took quite some time to complete on an individual basis.

Most of our patients were older, many into their 90's. All of course were most grateful to have the opportunity to have an eye exam and be provided with glasses, if needed. Besides receiving hugs, handshakes and kisses, we had patients bringing in bouquets of flowers to show their appreciation. One lady brought us a sack of plums, so ripe and so delicious.

Speaking of food, Romanians eat much slower than us Americans. We had our meals served in the Theological Seminary. We were provided with a four- course lunch on our first day of clinic. Nevertheless, some team members were gone for 1 ½ hours for lunch, while the remaining half of the team carried on a "slow" clinic. That had to stop! We argued with the chief! We had to teach him the "American" style! The next day we were served buffet for each meal. They provided such delicious food. Tomatoes, cheese, cold meats and hotdogs, eggs, cereal for breakfast. Ciorba, breads, meat and sausages, potatoes, desserts for lunch. We can't forget the strong coffee! And for dinner we were taken into the city for wonderful meals. We experienced a typical Romanian dinner one evening, where we were offered a glass of plum brandy around an outdoor bonfire prior to entering the restaurant. Our welcoming dinner was a marvelous buffet with the Rotary. Our departing evening we were hosted by the Rotary again, only this time it was in a beautiful State House where the government houses dignitaries. We were served a fantastic buffet and a violinist entertained us even playing "Turkey in the Straw" for us Americans. We felt like dignitaries!

When we completed clinic time we also were able to do the "Dracula" tour into the Carpathian Mountains to see some of the beautiful monasteries, castles, and ruins as you will only find in Europe. The Peles Castle, Sinaia, is an example of the extravagance in architecture. Began In 1866, it is now a state museum.

The mysterious stone streets reveal slender buildings and houses that have ignored the passing of time and now display their beauty. Their charm cannot easily be described in words. We also did a day visit into Bucharest to see the National Museum, which reflects the history of medieval and modern times; the People's Palace, the second largest building in the world; and the village museum, depicting various architecture of homes throughout entire Romania.

Missions into this area provide a person the best of both worlds, an opportunity to provide services to the underserved, and to revel in the history and architecture of the old world. It was great, especially when our generous host provided us with personal tour directors, Ioana and Tony, from Stefan's family. Thank you, thank you!

As many of you readers know, team involvement means developing friendships that last a lifetime, both from the team members and those you work with in other countries. Some continue to correspond with their friends from all over the world, and these friendships are what make a VOSH mission so special.

That They May See

By Dolores Gonos in a VOSH-Ohio mission in Dominican Republic
Reprinted from VOSH/International Newsletter, March 1998

High in the mountains, miles from the city of Santa Domingo, lies Guayabal, a small village with a population of less than a thousand. It's four hours by truck. The truck alternates between careening through the stony dirt roads and grinding to sudden halts before hitting the ditches.

As I took in the beauty of the trees, flowers and small streams, I could see how nature had bent its paths. You feel you can reach out and touch the clouds and the sun. God's creation became so alive. Children were running barefoot, scantily clothed, but bearing beautiful smiles and happy eyes. We waved to them and they waved back with a welcome to their village.

As we approached this remote, unspoiled area, the new volunteers became anxious, not knowing what to expect. It is my first mission and I waited eagerly to see what was ahead. There are no road signs, stop signs or street signs or street lights. We see the village and catch sight of tin and straw roofs, a few donkeys trudging by, some chickens and dogs running around.

The village people have been preparing for our visit for a long time. We see a small group gathered at the building where we will work. Everyone helps to unload the supplies and equipment. We meet our home sponsor and greeted with smiles. A foreign culture and language is not a barrier, and we can see the love in their expressions and understand the body language. The lady of the house where I stayed seemed to understand just what I attempted to convey to her, and she to me. I knew I had been touched by the love and beauty of their lives, and their eyes danced with joy. We are so graced to live in a land where everything is easy for us. Our hosts may be poor in material things, but very rich in God's love.

Upon arrival at their home, I felt an overwhelming sadness. They were giving me the best place to sleep, showing me through each room in their small dwelling and offering me everything they had. It was all perfect, clean and ready for me, their guest. My hostess was so proud to have me there. I met her husband, a teacher, who hugged me joyfully, and their three sons, ages 6, 8 and 10. There are no modern appliances. Their main diet is rice, beans, hard boiled eggs, some chicken and vegetables such as squash, turnips, yucca and some others I did not recognize. They know as many ways to cook rice as we do hamburger.

They use a wooden "pelone" to crush vegetables and cook them to a puree or soup. Coffee was special treat. Breakfast was sliced and fried bread, no butter, and bananas, which are in great supply. Whatever is not eaten at a meal was saved for the next meal. There was no waste, especially water. I was never hungry. They gave what they had and were proud to share it.

There are many outhouses, but not many indoor toilets, because the water supply is low, you can't flush very often. Bathing is done in a basin of cold water. My family was very good to me. I had hot water to bathe on two occasions.

As for alarm clocks, they aren't necessary. You wake to the sounds of roosters crowing, pigs snorting and dogs barking. My first morning, I sat up in bed and listened to a lengthy conversation between two roosters discussing the day's activities. What a refreshing change.

I must mention the funny little brooms. The first chore of the day at any household is to sweep out the entire house, right out into the road. The brooms have a short wood pole stuck into some straw and tied around the top. I'm sure it was made by the man of the house. Most of the houses are open, some have shutters, but because it is so dry and dusty, there is a need to sweep daily.

In preparation for the trip, we had meetings, received some training, got our shots for disease prevention, and prepared the glasses and equipment for the trip. You must take your own flashlight, soap, Kleenex, toilet tissue, insect repellant, and towels. The doctors are responsible for the examination equipment and medical supplies. The cases of glasses are worth more than gold to us, since this is where we find the right prescription for patients. The right Rx is important, but we try to find the right style and fit, too.

Villagers are screened in advance and given a number. These people are a study in patience. They come early in the morning, wait in the hot sun and sit on the ground.

They've given up their chores for the day and must make up for it later. They have no money for glasses and no eye doctors other than the VOSH doctors. We make lists for follow-up for surgical needs, and arrangements for a little girl whose eyelids are growing into her head to be brought to the states for surgery. A young mother brings her child to us in fear that the child may go blind. The child is treated. There are cases of glaucoma, and many suffering from diabetes. We give them medications, eye drops and instructions on how to use them. We treated over 600 people and gave sunglasses to field workers.

As we left, I thought how blessed I was to go on this trip. I had read about the less fortunate, but now I have seen it. I hope that we not only reached out, but lifted them up and gave them hope. My prayer was not that they saw the material things we had, but rather the love we brought them. We are no longer strangers, but all God's children and we care.

"Just" a Simple Pair of Eyeglasses
By Patti Fuhr, OD, PHD, VOSH-Alabama
Reprinted from VOSH/International Newsletter, Fall/Winter 2004-05

A pair of glasses can make the difference in driving a car, obtaining employment, or supporting a family. A simple pair of reading glasses can make a difference in being able to help a child with homework, reading a book or newspaper, cooking or sewing, seeing a watch, or making a craft. I want to tell you the story of many organizations and individuals coming together to help those in need, and in particular, I want to tell you the story of one family.

It takes a village to raise a child successfully, as stated by Hillary Clinton, former First Lady of the United States. It also take the concern and cooperation of individuals and organizations to provide eye and vision care to some of the one billion persons in the world who do not have access to those services. In fact, if you were one of those individuals, you would not be able to read this article.

In the spring of 2004, VOSH-Alabama joined with the District 34-O Lions of Alabama to deliver eye and vision care to over 3,000 needy persons in Mexico. Sites for the eye care services and transportation for those in need were arranged by the Lions Clubs of Mascota and Union de Tula, Mexico. The local Lions worked with the US volunteers and arranged housing, meals, and local transportation for the participants from the US. Eyeglasses for the mission came from a variety of sources. Recycled eyeglasses were donated by the Lions Eyeglass recycling Centers of Ocala and Silver Springs, Florida.

In one town a family with five children presented for eye care. A small boy held the hand of his father on one side, and a little sister on the other side; his mother held a baby and the hand of another young girl, while another child followed by her side. We found that the father was not able to read anything on the eye chart and three of his children could not recognize any targets on the children's eye chart. The father reported that he could not read, had never been to school, and had never worked. He also said that neither he nor his children had ever seen an eye doctor. This was their first opportunity to do so.

The young boy who led his father into the room had normal vision, as did the mother and the baby. However, the reason the father was led into the room became immediately clear to the doctors. The gentleman was extremely nearsighted, to the point that he could only appreciate object within one inch of his eyes. He had walked around in a very foggy world all of his life. Now, his children were doing so also. Three of the five children were highly nearsighted.

Because of this mission, these children and their dad will receive the eyeglasses they so desperately need. The children will be able to see better, will go to school and will be able to read. They will receive an education because they will be able to participate in school, and when they grow up, they will be able to contribute to their communities and families. . . . all because they now have a simple pair of eyeglasses.

One Memorable Patient
By Rita Cherian, fourth-year NECO intern in Armenia
Reprinted from VOSH/International Newsletter, Spring 2008

We were conducting eye exams in the village of Maralyk, in the outskirts of Armenia. Patients were lining up in swarms with documentation and passport in hand. An elderly Armenian woman sat at my station. As I started taking her case history, the woman explained that she was blind from glaucoma and that she had been taking pilocarpine drops. She said her left eye was completely blind and she could see only figures and light with her right eye.

I proceeded with the exam and pulled out my retinoscopy rack and retinoscope. The woman began frantically gesturing that each lens I moved was better than the previous one and then she started crying. She was extremely emotional since she had lost all hope of seeing. Tears streamed down her cheeks and mine as well. Before I even put the trial frame on her face, she was kissing my hands and thanking me. After all was done, she was a -3.00 diopter myope. I couldn't hold back the tears. We both embraced and I still fill up whenever I recount this story that makes optometry such a worthwhile profession.

Return to Samoa
By Richard Ryan, OD, and Kathy Rosier
Reprinted from "VOSHers Serve a Second time in Samoa," VOSH/International Newsletter, Winter/Spring 2002-03; Name and content edited

To serve a population of roughly 200,000, Samoa has one resident ophthalmologist, one six-month, college-trained, certified optometrist (more equivalent to a licensed dispensing optician who does refracting) and one optician.

We saw close to 3,000 patients over five days in two locations: Salialoga, Savaii, (their big island, primarily agricultural) and Apia Upolu (the capital city).

As in all VOSH trips, each of our 25 team members paid their own way to serve for a second time in Samoa. Lodging and food was provided by our hosts during the days of the clinic, as was transportation to and from work sites.

The most memorable patient we saw was a young woman who worked as a newspaper reporter. She had been "blind" since birth, but had never had an eye examination. It turned out she was -16.00, but even with deprivational amblyopia, we were able to achieve 20/200 with glasses. While still legally blind, she was far more able to see shapes of objects and colors after being treated at the clinic. Needless to say the woman was ecstatic, as were we. Her eyes filled when she mentioned being able to make out the bright colors on her mother's dress. (Her mom serves as her guide.)

On both islands, a large number of patients with old agricultural type eye injuries were diagnosed, as were a large number of UV-related eye pathologies. Although there is a high incidence of diabetes in Western Samoa (as in most South Pacific Island populations), the incidence of retinopathy was very low, lending credence to the idea that diets rich in antioxidants and fish may be protective for the retina.

Christianity is a way of life here. Each night at 6:30 PM a curfew is imposed in several of the villages. When the gong sounds, all go inside for evening prayer. When the gong sounds again at around 7 PM, people are free to continue their activities. Sundays are for church and "umu" feasts, name for the clay ovens in which the cooking is done. There is little refrigeration so food does not keep.

Our trip coincided with the fourth of July. The American Consulate invited our team to celebration. To our surprise, we found we were the guests of honor and we were soon joined by native islanders as well as diplomatic representatives of a number of countries including New Zealand and Australia. The Deputy Prime Minister of Western Samoa made a moving speech about the special qualities of the citizens of the United States. His words, along with remarks of the New Zealand Consular Representative, seemed to be a heartfelt attempt to say to the US citizens in attendance that, in spite of the tendency for foreign nationals to look at the US as an overbearing parent, individual efforts such as VOSH show in a microcosm the bigger picture of what the US is all about.

The Night Watchman Shoe Story
By Audrey Blondin, VOSH-Connecticut, 2017

Even though the focus of every VOSH-CT mission is obviously providing eye examinations and glasses as well as sunglasses to those who otherwise would have no access to eye care, over the years we have been able to help in other ways as well.

During our mission trips in the San Juan del Sur, Nicaragua area we hire local residents to act as security guards. We have had the same 4 security guards at the mission entrance gate for 16 years and they are each paid for their work. We also provide them with t-shirts, hats that say Security on them, and the latest are security vests which they love!!

Several years ago, a very nice young man appeared at the end of the first day of clinic and said he was the night security watchman. Even though he was not originally part of our security team, we included him in and paid him for the week and he has returned each year since. This year when he arrived, I happened to look down at his shoes and noticed they were completely threadbare. This sent us on a quest after clinic was finished one day to try and find a decent pair of work shoes in a place not known for having many if any shoe stores. We did manage to find a very nice pair of work shoes in his size, and another local person we knew had a planned trip to Managua where they managed to find a great pair of sneakers for him. We couldn't wait to give him his new shoes, and it was just so exciting when we did!! The ones he took off literally crumbled before our eyes and it just brings so much happiness and joy to see the look on his face and how proud he felt to walk around the clinic site in his new work shoes.

No one here in America who has not been outside our country to the third world can begin to understand what it is like to have nothing. The satisfaction we have all earned over the years in being able to not only provide services to those in need but to give back to those less fortunate is priceless. We are thankful each day for the opportunities that have been given to us by our work on behalf of VOSH-CT, and we look forward to being able to provide continued services to those in need in and around the San Juan del Sur, Nicaragua area.

Contacts Give Nelson a New Life
Daily Contact Lenses give Nelson a new life
By Robert Foote, OD
*Reprinted from the VOSH/International
Newsletter, Winter/Spring 2002-03*

Vistakon's major financial contributions to VOSH/International are not its sole commitment to VOSH efforts. Take the case of VOSH-Michigan and Nelson Moises Lolindres of Honduras.

Nelson Moises Lolindres was first seen by a VOSH-Michigan team during our 2001 eye mission to Tegucigalpa, Honduras. Six years old at the time, the child was diagnosed with Marfan's Syndrome. Surgery to correct his distorted vision from the dislocation of his crystalline lenses was not possible.

One of our team members, Dr. Mark Cook, OD, had brought along some Acuvue diagnostic lenses for someone with very high myopia. Nelson's Rx was found to be -16.00 for each eye, with resulting visual acuity of 20/40 for each eye. With the insertion of -11.00 one-day Acuvue lenses, we saw an amazing transformation. Nelson went from hanging on to his mother's dress to playing with the other children at the clinic site.

Dr. Heidi Schefferly taught Nelson's mother insertion and removal techniques, as well as use of solutions.

Upon returning home, I contacted my Vistakon representative who provided us with a year's supply of One Day Acuvue diagnostic 8.5/-12.00 lenses.

A Lion's club member in Tegucigalpa takes them to the local eye professional. She sees the child approximately every 2-3 months and gives Nelson additional lenses.

The VOSH-Michigan team checked Nelson again in 2002 when they held a clinic in La Esperanza, site of VOSH-Michigan's permanent eye care clinic. We were pleased to see that Nelson was successfully using the contacts and eyeglasses we had sent him. He uses the eyeglasses in school over his contacts to completely correct his myopia. We also made him a pair of spectacles to use when he is not wearing contacts.

We plan to check on Nelson again when we hold another clinic in Honduras in early 2003.

Do Self-Refracting Glasses Really Work?

An interesting innovation for making glasses onsite from Oxford, England
Published in VOSH/International Newsletter, Fall/Winter 2004-05

Josh Silver, PhD, inventor and physics professor from Oxford, England, traveled to Florida in June to talk to VOSH/

International Annual Meeting attendees about the adaptive liquid lenses he has invented.

How they work sounds pretty simple. The person puts on a pair of mass-produced, liquid-filled, spherical glasses, adjusts each eye for clear vision, seals each lens and then removes the adjusters. The fluid then congeals.

Possible prescriptions range from -6.00 to +6.00. While they can't correct everyone's vision, they can help a significant number of adults, noted Dr. Silver.

Cost to produce a pair of these self-prescribing lenses is presently under $2 a pair. The glasses are now in mass production and product trials are underway.

If indeed, the goal of WHO (World Health Organization) is to provide eye care to a billion people who presently have no access to it by the year 2020, Dr. Silver believes conventional models of service are inadequate. His, is an alternative approach, one which he believes can help tackle the problem. "Eye care is a world health issue that is also social and economic and it has largely been overlooked," said Dr. Silver.

Several weeks after Dr. Silver's presentation, newly-appointed VOSH/International Executive Director Harry Zeltzer, OD, traveled to Oxford to participate in an international conference of Affordable Vision Correction in Third-World Countries that was hosted by Dr. Silver.

Children Living in a Landfill
Edited from VOSH/International Newsletter, Spring 2006

A team from VOSH-Northwest recently traveled to Nandasmo, Nicaragua, lead by team leader Carl Sakovits, OD. He noted that he had heard of a community of orphans living off a landfill not far from the VOSH team's hotel in Jinotepe. Indeed, they would include the children in their combined medical clinic, but rather than try to set up a satellite site, they would hire a bus to transport the children to the clinic.

As the school bus rolled in, the sounds of a very excited group of youngsters reverberated throughout the site. Roughly 60 orphans spent the day with the VOSH-Northeast team, receiving medical, eye, audiology, and dental care. At the end of the day, as Dr. Sakovits was rounding up the VOSH team to head back to their hotel, he noticed the rental bus that was just departing.

Dr. Sakovits wrote of the moment: "The kids were still going strong, jumping, screaming, and smiling as they had upon their arrival. The one adult chaperone that accompanied them settle them down just long enough for them to say thank you and to serenade us with a departing song in Spanish. They were on their way home – back to the garbage dump."

Dr. Sakovits paused to absorb the harsh reality and reflected, "I hope I never forget this."

Candy's Story
By Joanne Hendrick, OD, VOSH-Colorado
Reprinted from VOSH/International Newsletter, Fall 2006

During our VOSH trip to Colima, Mexico, in April 2006, Candy was brought into our clinic by her grandmother. She was ten years old, had never worn a pair of glasses and had actually been told that glasses would hurt her eyes!

I examined Candy and determined that her prescription was -19.00 diopters in both eyes. Needless to say, we did not have glasses with us that were strong enough. I left her with a pair that was -10.00 diopters and promised to send her a pair from the United States as soon as possible.

Upon returning home, I made two pairs of glasses and proceeded to try to deliver them to Candy. First of all, because of import regulations, the frames could not be manufactured in China, nor the cases, so I chose Italian frames. PECH Optical lab fabricated Candy attractive, thin lenses. I used FedEx to mail the glasses to one of the women in Colima who had helped us with translation. I was unaware that taxes had to be paid upon receipt, so our translator Lucy and DIF paid the taxes. At that point it turned out that Candy's grandmother had not provided a complete address, so Lucy, our translator worked diligently to find Candy. DIF finally located her after two weeks of searching and Lucy and her daughter went to deliver the glasses. Candy, her mother and grandmother are thrilled.

In the US, we take for granted our access to health care. I was thrilled to play a role in transforming Candy's life and to participate in a little bit of international diplomacy as well. Lucy will check in with Candy every year and I will continue to provide her with eyewear as needed.

Blind from Explosion
A short story of triumph by Dr. Harry Zeltzer

In El Salvador, a disheveled man walked into the clinic with the aid of a cane. According to his history, an explosion during combat caused dense corneal scarring of both eyes and a displaced crystalline lens. After examining him with the slit lamp we found an irregular shaped area within the cornea that had some clarity of about two or three millimeters in diameter. Excitedly, we located an aphakic correction from the inventory. It increased his acuity from counting fingers at three feet to 20/40. Lo and behold another aphakic correction was found that allowed him to read newspaper print. Everyone in the clinic was so thrilled. We collected two hundred dollars and gave him numerous toys for his three children.

Two years later the gentleman re-appeared without a cane and was nicely dressed. We learned he was successfully selling lottery tickets on the street. The purpose of his second visit was to return the two hundred dollars!

A Cacophony of Eye Disease
By Mailynn Pham, third-Year VOSH-ICO
*Edited from "VOSH-Florida, Yeguarizo Paraguay" in the
VOSH/International Newsletter, Fall 2008*

Paraguay is a landlocked country surrounded by Argentina, Bolivia, and Brazil. It has a population of six and a half million with more than one-third of its population living in poverty.

Charles Covington, VOSH-Florida led a diverse team to Paraguay. They included participants from Florida, Minnesota, Texas, Illinois, Argentina, Canada, and New Zealand. Peace Corps workers joined the team on site.

Our team was up early as breakfast was at 7 AM and we still had to finish setting up before clinic opened at 8 AM. As we walked across the yard from the clinic and sleeping quarters to eat, to our surprise, there were many people already waiting to be seen by us. We had barely started clinic that morning when a very young crying and screaming boy was brought in by his mother. Upon observation, one eye was red, the eyelid swollen, and the boy could not open his eyes due to the pronounced edema. This young boy and his treatment for preseptal cellulitis set the tone of how clinic was going to be – long, difficult, educational, but very rewarding. Other notable cases that were seen included retinal detachments, albinism, toxoplasmosis, diabetic retinopathy, hypertensive retinopathy, glaucoma, cataracts, and strabismus. Day two proved to be even more rewarding. One man came in having been shot in the eye with the bullet having exited out of his head.

Probably our most memorable occurrence of the day was an elderly woman who brought in a jar with a long worm in it. Earlier in the day, she had coughed it up out of her mouth and she was so proud showing it off to everyone and she even posed for pictures with it. One patient came in with intraocular pressures of OD 79 mm Hg and OS 18 mm Hg. With repeated instillation of IOP-lowering drugs, the pressures were brought down to 28.

The clinic on day three brought a young boy who had suffered a machete accident when he was just a few years old. Interesting patients included one with posterior synechiae, a metallic foreign body that was removed by Dr. Spencer, and a patient suffering a seizure while trying to do visual acuities. New pathology on day four included Duane's retraction syndrome and a corneal abrasion from barbed wire. Finally on the last day, a young man had a Cloquet's canal running from his optic disc to his lens.

One night, after dinner, local dancers came to dance for us in their cultural dresses. We were all touched by their offer of appreciation.

Approximately 2500 patients later including 139 cataract referrals, it was difficult to comprehend how they all walked around in their daily lives with no refractive correction. Imagine a world without your glasses and imagine seeing a blurry image of your child every time you look and him/her. Something so simple such as clear vision that is taken for granted daily was so greatly appreciated by these patients. I will always carry in my heart the kindness, love, and compassion that my Paraguayan 'family' not only showed to the patients, but to each other as well. Witnessing their gratitude and appreciation for the difference that we made in their vision was incredibly rewarding.

(Courtesy of Dr. Dale Cole)

(Courtesy of Jeff Cowan)

(Courtesy of Dr. Dale Cole)

Postscript
Thank You for Saying "YES"!
Because it's so easy to say "No"

It's so easy to say "no" in a time when most families are two career families – when just making a living is all that one can do. It's easy to say no to people you don't know, or who live in other countries, or "no" to your VOSH Chapter or to VOSH/ International.

It's so easy to say "there is no time" because you have your own children to raise, because you are putting children through college, or because you are busy keeping your optometric practice alive.

It's easy to say "there is no time" to go on a VOSH mission, to help your VOSH chapter, or to recruit another volunteer who is busy like yourself.

It's easy to say "there is no time" to bring the gift of sight to hundreds of people who cannot afford or obtain such care. It's so easy to say the problems of helping those in need are someone else's responsibility.

For you, as a busy member of society, it would be easy to say "no" to all of these volunteer opportunities.

But you didn't! You said, "YES" to helping others in need, "YES" to helping people see better and "YES" to "bringing the world into focus!"

By saying "YES" you are not only defining yourself but defining the essence of VOSH itself. By saying "YES," you are answering, by your deeds, the question posed in the beginning, "Why would anyone put their life on hold, paying their own expenses, traveling to the other side of the world, to give others they don't even know, the gift of sight?"

I want to be thoroughly used up when I die,
for the harder I work the more I live. I rejoice in life for its own sake.
Life is no "brief candle" for me.
It is a sort of splendid torch which I have got hold of for the moment,
and I want to make it burn as brightly as possible
before handing it on to future generations.
-   George Bernard Shaw

APPENDIX

Sources

Primary Sources include the author's thirty-eight years of memories as a member from the beginning, recalling many VOSH incidents, concerns, issues, initiatives, meetings and missions from the many member volunteers who shared the vision. Additional records were provided by Dr. Dale Cole, Dr. Harry Zeltzer and Executive Director Natalie Venezia

Over two-thousand pages of VOSH published newsletters, meeting minutes, financial statements, notes and other archives handed down from the previous VOSH Historian Dr. Dale Cole

Interviews with VOSH founders Dr. Herb White and extensively Dr. O.R. Morlong. Dr. Morlong also shared some original photographs of the first ever VOSH Missions.

Interviews from most of the living Past Presidents of VOSH/ International

The Kansas Optometric Journal most helpful was the January-March 2004 issue dedicated to the formation of VOSH Kansas with Dr. Ellis Potter as its editor

The Journal of the American Optometric Association Letters from Presidents Ronald Reagan and George Bush

Perseverance: Missions to the World, by author Barbara Plaugher (available on Amazon)

Highlights in VOSH

1962-71 Early eye-care missions by Dr. Reynold F. Swanson and others

1968 Dr. Reynold F. Swanson of Florida led a mission to Haiti and brought Dr. Franklin Harms of Kansas with him

1968 "Student Optometric Services to Haiti (SOSH) Pennsylvania", a precursor to VOSH, took its first mission to Haiti led by Dr. Algernon Phillips

1970 At this time several other states were actively providing eye care to other countries on a locally sponsored basis. The participating states included Minnesota, Missouri, Iowa, Indiana, Nebraska, and South Dakota

1970 Dr. Harms sets Pre-organization meeting in Kansas to organize as a committee under Kansas Optometric Foundation

1972 March 21st: The name "Volunteer Optometric Services to Humanity" was adopted by an organizing committee under the purview of the Kansas Optometric Foundation (supported by the Kansas Optometric Association)

1972 October: First Kansas VOSH Project "Fly In" with two planes to Montemorelos, Mexico

1974 February: a nation-wide workshop on eye care mission work was conducted in Wichita, Kansas. All State Associations and interested parties were invited – 18 states were represented

1975 September: The name "VOSH/Interstate" was adopted at a VOSH organizational meeting in Kansas City. Officers were elected. Organization was to consist of separate State Chapters

1975 The American Optometric Association adopted the "VOSH Project Plan" as a supporter

1978 VOSH founder, Dr. Franklin Harms, dies of a heart attack

1979 July: VOSH/International formed, adopted Bylaws, and elected Dr. Russ Dorman as first VOSH/International President

1979 October: VOSH/International incorporated in the State of Indiana by Dr. Walter Marshall

1992 Our own VOSH/International Eyeglass Neutralization Site was established at the State Prison in Taylorville, Illinois, and was overseen by Dianne Johnson

1993 Dr David Krasnow (California VOSH) initiated a "sustainability" program for VOSH as well as developed the utilization of "outcome metrics" to indicate impact and progress

1996 VOSH-British Columbia, Canada was added as the first sustainable International Chapter. VOSH-BC was known as TWECS Third World Eye Care Society with President Dr. Marina Roma-March as President. It was followed in 1998 by the second continuously operational International Chapter VOSH-Honduras

1996 VOSH/International launched its first VOSH Web Page at wwwvosh.org it was informative but very basic. VOSH website expanded dramatically beginning in 2000.

1997 VOSH/International had its first joint multi-chapter Domestic Eye Mission in downtown Detroit at the Detroit Rescue

Mission which served 200 inner-city homeless – Dr. Carol Hunt was project coordinator, assisted by Dr. Nelson Edwards

1997 At our invitation, the American Optometric Association appointed a member of their Board, Dr. Gary Blackman of Illinois, to serve as an Ad Hoc member on the VOSH/International Board

2000 Dr. Larry Hookway (Ohio) initiated the work on the comprehensive global Presbyopia Study

2001 An effort was initiated to shift primary revenues from member/chapter dues to outside grants and other funding sources: A $20,000 grant was accepted from Vistakon (Johnson and Johnson)

2001 "VISION 2020" to end preventable blindness in the world is initiated by the World Health Organization (WHO) and joined by the World Council of Optometry (WCO), Volunteer Optometric Services to Humanity (VOSH) and twenty-six other NGO co-signers

2002 VOSH became a member of the "World Council of Optometry" – global networking with other international organizations became the operant paradigm of the time

2003 Director Clive Miller (Australia) of "Optometry Giving Sight" began a strong long-term partnership with VOSH/International

2004 The office of Executive Director is created to administer VOSH International. Dr. Harry Zeltzer was the first to serve as a volunteer. Natalie Venezia succeeded as Executive Director of VOSH/International in 2012

2006 The Franklin Harms Society was created to honor VOSHers who had served significantly having participated in at least ten VOSH missions

2006 VOSH formed the "Technical Transfer Program" (TTP) with support of Optometry Giving Sight (OGS). First Jeff Forrey and soon after, Dr. Michael DeRosier became Chairman of the program to get it started. Dr. David Stacy continues as director of the program today

2006 "Fellow of VOSH/International" (FVI) was created as a program to build an experienced cadre of informative optometrists to speak for VOSH. It was first directed by Dr. Stewart Frank and continued by Dr. Ann Slocum Edmonds

2005 Dr. Ruth McAndrews became VOSH's first woman International President

2011 VOSH Corps formed to endow an optometric educator to serve an internship in a developing foreign optometry school

2013 VOSH created a Disaster Relief Program that sends VOSH volunteers to areas in need

2016 VOSH Forms a new Optometry School in Port au Prince, Haiti under the initiative of Dr. David McPhillips and with the support of Optometry Giving Sight and others.

Chapters of VOSH/ International

**LIST OF VOSH CHAPTERS
JANUARY 2017**

<u>STATE OR REGIONAL VOSH CHAPTERS</u>

ALBERTA

ARIZONA

BRITISH COLUMBIA (TWECS)

CALIFORNIA

COLORADO

CONNECTICUT

GHANA

HONDURAS, FUNDACIÓN PARA SERVICIOS MÉDICOS VOLUNTARIOS

ILLINOIS

INDIA-MAHARASHTRA

INDIANA

IOWA

KANSAS

KENTUCKY

MICHIGAN

MINNESOTA

MISSOURI

NEBRASKA

NEW YORK

NORTHEAST (MD, RI)

NORTHWEST (WA, ID, AK, OR)

NORTH CAROLINA

OHIO

OKLAHOMA

ONTARIO

ONE (OF NEW ENGLAND) (CT, MA, ME, NH, RI, VT)

PENNSYLVANIA

PUERTO RICO

QUEBEC (SANTA CRUZ)

SOUTHEAST (AL, FL, GA, SC, MS)

SOUTH DAKOTA

TEXAS

VIRGINIA

WISCONSIN

WYOMING

STUDENT VOSH CHAPTERS

NORTH AMERICA:

UNIVERSITY OF WATERLOO SCHOOL
OF OPTOMETRY (WATERLOO)

AMERICAN UNIVERSITY OF PUERTO RICO (BAYAMON)

UNIVERSITY OF THE WEST INDIES (TRINIDAD)

UNIVERSITY OF ALABAMA AT BIRMINGHAM (BIRMINGHAM)

MIDWESTERN UNIVERSITY ARIZONA COLLEGE
OF OPTOMETRY (GLENDALE)

SOUTHERN CALIFORNIA COLLEGE OF OPTOMETRY AT
MARSHALL B. KETCHUM UNIVERSITY (FULLERTON)

UNIVERSITY OF CALIFORNIA - BERKELEY

WESTERN UNIVERSITY OF HEALTH SCIENCES (POMONA)

NOVA SOUTHEASTERN UNIVERSITY (FT LAUDERDALE)

ILLINOIS COLLEGE OF OPTOMETRY (CHICAGO)

INDIANA UNIVERSITY (BLOOMINGTON)

UNIVERSITY OF PIKEVILLE KENTUCKY
COLLEGE OF OPTOMETRY (PIKEVILLE)

MASSACHUSETTES COLLEGE OF PHARMACY
AND HEALTH SCIENCES (WORCESTER)

NEW ENGLAND COLLEGE OF OPTOMETRY (BOSTON)

MICHIGAN COLLEGE OF OPTOMETRY AT
FERRIS STATE UNIVERSITY (BIG RAPIDS)

UNIVERSITY OF MISSOURI AT ST. LOUIS (ST LOUIS)

STATE UNIVERSITY OF NEW YORK COLLEGE
OF OPTOMETRY (NEW YORK)

THE OHIO STATE UNIVERSITY (COLUMBUS)

NORTHEASTERN STATE UNIVERSITY OKLAHOMA
COLLEGE OF OPTOMETRY (TAHLEQUAH)

PACIFIC UNIVERSITY COLLEGE OF
OPTOMETRY (FOREST GROVE)

SALUS UNIVERSITY PENNSYLVANIA COLLEGE
OF OPTOMETRY (ELKINS PARK)

SOUTHERN COLLEGE OF OPTOMETRY (MEMPHIS)

UNIVERSITY OF HOUSTON COLLEGE
OF OPTOMETRY (HOUSTON)

UNIVERSITY OF THE INCARNATE WORD ROSENBERG
SCHOOL OF OPTOMETRY (SAN ANTONIO)

MEXICO, CENTRAL AND SOUTH AMERICA:

UNIVERSIDAD AUTONOMA DURANGO

UNIVERSIDAD NACIONAL DE LA PLATA

OPTOMETRY SCHOOL OF CENTRO DE
EDUCACION PROFESIONAL, FILADELFIA

UNIVERSIDAD DE LA SALLE

UNIVERSIDAD SANTO TOMÁS

UNIVERSIDAD EL BOSQUE

UNIVERSIDAD FUNDACIÓN DE AREA ANDEAN

METROPOLITANA ECUADOR

UNAM FES IZTACALA

UNIVERSIDAD AUTONOMA DE SINOLOA

UNIVERSIDAD NACIONAL AUTONOMA DE NICARAGUA

IESTPOO INSTITUTO DE OPTOMETRIA Y OPTICA

INSTITUTO EUROHISPANO

AFRICA:

UNIVERSITY OF GONDAR OPTOMETRY DEPARTMENT

KWAME NKRUMAH UNIV OF SCIENCE & TECHNOLOGY

UNIVERSITY OF CAPE COAST

MZUZU UNIVERSITY

MALAWI COLLEGE OF HEALTH SCIENCES
DEPARTMENT OF OPTOMETRY

UNIVERSITY OF BENIN DEPARTMENT OF OPTOMETRY

ABIA STATE UNIVERSITY DEPARTMENT OF OPTOMETRY

PHILIPPINES:

MANILA CENTRAL UNIVERSITY COLLEGE OF OPTOMETRY

VOSH Mission

VOSH/International believes in the freedom to see providing the gift of vision and eye health to people worldwide. We facilitate the provision and the sustainability of vision care anywhere for people who can neither afford nor obtain such care. Our goal is to increase our global impact whenever possible by supporting sustainable eye clinics, optometry schools and optometric educators in areas lacking sufficient eye care.

Printed in the United States
By Bookmasters